Organization Theory *is boring*

From Chester Barnard to the Present and Beyond

Expanded Edition

Edited by
OLIVER E. WILLIAMSON

New York   Oxford
OXFORD UNIVERSITY PRESS
1995

Oxford University Press

Oxford   New York
Athens   Auckland   Bangkok   Bombay
Calcutta   Cape Town   Dar es Salaam   Delhi
Florence   Hong Kong   Istanbul   Karachi
Kuala Lumpur   Madras   Madrid   Melbourne
Mexico City   Nairobi   Paris   Singapore
Taipei   Tokyo   Toronto

and associated companies in
Berlin   Ibadan

Library of Congress Cataloging-in-Publication Data
Organization theory : from Chester Barnard to the present
and beyond / edited by Oliver E. Williamson. — Expanded ed.
p.   cm.
Includes bibliographical references and index.
ISBN 0-19-509830-7 (pbk.)
1. Industrial organization–History.
2. Organizational behavior–History.
I. Williamson, Oliver E.
HD31.0753   1995
302.3′5′01—dc20   95-7974

3 4 5 6 7 8 9

Printed in the United States of America
on acid-free paper

Preface

The chapters appearing in this volume were originally prepared as lectures for a seminar held at the University of California, Berkeley, during the spring of 1988. I had a visiting appointment in the Economics Department and the (now) Haas School of Business at that time and was asked to organize an interdisciplinary seminar in that connection.

Of the several possible seminar themes considered, we decided to implement the one in which Chester Barnard's classic book *The Functions of the Executive* was used as the unifying theme. Not only was it unanimously agreed that *The Functions of the Executive* was an important book with wide interdisciplinary reach, but 1988 celebrated the fiftieth anniversary of its publication. Significant interim research developments notwithstanding, the book had a timeless character, and its current research significance was undervalued.

I was responsible for the first several sessions. The main object of these was to remind older students of and familiarize newer students with the key contributions of Barnard. Thereafter, each speaker was asked to explicate that area of research with which his or her research was principally concerned. Each was asked also to indicate where and how, if at all, Barnard had a bearing on this line of work.

Not only were students and faculty at Berkeley enthusiastic about the idea for a Barnard seminar series, but every invitation to make a seminar presentation, save one, was accepted. Although I mentioned during initial discussions with the seminar speakers that a subset of the seminar presentations might subsequently be written up and published as a book, the central purpose of the seminar was to conduct an active dialogue with seminar participants. Publication of a volume could be decided later, and speakers were merely asked to save their notes.

A group of about seventy students and faculty attended the seminar. Not only were large numbers of students and faculty from the Economics Department and the Business School in attendance, but political science, sociology, law, agricultural economics, and public policy were represented as well.

Initial doubts about the merits of celebrating a fifty-year-old book were quickly dispelled. A sustained dialogue was set up and the research interests of seminar participants were engaged. Insistence on pulling the lectures together as a book spontaneously began to build. This volume took shape.

That Barnard not only had but continues to have far-reaching and lasting impact on the study of organization is evident from the chapters in this book. Unlike the 1930s, moreover, the relevant social sciences have more recently become involved in an interdisciplinary dialogue. Given the complex and interdisciplinary nature of organizations and organization theory, that is as it should be. Occasional acrimony aside (which, however, adds to the interest), a productive research future for the study of organizations is in prospect.

Berkeley, California   O.E.W.
August 1989

Contents

Contributors

Glenn R. Carroll is professor of business administration at the University of California, Berkeley. Carroll is currently studying the organizational ecology of brewing industries. With collaborators in West Germany, he is studying the historical evolution of beer brewing in the United States, Germany, Austria, and Czechoslovakia.

Mary Douglas is professor emeritus at Northwestern University and resides in London. Her research applies cultural theory to economic and social problems, with particular emphasis on the cultures of labor markets.

Oliver Hart is professor of economics at the Massachusetts Institute of Technology. His research deals with contract theory, the theory of organizations, and the financial structure of firms.

Barbara Levitt is NIMH post-doctoral fellow at the University of California, Berkeley. She is doing research on organizational learning and decision making, professional socialization, and gender in organizations.

James G. March is Fred H. Merrill professor of management and professor of political science and sociology at Stanford University. His research focuses on decision making and leadership in organizations.

Terry M. Moe is professor of political science at Stanford University. His research is concerned with the organization of and purposes served by public sector bureaucracies from a rational choice perspective.

Jeffrey Pfeffer is Thomas D. Dee II professor of organizational behavior at Stanford University. His research interests are in the causes and consequences of wage structures in organizations, with a particular focus on wage dispersion, pay for performance, and the social psychology of social comparison processes.

W. Richard Scott is professor of sociology and director of the Stanford Center for Organizations Research at Stanford University. Scott is interested in examining the ways in which the technical and institutional environments of organizations influence the structure and function of individual organizations and of organizational fields.

Oliver E. Williamson is Transamerica professor of business, economics, and law at the University of California, Berkeley. Williamson is engaged in the study of transaction cost economics—in conceptual, theoretical, and public policy respects—with reference to the study of capitalist and, more recently, socialist economic organization.

Organization Theory

Introduction

OLIVER E. WILLIAMSON

Chester I. Barnard's remarkable and still influential book *The Functions of the Executive* was first published in 1938. The golden anniversary of that publication was celebrated with a seminar series of lectures held at the University of California, Berkeley, in the spring of 1988. Eight of those lectures were subsequently written down as essays and, with the exception of chapter 1, are published here for the first time.

This introduction is in two parts. The first section is concerned with Barnard—the man, his book, and his influence. The second section contains a précis of each of the eight essays.

CHESTER BARNARD

Barnard came to his subject with a keen intelligence, an uncommon intuition, and "thirty years . . . [of] intimate and continuous experience" in large, complex organizations (1938, p. xii). Upon leaving college (without a degree), he took a job with the American Telephone and Telegraph Company. He was the president of the New Jersey Bell Telephone Company at the time he wrote *The Functions of the Executive*.

Barnard retired from that position to become president of the Rockefeller Foundation in 1948. In the meantime he had served the U.S. government in a variety of civilian positions during World War II. Thereafter he served as president of the National Science Foundation (1952–54) and as chairman of the National Science Board (1950–56).

Not many academics write scholarly books. Not many scholarly books have a lasting impact on a field of study. *The Functions of the Executive* is a scholarly book that has had a significant and lasting influence on the study of organizations. Noteworthy, in this connection, is the fact that Barnard saw the job as just beginning. He remarked, in his closing chapter, on the unrealized (and even unrecognized) need for a science of organization. Despite a long gestation period, a science of organization is gradually taking shape. The resulting new science is recognizably inspired, moreover, by Barnard.

To be sure, others have been influential in this new science of organization. Interestingly, several of the more important contributions were also written in the 1930s. With the benefit of hindsight, we can see that was a fecund decade. Of special significance are contributions by Karl Llewellyn (1931) and Eugen Ehrlich (1936) in law, and by John R. Commons (1934) and Ronald Coase (1937) in economics.

Indeed, although others might describe it differently, the new science of organization to which I refer involves a joinder of law, economics, and organization theory. Economics and organization theory form the axis, to which contract law provides added support. Barnard anchors the organization theory member of this triad.

Although Barnard specifically acknowledges the influence Ehrlich had on his work and makes reference to (even if not much use of) Commons, *The Functions of the Executive* is mainly the product of Barnard's introspection coupled with a keen economic intuition and his grave dissatisfaction with the state of organization theory in the 1930s. Barnard consulted his own extensive experience as an executive and remarked that executives from other companies with whom he met were "able to understand each other with very few words when discussing essential problems of organization" (1938, p. vii). Arguably there was a common core from which he and these other executives worked. If so, the tacit knowledge that informed that core ought to be articulated. When he went to the literature, however, Barnard found that neither organization theory nor the contiguous social sciences were of much help.

Organization theory at that time was too mechanistic and abstract. The early subtleties of F. W. Taylor's scientific management had mainly given way to a "machine model," while the abstract principles of administration advanced by Henri Fayol and others failed to engage the issues as Barnard experienced them. The related social sciences, moreover, paid little heed to the formal and purposeful features of organization to which Barnard ascribed special importance: "there was lacking much recognition of formal organization as a most important characteristic of social life" (1938, p. ix).

Having sensed that organizations possessed a common conceptual core, and finding little in the literature that helped explicate that condition, Barnard set about addressing it himself. A remarkable transformation of the study of organization resulted. As Thomas Kuhn and others have observed, new paradigms are often associated with those who are young or new to a crisis-ridden field (Kuhn, 1970, p. 144); Barnard's relation to and impact on organization theory is an illustration.

That I ascribe a keen economic intuition to Barnard comes as a surprise to some and is disputed by others. After all, Barnard expressed great dissatisfaction with the state of economics in the 1930s, and professed that it was not until he had "relegated economic theory and economic interest to a secondary . . . place" that he was able to understand organizations (1938, p. xi). Surely it was Barnard's keen *non*economic intuition that disclosed that "economic man" was a superficial construction, whereupon "organizational man" became the relevant entity upon which to base the analysis.

I submit, however, that if an economic intuition is understood to be one that brings a "rational spirit" (broadly conceived) to bear on puzzling economic and organizational phenomena—which is the way Kenneth Arrow has described it (1974, p. 16)—then the apparent contradiction vanishes. Barnard combined a curious mind with a rational spirit to a superlative degree.

Thus, although many students of organization find that neither orthodox economics nor rationality engage the issues, Barnard was able to separate orthodoxy from rationality and employed the latter. Specifically, Barnard brought a powerful rationality orientation to the study of formal organization, the latter being defined as "that kind of cooperation among men that is conscious, deliberate, purposeful" (1938, p. 4). At the same time, Barnard made provision for both the cognitive limitations and the social attributes of human actors. Wanting to explicate how complex organization worked and why, he was concerned principally with the anatomy and physiology, rather than the pathology, of organization.

Despite this rationality emphasis, Barnard's influence went beyond what came to be known as the "rational systems" school to include the "natural systems" school of organization theory as well. Thus, the study of formal organization, communication, the authority relation, zones of acceptance, and so on were all featured in Herbert Simon's book, *Administrative Behavior* (1947), which relies on and explicates Barnard and gave impetus to the rational systems approach to organization. But Philip Selznick (1957; 1969) was likewise inspired by Barnard. For Selznick, however, it was Barnard's treatments of informal organization, leadership, goal formation, the inculcation of a moral order, and other factors—concerns that are central to the natural systems tradition—that were important. Not only, therefore, was *The Functions of the Executive* an important (albeit difficult and sometimes obscure) book in itself, but Barnard inspired some of the very best work in organization theory that followed.

Still, the science of organization to which Barnard referred did not quickly materialize. Partly that was because the follow-on work was concerned almost entirely with the science of *administration* rather than the science of organization. Also, an appreciation for the relations among law, economics, and organization has taken a very long time to develop—indeed, is still in the process of developing.

A science of administration is predominantly concerned with internal organization. Viewed normatively, the focus is on hierarchical structure, internal incentives and controls, communication and information processing, ascribed goals, workplace democracy, and the like. The positive analysis of internal organization is concerned with bureaucratic and other "un-anticipated consequences" of hierarchical structures, demands for control, information disparities, conditions of dependency, and the like. A unified science of organization requires that internal (administrative) and market modes be treated in a unified way. One way to accomplish this unification is to regard markets, hierarchies, and hybrid modes of contracting as alternative GOVERNANCE STRUCTURES for organizing the same transactions. The governance of contractual relations, with special emphasis on private ordering, thus becomes the object of analysis. The joinder of law, economics, and organization to which I referred earlier is thereby engaged.

Interestingly, Barnard was attracted to the view that law is responsive rather than imposed: "all law arises from the formal and especially the informal understandings of the people as socially organized" (1938, p. x). In effect, a consensual approach (in which informal organization plays a major role) is what Barnard used to examine authority and describe the employment relation. As it turns out, this approach, together with the purposive orientation out of which Barnard worked, can be applied to the study of contracting more generally. That is what has materialized.

THE ESSAYS

Barnard's greatest influence has been in the area of organization theory. But organization theory has been changing, and the reach of Barnard's influence has been increasing. Thus whereas four of the chapters in the book are written by organization theorists (from quite different perspectives), the other four are by nonorganization theorists (two economists, one anthropologist, and one political scientist). Considering these chapters and other work in progress, there is reason to believe an incipient science of organization is taking shape. The next decade should decide whether Barnard's aspiration succeeds or fails.

The eight chapters in this book are grouped with the organization theorists (Barbara Levitt and James March, W. Richard Scott, Glenn Carroll, and Jeffrey Pfeffer) placed first, followed by the related social scientists (Mary Douglas, anthropology; Terry Moe, political science; Oliver Hart and Oliver Williamson, economics). The chapter by Levitt and March characterizes *The Functions of the Executive* as poetic and evocative (rather than precise and definitive), and distinguishes between the aforementioned rational systems and natural systems schools.

The first of these is more instrumental and appeals more to economists; the second invites consideration of how the preferences of participants in an organization are transformed and a moral order is constructed. The Levitt and March chapter is closer to the second of these themes—although, as they point out, these two conceptions ought to inform each other. The appendix to Barnard's book (which is often neglected) is of special interest to Levitt and March. Here Barnard distinguishes between logical and nonlogical mental processes and invites the examination of "alternative forms of organizational intelligence." The Levitt and March chapter examines the strengths and weaknesses of "experiential learning" as it relates to the development of organizational intelligence.

Scott's chapter, titled "Symbols and Organizations: From Barnard to the Institutionalists," similarly emphasizes the "natural systems" rather than the "rational systems" side of Barnard's work. As Scott points out, the fact that Barnard was able to work in both domains—insisting, for example, that formal and informal organization are nonseparable—speaks to his deep organizational insights and genius.

Scott distinguishes between "technical invironments" and "institutional environments"—the first of these referring to the ease of metering the product of work (mainly entailing output controls) while the second involves the elaboration of rules. Weak and strong distinctions within each type of environment are made, whence a four-way classification of organizations and socioeconomic activities is possible. This helps to clarify differences among organizations and highlights, among other things, why activities in the quadrant where both the technical and institutional environments are weak (personal service units, e.g., health clubs and child care services) are especially hard to organize. Further study of the implications of the institutional perspective is proposed.

Contrary to the widespread belief that Barnard and the organizational ecology perspectives are disjointed, Carroll finds numerous ecological insights in Barnard—some of which are vital—in his chapter titled "On the Organizational Ecology of Chester I. Barnard." Barnard's recognition that most cooperative effects fail mainly because they are unable to adapt effectively to outside disturbances is the most important of these insights. Related to this is Barnard's assertion that survival is the only meaningful measure of an organization's efficiency. Thus, although it would be unwarranted to call Barnard the father of the large, growing, and influential body of literature in population ecology, he nonetheless possessed many of the requisite instincts.

Combining a short-term *adaptive* approach to *individual* organizations with a longer-term *selective* approach to *populations* of organizations, Carroll argues that ecological analysis can be fruitfully brought to bear on such issues as the composition of "strategic groups," which has been of special interest in the burgeoning literature on strategic management. This insight, too, invites further research.

Pfeffer examines "Incentives in Organizations: The Importance of Social Relations." A chronic source of strain between economists and organization theorists is that the former place much greater weight on monetary incentives than noneconomists think appropriate. This disproportionate emphasis on monetary incentives was a concern of Barnard, who found it necessary to relegate "economic theory and economic interests to a secondary . . . place" (1938, p. xi) in order to develop his understanding of organization.

Pfeffer agrees that material incentives are much too narrow a basis for the study of incentives, and instead adopts a "social relations" orientation. This is plainly consonant with Barnard's rich characterization of incentives and is the approach to the study of incentives that has inspired a wide range of recent work in this area—which Pfeffer both summarizes and interprets. Better theories and practice "more closely attuned to the social realities in organization," which emphasize comparative equity, are in prospect.

Douglas, in her chapter on "Converging on Autonomy: Anthropology and Institutional Economics," maintains that a cultural theory is needed to understand how goals of individuals and organizations are formed. A problem she has with Barnard, and with recent work in institutional economics, is that both work out of the framework of methodological individualism. She suggests instead an embeddedness approach.

Specifically, she suggests that the grid/group approach that informs her work and that of others can usefully be brought to bear on the study of economic organization. With reference to the group dimension, the question is whether the membership demands of a group are slight or great. The grid dimension is variously defined. One definition is in terms of roles: Can roles be achieved or are they ascribed? A four-way classification obtains. To know whether an individual is located in grid/group terms is to know his or her preferences and goals. This theory both can and should inform the study of economic organization.

Moe is concerned with "The Politics of Structural Choice: Toward a Theory of Public Bureaucracy." He observes that, whereas public administration and organization theory once developed in tandem (recall that this was Herbert Simon's background), public administration has since fallen on hard times. Furthermore, political scientists have generally neglected the study of bureaucracy in favor of social choice, voting, and legislative institutions.

Moe argues for a genuinely political theory of public bureaucracy in which the influence of interest groups, legislators, bureaucrats, and the presidency are all recognized. Working off of the new economics of organization, Moe adopts a contractual approach in which incomplete contracting is featured. Specifically, Moe appeals to the concept of "incomplete contracting *in its entirety*" for the purposes of studying bureaucracy. This leads to a number of bureaucratic design insights and promises to be a rich basis for follow-up research. Combining economics and politics in this way, Moe urges that political scientists come back to being organization theorists.

Hart develops "An Economist's Perspective on the Theory of the Firm." A chronic problem with the older neoclassical theory of the firm and with the more recent principal-agent theory of contract is that both disallow any role for organization. That is because the first of these treats the firm in technological terms while the second concentrates all of the relevant contracting action on the ex-ante contractual agreement.

Transaction cost economics takes exception to that view, insisting that all complex contracts are unavoidably incomplete. The formal modeling of incomplete contracts is formidably difficult, however, which explains why the shift to an incomplete contracting set-up was so long resisted. Hart (together with Sanford Grossman) broke with that tradition in 1986, when their paper on "the Costs and Benefits of Ownership" was published. As Hart's chapter discloses, the formal modeling of incomplete contracting has since become an uncommonly productive research arena. The incipient science of organization appears to have crossed a threshold from which there is no return.

What was, in the 1990 edition of this book, the last chapter, is titled "Chester Barnard and the Incipient Science of Organization." Some of the salient organization theory contributions of Barnard and of follow-up research (especially that of Simon) are summarized. Transaction cost economics selectively draws on Barnard–Simon, combining this with economics and aspects of the law in an effort to reconceptualize the problem of economic organization.

I have continued to work on these combined issues of economics and organization, however, and this edition includes a new (and now final chapter) on "Transaction Cost Economics and Organization Theory." In it I examine the numerous ways in which organization theory has influenced transaction cost economics and indicate how transaction cost economics adds value to organization theory in return. Some of the unrelieved strains are also discussed.

I remain optimistic that a microanalytic comparative institutional, economizing approach to the study of economic organization will continue to develop. Not only are economists now prepared to concede a place of importance to organization theory, but organization theorists now concede value in the economizing approach. Kenneth Arrow speaks to the first of these: the successes of the New Institutional Economics are largely attributable to its more microanalytic orientation (1987, p. 734). And Mayer Zald speaks to the second: organization theorists have begun to come to terms with economizing (1987). A fruitful dialogue between economics and organization is progressively taking shape.

Whether the long-awaited science of organization to which Barnard alluded in 1938 will materialize before the end of the century remains to be seen. The prospects for such a result appear to have been improved, however, by the microanalytic-economizing joinder to which I refer. Considering the astonishing quality of the research talents that are currently being applied to the new economics of organization/institutions/contracting, cautious optimism is warranted, at the very least.

REFERENCES

Arrow, Kenneth. 1974. *The Limits of Organization.* New York: W. W. Norton.
———. 1987. "Reflections on the Essays," in George Feiwel, ed., *Arrow and the Foundations of the Theory of Economic Policy.* New York: New York University Press, pp. 727–34.
Barnard, Chester. 1938. *The Functions of the Executive.* Cambridge, Mass.: Harvard University Press (Reprinted, 1962).
Coase, Ronald. 1952. "The Nature of the Firm," *Economica N.S.,* 4 (1937): 386–405. Reprinted in G. J. Stigler and K. E. Boulding, eds., *Readings in Price Theory.* Homewood, Ill.: Richard D. Irwin.
Commons, John. 1934. *Institutional Economics.* Madison: University of Wisconsin Press.
Erhlich, Eugen. 1936. *Fundamental Principles of the Sociology of Law.* Cambridge, Mass.: Harvard University Press.
Grossman, Sanford, and Oliver Hart. 1986. "The Costs and Benefits of Ownership: A Theory of Vertical and Lateral Integration," *Journal of Political Economy,* 94 (August): 691–719.
Henderson, James, and Richard Quandt. 1971. *Microeconomic Theory: A Mathematical Approach.* 2nd ed. New York: McGraw-Hill.
Kuhn, Thomas. 1970. *The Structure of Scientific Revolutions.* Chicago: University of Chicago Press.
Llewellyn, Karl. 1931. What price contract? An essay in perspective. *Yale Law Journal* 40: 704–51.
Selznick, Philip. 1957. *Leadership in Administration.* New York: Harper & Row.
———. 1969. *Law, Society, and Industrial Justice.* New York: Russell Sage Foundation.
Simon, Herbert. 1947. *Administrative Behavior.* New York: Macmillan.
Zald, Mayer. 1987. "Review Essay: The New Institutional Economics," *American Journal of Sociology,* 93 (November): 701–8.

1

Chester I. Barnard
and the Intelligence of Learning

BARBARA LEVITT and JAMES G. MARCH

WHAT BARNARD SAID

This volume honors a book by Chester I. Barnard (1938), *The Functions of the Executive*, which has had an enduring influence. The book contains seeds of several of the more important developments in organization theory over the past fifty years. It is poetic and evocative rather than precise and definitive, and in honoring Barnard we also honor those inspired by him. Through the imagination of people like Herbert A. Simon and Oliver Williamson, for example, Barnard's master work has become an enriched and somewhat stylized script.

We have institutionalized the socially constructed meaning of a socially annointed classic, but neither the interpretation nor the identification of *The Functions of the Executive* as a classic is arbitrary. Barnard anticipated the broad outlines of much of contemporary treatments of organizations in information economics and agency theory. These were central ideas for him and for disciplines concerned with organizations.

The Problem of Organizing

Barnard's primary concern was the problem of organizing, the complexities involved in coordinating numerous actors of potentially divergent interests under conditions of environmental uncertainty and instability. His approach to this problem fits comfortably within the traditions of economics and political science and has found most favor there, but it also has general appeal.

The second part of this paper was originally published in the *Annual Review of Sociology*, 14 (1988) 319–40. Reproduced, with permission, from the *Annual Review of Sociology*, Vol. 14 © 1988 by Annual Reviews Inc.

In effect, Barnard distinguished conflict systems from cooperative systems. A conflict system is one in which individuals have objectives that are not jointly consistent. It organizes through exchanges and other interactions among strategic actors. A cooperative system is one in which individuals act rationally in the name of a common objective. The problem of organizing was seen as one of transforming a conflict (political) system into a cooperative (rational) system

Barnard recognized that such a transformation was a nontrivial problem. He was conscious of the numerous ways in which actual attempts at organizing could be frustrated and the frequency of failure. Until such failures became particularly salient to theories of selection, many students of organizations did not appreciate the significance of the high failure rate in organizing; often not recognizing (as Barnard clearly did) that since failures disappear and successes remain, the relative frequency of the latter is systematically exaggerated.

Barnard's analysis of this problem of organizing anticipated much of the discussion in contemporary theories of organizations. In particular, he emphasized that cooperative rationality presumed knowledge, and he saw the limits of organization in securing and attending to information. Thus, he is correctly seen as a forerunner of those parts of organization theory that emphasize the cognitive limits on information processing in organizations.

Even more, he anticipated the complications of conflict. He saw the significance of strategic action on the part of self-interested actors in organizations and the difficulties of discovering and negotiating jointly satisfactory sets of exchanges and agreements. His discussions of inducements and contributions in the employment contract clearly make Barnard an early agency theorist. A consistent theme is the need to find a set of incentives such that self-interested actors act cooperatively in the interest of the organization. Moreover, he anticipated the recent interest among economic theorists of cooperative games in faith and trust as important elements in developing incentive structures.

These ideas have been the basis of the giants of contemporary economic theories of organization, associated particularly with names such as Coase, von Neumann and Morgenstern, Simon, and Marschak and Radner. Standard interpretations of *The Functions of the Executive* capture central themes of the text, and those themes are reflected in much contemporary work in organization theory.

Preferences as Instruments of Organizing

After fifty years of interpretation and honor, however, it may be useful to note that there are important things to which Barnard devoted considerable attention but writers in the "Barnard tradition" have largely overlooked. One obvious way the Barnard tradition deviates from the Barnard text is in the treatment of individual preferences. Writers on organizations in the Barnard economics tradition, for the most part, treat preferences as given. Individuals come to the organization with preferences that are in conflict; they are induced to act cooperatively through a set of incentives that make their actions mutually consistent; but their underlying values or utility functions are treated as exogenous and fixed. In this perspective, preferences are important premises of organizing, but they are not instruments of organizing.

The Barnard strategy for organizing includes such efforts, but it explicitly goes beyond them to include conscious attention to the transformation of preferences. Changing motives is seen to be an important part of management, as is the creation of new moral codes. In modern terms, Barnard proposed that an executive create and sustain a culture of beliefs and values that would support cooperation. The appeal is not to exchanges, Pareto optimality, or the search for incentive schemes; it is to the construction of a moral order in which individual participants act in the name of the institution—not because it is in their self-interest to do so, but because they identify with the institution and are prepared to sacrifice some aspects of themselves for it.

Since Barnard treated both the management of coalitions based on prior preferences and the transformation of preferences as obvious strategies, he probably did not anticipate that the first would come to dominate the major part of his heritage and the second another part. The inducements–contributions schema has come to be used primarily to describe relations among individuals with static preferences. The possible interrelations between adapting to preferences and shaping them, the subtleties of simultaneously feeding a hunger and changing it, have been largely lost.

Alternative Routes to Intelligence

A second major way in which the Barnard tradition deviates from his text is in the treatment of the relationship between reason and intelligence. As we have already noted, Barnard saw the problem of organizing as one of transforming a multitude of conflicting, self-interested, strategic actors into a single rational system that can act consistently in the name of future consequences evaluated with respect to future preferences. He saw substantial gains to be achieved through such a transformation.

At the same time, however, he did not equate the processes of reason or rationality with intelligence. He saw reason (in practice) as flawed and its claim to intelligence as limited. From this point of view, probably the most revealing feature of *The Functions of the Executive* is Barnard's decision to reprint his 1936 Cyrus Fogg Brackett Lecture at Princeton University on "Mind in Everyday Affairs." This essay distinguishes between "logical" and "nonlogical" mental processes and makes a case for the intelligence of the latter and the limitations of the former.

The argument regarding logic or reason is largely that it is an inadequate instrument in human hands (minds). Barnard writes: "It is my belief that if an inventory of the reasonings of competent intellects could be made it would be found that an extremely high percentage was in error" (1938, p. 303). Barnard honors reason and believes that others should do so also, but he sees the many ways it can lead to unintelligent actions. Specifically, he focuses on the information-processing limitations of human actors and on limitations human actors exhibit as they process preferences.

The argument regarding nonlogical processes focuses on "good judgment" or "good sense." Barnard does not attempt to define exactly what these processes consist of, but it is clear that one thing he has in mind is the coding of experience and knowledge, the way intelligence consults history. He describes some of the advantages of such processes, some of the circumstances in which they have advantages over rationality. He also describes some of their limitations. He is not an unconditional enthusiast for unreason, but a cautious observer of the lack of any perfect process for intelligence.

Thus, *The Functions of the Executive* is an invitation to examine alternative forms of organizational intelligence, different processes by which organization might respond to situations in which they find themselves, as those processes are actually exhibited by real individuals and organizations. Under what conditions, and with what qualifications, will we find intelligence in the anticipatory calculation of rationality? In coalition formation and bargaining? In imitation? In adaptation to experience through selection or learning?

The Barnard economics tradition has largely ignored the invitation, preferring to focus on an elaboration of our understanding of rational processes. In particular, Barnard's heirs have spawned an extensive examination of the limitations of rationality. We are now reasonably confident that Barnard was right in observing that rationality, in practice, frequently leads organizations astray.

The normative response to the limitations of rationality has, for the most part, been twofold. First, there have been efforts to remove the limitations seen as restricting the effectiveness of reason. For example, the computer has been seen as a basis for a new form of information system that relaxes some of the restrictions on reason. Barnard saw the difficulties with reason as fundamental, but the first instinct has been to redefine them as technical and relatively easily ameliorated. Second, there have been efforts to embrace alternative visions of organizational intelligence, to see various forms of nonrational action as central to sensible action. In particular, it has been suggested that learning is a route to intelligence that matches organizational capabilities better than rationality. Barnard saw experiential learning and other forms of nonrational processes as essential though imperfect, but this second instinct embraces them without much attention to the many ways in which the same processes that produce good outcomes can also lead to poor ones.

Thus, though his ideas were not always fully developed, Barnard was right in a number of very important ways that have been largely over-looked. He saw more clearly than others that organizations often fail, though he did not see so clearly the role of failure in adaptation. He saw more clearly than others that preferences were instruments of organization as well as premises for it, though he probably did not recognize the full significance of endogenous preferences for theories of cooperative behavior. He saw more clearly than others the existence of alternative routes to intelligence in organizations and that no route was perfect, though his elaboration of the prospects for and difficulties with logical, rational processes was more complete than his analysis of alternative intelligences.

This chapter follows this last Barnard tradition. It accepts the idea that rational processes are not perfect, that under some circumstances they may be less intelligent than alternative processes. But it emphasizes the other side of the Barnard approach to alternative intelligences, seeking to understand their strengths and weaknesses. In particular, we examine experiential learning as an alternative process of organizational intelligence. We ask how such processes function in an organization and whether and when they might be intelligent.

PROCESSES OF ORGANIZATIONAL LEARNING

Theories of organizational learning can be distinguished from theories of analysis and choice, which emphasize anticipatory calculation and intention (Machina 1987), from theories of conflict and bargaining, which emphasize strategic action, power, and exchange (Pfeffer 1981), and from theories of variation and selection, which emphasize differential birth and survival rates of invariant forms (Hannan & Freeman 1977). Although the actual behavioral processes and mechanisms of learning are sufficiently intertwined with choice, bargaining, and selection to make such theoretical distinctions artificial at times, ideas about organizational learning are distinct from, and framed by, ideas about the other processes (Grandori 1987; Scott 1987).

Basic Framework

Our interpretation of organizational learning builds on three classical observations drawn from behavioral studies of organizations. The first is that behavior in an organization is based on routines (Cyert & March 1963; Nelson & Winter 1982). Action stems from a logic of appropriateness or legitimacy more than a logic of consequentiality or intention. It involves matching procedures to situations more than calculating choices. The second observation is that organizational actions are history dependent (Lindblom 1959; Steinbruner 1974). Routines are based on interpretations of the past more than anticipations of the future. They adapt to experience incrementally in response to feedback about outcomes. The third observation is that organizations are oriented to targets (Simon 1955; Siegel 1957). Their behavior depends on the relation between the outcomes they observe and their aspirations for those outcomes. Sharper distinctions are made between success and failure than among gradations of either.

Within such a framework, organizations are seen as learning by encoding inferences from history into routines that guide behavior. The generic term *routines* includes the forms, rules, procedures, conventions, roles, strategies, and technologies around which organizations are constructed and through which they operate. It also includes the structure of beliefs, frameworks, paradigms, codes, cultures, and knowledge that buttress, elaborate, and contradict the formal routines. Routines are independent of the individual actors who execute them and are capable of surviving considerable turnover in individuals.

The experiential lessons of history are captured by routines in a way that makes the lessons, but not the history, accessible to organizations and organizational members who have not themselves experienced the history. Routines are transmitted through socialization, education, imitation, professionalization, personnel movement, mergers, and acquisitions. They are recorded in a collective memory that is often coherent but is sometimes jumbled, that often endures but is sometimes lost. They change as a result of experience within a community of other learning organizations. These changes depend on interpretations of history, particularly on the evaluation of outcomes in terms of targets.

In the remainder of this chapter we examine such processes of organizational learning. The perspective is narrower than that used by some (Starbuck 1976; Hedberg 1981; Fiol & Lyles 1985) and differs conceptually from that used by others. In particular, the emphases on both routines and ecologies of learning distinguish the present formulation from treatments that deal primarily with individual learning within single organizations (March & Olsen 1975; Argyris & Schön 1978) and place this chapter closer to the traditions of behavioral theories of organizational decision making (Winger 1986; House & Singh 1987) and to population level theories of organizational change (Carroll 1984; Astley 1985).

Learning from Direct Experience

Mechanisms   Routines and beliefs change in response to direct organizational experience through two major mechanisms. The first is trial-and-error experimentation. The likelihood that a routine will be used increases when it is associated with success in meeting a target, and decreases when it is associated with failure (Cyert & March 1963). The underlying process by which this occurs is left largely unspecified. The second mechanism is organizational search. An organization draws from a pool of alternative routines, adopting better ones when they are discovered. Since the rate of discovery is a function of both the richness of the pool and the intensity and direction of search, it depends on the history of success and failure of the organization (Radner 1975).

Learning by doing   The purest example of learning from direct experience is found in the effects of cumulated production on productivity in manufacturing (Dutton, Thomas & Butler 1984). Research on aircraft production, first in the 1930s (Wright 1936) and subsequently during World War II (Adher 1956), indicated that direct labor costs in producing airframes declined with the accumulated number of airframes produced. If C_i is the direct labor cost of the i_{th} airframe produced, and a is a constant, then the empirical results are approximated by $C_n = C_1 n^{-a}$. This equation, similar to learning curves in individuals and animals, has been shown to fit production costs (in constant dollars) reasonably well in a relatively large number of products, firms, and nations (Yelle 1979). Much of the early research involved only simple graphical techniques, but more elaborate analyses have largely confirmed the original results (Rapping 1965). Estimates of the learning rate, however, vary substantially across industries, products, and time (Dutton & Thomas 1984).

Empirical plots of experience curves have been buttressed by three kinds of analytical elaborations. First, there have been attempts to decompose experience curves into several intercorrelated causes and to assess their separate contributions to the observed improvements in manufacturing costs. Although it has been argued that important elements of the improvements come through feedback from customers who use the products, particularly when products are complex (Rosenberg 1982), most of the research on experience curves has emphasized the direct effects of cumulative experience on production efficiency. Most studies indicate that the effects of cumulative production are greater than those of changes in the current scale of production, transformation of the technology, increases in the experience of individual production workers, or the passage of time (Preston & Keachie 1964; Hollander 1965; Argote, Beckman, & Epple 1987); there is evidence, however, that the latter effects are also involved (Dutton & Thomas 1984; 1985). Second, attempts to use experience curves as a basis for marketing strategies have led to some well-publicized successes, but also to some failures attributable to inadequate specification of the basic model, particularly as it relates to the sharing of experience across organizations (Day & Montgomery 1983; Dutton & Freedman 1985). Third, attempts have been made to define models that not only predict the general log-linear result but also accommodate some of the small but theoretically interesting departures from that curve (Muth 1986). These efforts are, for the most part, variations on themes of trial-and-error learning or organizational search.

Competency traps   In simple discussions of experiential learning based on trial-and-error learning or organizational search, organizations are described as gradually adopting routines, procedures, or strategies that lead to favorable outcomes; but the routines themselves are treated as fixed. In fact, routines are transformed at the same time the organization learns which to pursue, and discrimination among alternative routines is affected by their transformations (March 1981; Burgelman 1988).

The dynamics are exemplified by cases in which each routine is itself a collection of routines, and learning takes place at several nested levels. In such multilevel learning, organizations learn simultaneously both to discriminate among routines and to refine those routines by learning within them. A familiar contemporary example is the way in which organizations learn to use certain software systems and simultaneously refine their skills on these systems. As a result of such learning, efficiency with any particular procedure increases with use, and differences in success with different procedures reflect not only differences in the performance potentials of the procedures but also an organization's current competences with them.

Multilevel learning typically leads to specialization. Improving competencies within frequently used procedures increases the frequency with which those procedures result in successful outcomes, and thereby increases their use. Provided this process leads the organization both to improve the efficiency and to increase the use of the procedure with the highest potential, specialization is advantageous. However, a competency trap can occur when a favorable performance with an inferior procedure keeps an organization from gaining enough experience with a superior procedure to make it worth using. Such traps are well known in both new technologies (Cooper & Schendel 1976) and new procedures (Zucker 1977).

Competency traps are particularly likely to lead to maladaptive specialization if newer routines are better than older ones. One case is the sequential exposure to new procedures in a developing technology (Barley 1988). Later procedures are improvements, but organizations have problems overcoming the competences they have developed with earlier ones (Whetten 1987). The likelihood of such persistence with inferior procedures depends on the difference between the potentials of the alternatives. The status quo is unlikely to be stable if the difference between existing routines and new ones is substantial (Stinchcombe 1986). The likelihood of falling into a competency trap also depends on learning rates. Fast learning among alternative routines tends to increase the risks of maladaptive specialization, while fast learning within a new routine tends to decrease the risk (Herriott, Levinthal & March 1985).

The broader social and evolutionary implications of competency traps are considerable. In effect, learning produces increasing returns to experience (thus typically to scale) and leads an organization, industry, or society to persist in using a set of procedures or technologies that may be far from optimal (Arthur 1984). Familiar examples are the standard typewriter keyboard and the use of internal combustion gasoline engines to power motor vehicles. Competency traps result in organizational histories for which broad functional or efficiency explanations are inadequate.

Interpretation of Experience

The lessons of experience are drawn from a relatively small number of observations in a complex, changing ecology of learning organizations. What has happened is not always obvious, and the causality of events is difficult to untangle. What an organization should expect to achieve, and thus the difference between success and failure, is not always clear. Nevertheless, people in organizations form interpretations of events and come to classify outcomes as good or bad (Thompson 1967).

Certain properties of this interpretation of experience stem from features of individual inference and judgment. As has frequently been observed, human beings are not perfect statisticians (Kahneman, Slovic & Tversky 1982). They make systematic errors in recording the events of history and in making inferences from them. They overestimate the probability of events that occur and that are available to attention because of their recency or saliency. They are insensitive to sample size. They exaggerate the influence of intentional actions of individuals on events. They use simple linear and functional rules, associate causality with spatial and temporal contiguity, and assume that big effects must have big causes. These attributes of individuals as historians are important to the present topic because they lead to systematic biases in interpretation, but because they have been reviewed in several previous publications (Slovic, Fischhoff & Lichtenstein 1977; Einhorn & Hogarth 1986; Starbuck & Milliken 1988) they are not discussed here.

Stories, paradigms, and frames   Organizations devote considerable energy to developing collective understandings of history. These interpretations of experience depend on the frames within which events are comprehended (Daft & Weick 1984). They are translated into, and developed through, storylines that are broadly, but not universally, shared (Clark 1972; Martin, Sitkin & Boehm 1985). This structure of meaning is normally suppressed as a conscious concern, but learning occurs within it. As a result, some of the more powerful phenomena in organizational change surround the transformation of givens—the redefinition of events, alternatives, and concepts through consciousness raising, culture building, double-loop learning, or paradigm shifts (Argyris & Schön 1978; Brown 1987; Beyer 1981).

It is imaginable that organizations will discard ineffective interpretive frames in the very long run, but the difficulties in using history to discriminate intelligently among alternative paradigms are profound. Where multiple, hierarchically arranged levels of simultaneous learning exist, their interactions are complex, and it is difficult to evaluate higher-order alternatives on the basis of experience. Alternative frames are flexible enough to allow change in operational routines without affecting organizational mythology (Meyer & Rowan 1977; Krieger 1979), and organizational participants collude in support of interpretations that sustain the myths

(Tirole 1986). As a result, stories, paradigms, and beliefs are conserved in the face of considerable potential disconfirmation (Sproull 1981); what is learned appears to be less influenced by history than by the frames applied to that history (Fischhoff 1975; Pettigrew 1985).

Although frameworks for interpreting experience within organizations are generally resistant to experience—indeed may enact experience (Weick 1979)—they are vulnerable to paradigm peddling and paradigm politics. Ambiguity sustains the efforts of theorists and therapists to promote their favorite frameworks, and the process by which interpretations are developed makes it relatively easy for conflicts of interest within an organization to spawn conflicting interpretations. For example, leaders of organizations are inclined to accept paradigms that attribute organizational successes to their own actions and organizational failures to the actions of others or to external forces, while opposition groups have the converse principle for attributing causality (Miller & Ross 1975). Similarly, advocates of a particular policy, but not their opponents, are likely to interpret failures as an indication that it has not been pursued vigorously enough while their opponents see it as a symptom that the policy was incorrect (Ross & Staw 1986). As a result, disagreements over the meaning of history are possible, and different groups develop alternative stories that interpret the same experience quite differently.

The ambiguity of success   Both trial-and-error learning and incremental search depend on the evaluation of outcomes as successes or failures. There is a structural bias toward postdecision disappointment in ordinary decision making (Harrison & March 1984), but individual decision makers often seem to be able to reinterpret their objectives or the outcomes in such a way as to make themselves successful even when the shortfall seems large (Staw & Ross 1978).

The process is similar in organizational learning, particularly when the leadership is stable and the organization is tightly integrated (Ross & Staw 1986). But when such conditions do not hold, differences often stem from the political nature of an organization. Goals are ambiguous, and commitment to them is confounded by their relation to personal and subgroup objectives (Moore & Gates 1986). Conflict and decision advocacy within putatively rational decision processes lead to inflated expectations and problems of implementation, and thus to disappointments (Olsen 1976; Sproull, Weiner & Wolf 1978). Different groups in an organization often have different targets and evaluate the same outcome differently. Simple euphoria is constrained by the presence of individuals and groups who opposed the direction being pursued, or who at least feel no need to accept responsibility for it (Brunsson 1985). New organizational leaders are inclined to define previous outcomes more negatively than their predecessors (Hedberg 1981). As a result, evaluations of outcomes are likely to be more negative or mixed in organizations than they are for individuals.

Organizational success is ordinarily defined in terms of the relationship between performance outcomes and targets. Targets, however, change over time in two ways. First, the indicators of success are modified. Accounting definitions change (Burchell, Colin & Hopwood 1985); social and policy indicators are redefined (MacRae 1985). Second, levels of aspiration change with respect to particular indicators. The most common assumption is that a target is a function of some kind of moving average of past achievement, the gap between past achievement and past targets, or the rate of change of either (Cyert & March 1963; Lant 1987).

Superstitious learning   Superstitious learning occurs when the subjective experience of learning is compelling, but the connections between actions and outcomes are misspecified. Numerous opportunities exist for such mis-understandings in learning from experience in organizations. For example, it is easy for technicians to develop superstitious perceptions of a new technology from their experience with it (Barley 1988). Cases of superstition that are of particular interest to students of organizations are those that stem from special features of life in hierarchical organizations. For example, promotion of managers on the basis of performance produces self-confidence among top executives that is partly superstitious, leading them to overestimate the extent to which they can control the risks their orga-nizations face (March & Shapira 1987).

Superstitious learning often involves situations in which subjective eval-uations of success are insensitive to the actions taken. During very good times, when postoutcome euphoria reinterprets outcomes positively, or when targets are low, only exceptionally inappropriate routines lead an organi-zation to experience failure. In like manner, during very bad times, when postoutcome pessimism reinterprets outcomes negatively, or when targets are high, no routine leads to success. Evaluations that are insensitive to actions can also result from adaptive aspirations. Targets that adapt very rapidly are close to the current performance level. This makes being above or below the target an almost chance event. Very slow adaptation, on the other hand, is likely to keep an organization either successful or unsuc-cessful for long periods of time. A similar result occurs if targets adapt to the performance of other organizations. For example, if each firm in an industry sets its target equal to the average performance of firms in that industry, some firms are likely to be persistently above the target and oth-ers persistently below it (Levinthal & March 1981; Herriott, Levinthal & March 1985).

Each of these situations produces superstitious learning. In an organi-zation that is invariably successful, routines that are followed are associ-ated with success and reinforced; other routines are inhibited. The orga-nization becomes committed to a particular set of routines, but these routines are determined more by early, relatively arbitrary, actions than by infor-mation gained from the learning situation (Nystrom & Starbuck 1984). Alternatively, if failure is experienced regardless of the particular routine that is used, these routines are changed frequently in a fruitless search for

some that work. In both cases, the subjective feeling of learning is powerful, but it is misleading.

Organizational Memory

Organizational learning depends on features of individual memories (Hastie, Park & Weber 1984; Johnson & Hasher 1987), but our present concern is with organizational aspects of memory. Routine-based conceptions
of learning presume that the lessons of experience are maintained and accumulated within routines despite the turnover of personnel and the passage of time. Rules, procedures, technologies, beliefs, and cultures are conserved through systems of socialization and control. They are retrieved
through mechanisms of attention within a memory structure. Such organizational instruments not only record history but shape its future path,
and the details of that path depend to a significant degree on the processes
through which the memory is maintained and consulted. An accounting
system, whether viewed as the product of design or the residue of historical development, affects the recording and creation of history by an organization (Johnson & Kaplan 1987; Røvik 1987). The ways in which military routines are changed, maintained, and consulted contribute to the
likelihood and orchestration of military engagement (Levy 1986).

Recording of experience   Inferences drawn from experience are recorded
in documents, accounts, files, standard operating procedures, and rule books;
the social and physical geography of organizational structures and relationships; standards of good professional practice; the culture of organizational stories; and shared perceptions of "the way things are done around
here." Relatively few details are known about the process by which organizational experience is accumulated in a structure of routines, but it is
clearly one that yields different kinds of routines in different situations and
is only partly successful in imposing internal consistency on organizational
memories.

   Not everything is recorded. The transformation of experience into routines and the recording of those routines involve costs. The costs are sensitive to information technology, and a common observation is that modern computer-based technology encourages the automation of routines by
substantially reducing the costs of recording them. Even so, a good deal of
experience is unrecorded simply because the costs are too great. Organizations also often distinguish between outcomes that are considered relevant for future actions and those that are not. The distinction may be
implicit—for example, when comparisons between projected and realized
returns from capital investment projects are ignored (Hägg 1979)—or it
may be explicit—as when exceptions to the rules are declared not to be
precedents for the future. By creating a set of actions that are not precedents, an organization gives routines both short-term flexibility and long-
term stability (Powell 1986).

Organizations vary in the emphasis they place on formal routines. Craft-based organizations rely more heavily on tacit knowledge than bureaucracies (Becker 1982). Organizations facing complex uncertainties rely on informally shared understandings more than organizations dealing with simpler, more stable environments (Ouchi 1980). Variation also exists within organizations. Higher-level managers rely more on ambiguous information (relative to formal rules) than lower-level managers (Daft & Lengel 1984).

Experiential knowledge, whether in tacit form or in formal rules, is recorded in an organizational memory. That memory is orderly, but it exhibits inconsistencies and ambiguities. Some of the contradictions are a consequence of inherent complications in maintaining consistency in inferences drawn sequentially from a changing experience. Some, however, reflect differences in experience, the confusions of history, and conflicting interpretations of that history. These latter inconsistencies are likely to be organized into deviant memories, maintained by subcultures, subgroups, and subunits (Martin, Sitkin, & Boehm 1985). With a change in the fortunes of the dominant coalition, the deviant memories become more salient to action (Martin & Siehl 1983).

Conservation of experience   Unless the implications of experience can be transferred from those who experienced it to those who did not, the lessons of history are likely to be lost through turnover of personnel. Written rules, oral traditions, and systems of formal and informal apprenticeships implicitly instruct new individuals in the lessons of history. Under many circumstances, the transfer of tradition is relatively straightforward and organizational experience is substantially conserved. For example, most police officers are socialized successfully to actions and beliefs recognizable as acceptable police behavior, even when those actions and beliefs are substantially different from those that led the individual to the career (Van Maanen 1973).

Under other circumstances, however, organizational experience is not conserved. Knowledge disappears from an organization's active memory (Neustadt & May 1986). Routines are not conserved because of limits on the time or legitimacy of the socializing agents, for example, in deviant subgroups or when the number of new members is large (Sproull, Weiner & Wolf 1978); because of conflict with other normative orders, for example, with new organization members who are also members of well-organized professions (Hall 1968); or because of the weaknesses of organizational control, for example, in implementation across geographic or cultural distances (Brytting 1986).

Retrieval of experience   Even within a consistent and accepted set of routines, only part of an organization's memory is likely to be evoked at a particular time, or in a particular part of the organization. Some parts of organizational memory are more available for retrieval than others. Availability is associated with a routine's frequency of use, the recency of its use, and its organizational proximity. Recently and frequently used routines are more easily evoked than those that have been used infrequently. Thus, organizations have difficulty retrieving relatively old, unused knowledge or skills (Argote, Beckman & Epple 1987). In cases in which routines are nested within more general routines, the repetitive use of lower-level routines tends to make them more accessible than the more general routines to which they are related (Merton 1940). The effects of proximity stem from the ways the accumulation of history is linked to regularized responsibility. The routines that record lessons of experience are organized around organizational responsibilities and are retrieved more easily when actions are taken through regular channels than when they occur outside those channels (Olsen 1983). At the same time, organizational structures create advocates for routines. Policies are converted into responsibilities that encourage rule zealotry (Mazmanian & Nienaber 1979).

Availability is also partly a matter of the direct costs of finding and using what is stored in memory. Particularly when there are large numbers of routines bearing on relatively specific actions, modern information technology has reduced those costs and made the routinization of relatively complex organizational behavior economically feasible, for example, in preparing reports or presentations, scheduling production or logistical support, designing structures or engineering systems, or analyzing financial statements (Smith & Green 1980). Such automation of the recovery of routines makes retrieval more reliable. Reliability is, however, a mixed blessing. It standardizes retrieval and thus typically underestimates the conflict of interest and ambiguity over preferences in an organization. Expert systems of the standard type have difficulty capturing the unpredictable richness, erratic redundancy, and casual validity checking of traditional retrieval procedures, and they reduce or eliminate the fortuitous experimentation of unreliable retrieval (Simon 1971; Wildavsky 1983). As a result, they can easily make learning more difficult for an organization.

Learning in More Complicated Worlds

Learning from the experience of others   Organizations capture the experience of other organizations through the transfer of encoded experience in the form of technologies, codes, procedures, or similar routines (Dutton & Starbuck 1978). This diffusion of experience and routines from other organizations within a community of organizations complicates theories of routine-based learning. It suggests that understanding the relationship between experiential learning and routines, strategies, or technologies in organizations requires attention to organizational networks (Håkansson 1987) as well as to the experience of the individual organization. At the same time, it makes the derivation of competitive strategies (e.g., pricing strategies) more complex than it would otherwise be (Hilke & Nelson 1987).

The standard literature on the epidemiology of disease or information distinguishes three broad processes of diffusion. The first is diffusion involving a single source broadcasting a disease to a population of potential, but not necessarily equally vulnerable, victims. Organizational examples include rules promulgated by governmental agencies, trade associations, professional associations, and unions (Scott 1985). The second process is diffusion involving the spread of a disease through contact between a member of the population who is infected and one who is not, sometimes mediated by a host carrier. Organizational examples include routines diffused by contacts among organizations, by consultants, and by the movement of personnel (Biggart 1977). The third process is two-stage diffusion involving the spread of a disease within a small group by contagion and then by broadcast from them to the remainder of a population. Organizational examples include routines communicated through formal and informal educational institutions, experts, and trade and popular publications (Heimer 1985a). In the organizational literature, these three processes have been labeled coercive, mimetic, and normative (DiMaggio & Powell 1983). All three are involved in a comprehensive system of information diffusion (Imai, Nonaka & Takeuchi 1985).

The possibilities for learning from the experience of others, as well as some of the difficulties, can be illustrated by looking at the diffusion of innovations among organizations. We consider here only some issues that are particularly important for organizational learning. For more general reviews of the literature, see Rogers & Shoemaker (1971) and Kimberly (1981).

Although it is not easy to untangle the effects of imitation from other effects that lead to differences in the time of adoption, studies of the spread of new technologies among organizations seem to indicate that diffusion through imitation is less significant than variation in the match between the technology and the organization (Mansfield 1968), especially as that match is discovered and molded through learning (Kay 1979). Imitation, on the other hand, has been credited with contributing substantially to diffusion of city manager plans among American cities (Knoke 1982) and multidivisional organizational structures among American firms (Fligstein 1985). Studies of the adoption of civil service reform by cities in the United States (Tolbert & Zucker 1983) and of high-technology weaponry by air forces (Eyre, Suchman & Alexander 1987) both show patterns of adoption in which features of the match between the procedures and the adopting organizations are more significant in explaining early adoptions than later ones, which seem to be better interpreted as due to imitation. The latter result is also supported by a study of the adoption of accounting conventions by firms (Mezias 1987).

The underlying ideas in the literature on the sociology of institutionalization are less epidemiological than functional, but the diffusion of practices and forms is one of the central mechanisms considered (Zucker 1987). Pressure on organizations to demonstrate that they are acting on collectively valued purposes in collectively valued ways leads them to copy ideas and practices from each other. The particular professions, policies, programs, laws, and public opinion that are created in the process of producing and marketing goods and services become powerful, institutionalized myths, which organizations adopt to establish legitimacy and ensure public support (Meyer & Rowan 1977; Zucker 1977). The process diffuses forms and procedures, and thereby tends to diffuse organizational power structures as well (Fligstein 1987).

The dynamics of imitation depend not only on the advantages that come to an organization as it profits from the experience of others, but also on the gains or losses that accrue to those organizations from which the routines or beliefs are drawn (DiMaggio & Powell 1983). In many (but not all) situations involving considerations of technical efficiency, diffusion of experience has negative consequences for organizations that are copied. This situation is typified by the case of technical secrets, in which sharing leads to loss of competitive position. In many (but not all) situations involving considerations of legitimacy, diffusion of experience has positive consequences for organizations that are copied. This situation is typified in accounting practices, in which case sharing leads to greater legitimacy for all concerned.

The critical factor for the dynamics is less whether the functional impetus is a concern for efficiency or legitimacy than whether the feedback effects are positive or negative (Wiewel & Hunter 1985). Where concerns for technical efficiency are associated with positive effects of sharing—for example, in many symbiotic relationships within an industry—the process unfolds in ways similar to the process of institutionalization. Where concerns for legitimacy are associated with negative effects of sharing—for example, in cases of diffusion in which mimicking by lower-status organizations reduces the lead organization's status—the process unfolds in ways similar to the spread of secrets.

Ecologies of learning   Organizations are collections of subunits learning in an environment that consists largely of other collections of learning subunits (Cangelosi & Dill 1965). The ecological structure is a complication in two senses. First, it complicates learning. Because of the simultaneously adapting behavior of other organizations, a routine may produce different outcomes at different times, or different routines may produce the same outcome at different times. Second, an ecology of learners complicates the systematic comprehension and modeling of learning processes. Environments change endogenously, and even relatively simple conceptions of learning become complex.

Ecologies of learning include various types of interactions among learners, but the classical type is a collection of competitors. Competitors are linked partly through the diffusion of experience; and to understand learning within competitive communities of organizations involves seeing how experience, particularly secrets, is shared (Sitkin 1986), and how organizational actors come to trust one another, or not (Zucker 1986). Competitors are also linked through the effects of their actions on each other. One organization's action is another's outcome. As a result, even if learning by an individual organization did not involve diffusion, it could be comprehended only by specifying the competitive structure.

Suppose competitors learn how to allocate resources to alternative technologies (strategies, procedures) in a world in which the return received by each competitor from the several technologies is a joint consequence of the potentials of the technologies, the changing competences of the several competitors within the technologies, and the allocations of effort by the several competitors among the technologies (Khandwalla 1981). In a situation of this type, it has been shown that there are strong ecological effects (Herriott, Levinthal & March 1985). The learning outcomes depend on the number of competitors, the rates at which they learn from their own experience, the rates at which they adjust their targets, the extent to which they learn from the experience of others, and the differences in the potentials of the technologies. Organizations tend to specialize, and faster learners often specialize in inferior technologies.

Learning itself can be viewed as one of the technologies within which organizations develop competence through use and among which they choose on the basis of experience. The general (nonecological) expectation is that learning procedures will become common when they lead to favorable outcomes and organizations will become effective at learning when they use learning routines frequently. The ecological question is whether properties of the relations among interacting organizations may lead some of them to learn to learn and not others.

In competitive situations, small differences in competence at learning tend to accumulate through the competency multiplier, driving slower learners to other procedures. If some organizations are powerful enough to create their own environments, weaker organizations learn to adapt to the dominant ones; that is, they learn to learn (Heimer 1985b). By the same token, powerful organizations, by virtue of their ability to ignore competition, are less inclined to learn from experience and less competent at doing so (Engwall 1976). The circumstances under which these learning disabilities produce a disadvantage, rather than an advantage, are more complicated than might appear, but there is a chance that a powerful organization will become incapable of coping with an environment it cannot arbitrarily enact (Hannan & Freeman 1984).

LEARNING AND INTELLIGENCE

Organizational learning from experience is not only a useful perspective from which to describe organizational change; it is also an important instrument of organizational intelligence. The speculation that learning can

improve the performance and thus the intelligence of organizations is confirmed by numerous studies of learning by doing, case observations, and
theoretical analyses.

Since we have defined learning as a process rather than an outcome, the
observation that learning is beneficial to organizations is not empty. It has
become commonplace to emphasize learning in the design of organizations, to argue that some important improvements in organizational intelligence can be achieved by giving organizations capabilities to learn quickly
and precisely (Starbuck & Dutton 1973; Duncan & Weiss 1979).

Structural Problems in Learning from Experience

Learning is often a form of organizational intelligence, but the complications in using learning are substantial. Moreover, those problems are not
due exclusively to avoidable individual and organizational inadequacies.
There are structural difficulties in learning from experience. The past is
not a perfect predictor of the future, and the experimental designs generated by ordinary life are far from ideal for casual inference (Brehmer 1980).

Making organizational learning effective as a tool for comprehending
history involves confronting several problems in the structure of organizational experience.

The paucity-of-experience problem   Learning from experience in organizations is compromised by the fact that nature provides inadequate experience relative to the complexities and instabilities of history, particularly
when the environment is changing rapidly or involves many dangers or
opportunities, each of which is very unlikely.

The redundancy-of-experience problem   Ordinary learning tends to lead
to stability in routines and extinguish the experimentation required to make
a learning process effective.

The complexity-of-experience problem   Organizational environments involve complicated causal systems, as well as interactions among learning
organizations. The various parts of the ecology fit together to produce
learning outcomes that are hard to interpret.

The problems of paucity, redundancy, and complexity in experience cannot
be eliminated, but they can be ameliorated. One response to the paucity
of experience is to augment direct experience through the diffusion of routines. Diffusion increases the amount of experience from which an organization draws and reduces vulnerability to local optima. However, sharing experience through diffusion can lead to remarkably incomplete or
flawed understandings. For example, if the experiences that are combined
are not independent, the advantages of sharing are attenuated, and organizations are prone to exaggerate the experience base of the encoded in-

formation. Indeed, part of what each organization learns from others is likely to echo its own previous knowledge (Andersen 1848).

Patience is a virtue. There is considerable evidence that organizations often change through a sequence of small, frequent changes and inferences from these experiences (Zald 1970). Since frequent changes accentuate the sample size problem by modifying a situation before it can be comprehended, such behavior is likely to lead to random drift rather than improvement (Lounamaa & March 1987). Reducing the frequency or magnitude of change, therefore, often aids comprehension, though the benefits of added information about one situation are purchases at the cost of reducing the information about others (Levinthal & Yao 1988).

The sample size problem is particularly acute in learning from low-probability, high-consequence events. Not only is the number of occurrences small, but the organizational, political, and legal significance of the events, if they occur, often muddies the inferences made about them with conflict over formal responsibility, accountability, and liability. One strategy for moderating the effects of these problems is to supplement history with histories of hypothetical events (Tamuz 1987). Such histories draw on a richer, less politically polarized set of interpretations, but their hypothetical nature introduces error.

Difficulties in overcoming the redundancy of experience and ensuring adequate variety of experience is a familiar theme for students of organizational change (Tushman & Romanelli 1985). Organizational slack facilitates unintentional innovation (March 1981), and success provides self-confidence in managers that leads to risk-taking (March & Shapira 1987); but in most other ways success is the enemy of experimentation (Maidique & Zirger 1985). Thus, concern for increasing experimentation in organizations focuses attention on mechanisms that produce variations in the failure rate, preferably independent of the performance level. One mechanism is noise in the measurement of performance. Random error or confusion in performance measurement produces arbitrary experiences of failure without a change in (real) performance (Hedberg & Jvnsson 1978). A second mechanism is aspiration level adjustment. An aspiration level that tracks past performance (but not too closely) produces a failure rate—and consequently a level of search and risk taking—that is relatively constant regardless of the absolute level of performance (March 1988).

A second source of experimentation in learning comes from imperfect routine maintenance: failures of memory, socialization, or control. Incomplete socialization of new organizational members leads to experimentation, as do errors in execution of routines or failures of implementation (Pressman & Wildavsky 1973). Although it seems axiomatic that most new ideas are bad ones (Hall 1976), the ideology of management and managerial experience combine to make managers a source of experimentation. Leaders are exhorted to introduce change; they are supposed to make a difference (MacCrimmon & Wehrung 1986). At the same time, individuals who have been successful in the past are systematically more likely to reach top-level positions in organizations that are individuals who have not. Their experience gives them an exaggerated confidence in the chances of success from experimentation and risk taking (March & Shapira 1987).

Overcoming the worst effects of complexity in experience involves improving the experimental design of natural experience. In particular, it involves making large changes rather than small ones and avoiding multiple simultaneous changes (Miller & Friesen 1982; Lounamaa & March 1987). From this point of view, the standard version of incrementalism—with its emphasis on frequent, multiple, small changes—cannot, in general, be a good learning strategy, particularly since it also violates the patience imperative discussed earlier (Starbuck 1983). Nor, as we have previously suggested, is it obvious that fast, precise learning is guaranteed to produce superior performance. Learning that is somewhat slow and somewhat imprecise often provides an advantage (Levinthal & March 1981; Herriott, Levinthal & March 1985).

The Intelligence of Learning

The concept of intelligence is ambiguous when action and learning occur simultaneously at several nested levels of a system (March 1987). For example, since experimentation often benefits those who copy successes more than it does the experimenting organization, managerial illusions of control, risk taking, and playful experimentation may be more intelligent from the point of view of a community of organizations than from the point of view of organizations that experiment. Although legal arrangements, such as patent laws, attempt to reserve certain benefits of experimentation to those organizations that incur the costs, these complications are generally not resolved by explicit contracts but through sets of evolved practices that implicitly balance the concerns of the several levels (March 1981). The issues involved are closely related to similar issues that arise in variation and selection models (Holland 1975; Gould 1982).

Even within a single organization, there are severe limitations to organizational learning as an instrument of intelligence. Learning does not always lead to intelligent behavior. The same processes that yield experiential wisdom produce superstitious learning, competency traps, and erroneous inferences. Problems in learning from experience stem partly from inadequacies of human cognitive habits, partly from features of organization, and partly from characteristics of the structure of experience. There are strategies for ameliorating some of those problems, but ordinary organizational practices do not always generate behavior that conforms to such strategies.

The pessimism of this description must, however, be qualified by two caveats. First, adequate evidence exists that the lessons of history encoded in routines are an important basis for the intelligence of organizations. Despite the problems, organizations learn. Second, learning needs to be compared with other serious alternatives, not with an ideal of perfection. Processes of choice, bargaining, and selection also make mistakes. If we calibrate the imperfections of learning by the imperfections of its competititors, it is possible to see a role for routine-based, history-dependent, target-oriented organizational learning. To be effective, however, the design of learning organizations must recognize the difficulties of the process, and in particular both the extent to which intelligence in learning is often frustrated and the extent to which a comprehension of history may involve slow rather than fast adaptation, imprecise rather than precise responses to experience, and abrupt rather than incremental changes.

REFERENCES

Andersen, H. C. 1848. Det er ganske vist. In *H. C. Andersens Eventyr* (1985), ed. P. Høybe, pp. 72–75. Copenhagen: Forlaget Notabene.

Argote, L., S. Beckman, and D. Epple. 1987. The persistence and transfer of learning in industrial settings. Paper presented at the St. Louis meetings of the Institute of Management Sciences (TIMS) and the Operations Research Society of America (ORSA).

Argyris, C., and D. Schön. 1978. *Organizational Learning.* Reading, Mass.: Addison-Wesley.

Arthur, W. B. 1984. *Competing technologies and economic prediction.* IIASA Options, No. 2:10–13.

Asher, H. 1956. *Cost–Quantity Relationships in the Airframe Industry.* Santa Monica, Calif.: Rand.

Astley, W. G. 1985. The two ecologies: population and community perspectives on organizational evolution. *Administrative Science Quarterly* 30:224–41.

Barley, S. R. 1988. The social construction of a machine: ritual, superstition, magical thinking and other pragmatic responses to running a CT scanner. In *Biomedicine Examined,* ed. M. Lock and D. Gordon. Dordrecht: Kluwer.

Becker, H. S. 1982. *Art Worlds.* Berkeley: University of California Press.

Beyer, J. M. 1981. Ideologies, values, and decision making in organizations. See Nystrom and Starbuck 1981, 2:166–202.

Biggart, N. W. 1977. The creative-destructive process of organizational change: the case of the post office. *Administrative Science Quarterly,* 22:410–26.

Brehmer, B. 1980. In one word: not from experience. *Acta Psychologica* 45:223–41.

Brown, R. H. 1978. Bureaucracy as praxis: toward a political phenomenology of formal organizations. *Administrative Science Quarterly* 23:365–82.

Brunsson, N. 1985. *The Irrational Organization: Irrationality as a Basis for Organizational Action and Change.* Chichester: Wiley.

Brytting, T. 1986. The management of distance in antiquity. *Scandinavian Journal of Management Studies* 3:139–55.

Burchell, S., C. Colin, and A. G. Hopwood. 1985. Accounting in its social context:

towards a history of value added in the United Kingdom. *Accounting, Organizations and Society* 10:381–413.

Burgelman, R. A. 1988. Strategy-making as a social learning process: the case of internal corporate venturing. *Interfaces* 18:74–85.

Cangelosi, V. E., and W. R. Dill. 1965. Organizational learning: observations toward a theory. *Administrative Science Quarterly* 10:175–203.

Carroll, G. R. 1984. Organizational ecology. *Annual Review of Sociology* 10:71–93.

Clark, B. R. 1972. The organizational saga in higher education. *Administrative Science Quarterly* 17:178–84.

Cooper, A. C., and D. E. Schendel. 1976. Strategic responses to technological threats. *Business Horizons* 19 (1): 61–63.

Cyert, R. M., and J. G. March. 1963. *A Behavioral Theory of the Firm.* Englewood Cliffs, N.J.: Prentice-Hall.

Daft, R. L., and R. H. Lengel. 1984. Information richness: a new approach to managerial behavior and organization design. In *Research in Organizational Behavior,* eds. B. M. Staw and L. L. Cummings, 6:191–223. Greenwich, Conn.: JAI Press.

Daft, R. L., and K. E. Weick. 1984. Toward a model of organizations as interpretation systems. *Academy of Management Review* 9:284–95.

Day, G. S., and D. B. Montgomery. 1983. Diagnosing the experience curve. *Journal of Marketing* 47:44–58.

DiMaggio, P. J., and W. W. Powell. 1983. The iron cage revisited: institutional isomorphism and collective rationality in organizational fields. *American Sociological Review* 48:147–60.

Duncan, R., and A. Weiss. 1979. Organizational learning: implications for organizational design. In *Research in Organizational Behavior,* ed. B. M. Staw, 1:75–123. Greenwich, Conn.: JAI Press.

Dutton, J. M., and R. D. Freedman. 1985. External environment and internal strategies: calculating, experimenting, and imitating in organizations. In *Advances in Strategic Management,* ed. R. B. Lamb, 3:39–67. Greenwhich, Conn.: JAI Press.

Dutton, J. M., and W. H. Starbuck. 1978. Diffusion of an intellectual technology. In *Communication and Control in Society,* ed. K. Krippendorff, pp. 489–511. New York: Gordon and Breach.

Dutton, J. M., and A. Thomas. 1984. Treating progress functions as a managerial opportunity. *Academy of Management Review* 9:235–47.

Dutton, J. M., and A. Thomas. 1985. Relating technological change and learning by doing. In *Research on Technological Innovation, Management and Policy,* ed. R. S. Rosenbloom, 2:187–224. Greenwich, Conn.: JAI Press.

Dutton, J. M., A. Thomas, and J. E. Butler. 1984. The history of progress functions as a managerial technology. *Business History Review* 58:204–33.

Einhorn, E. J., and R. M. Hogarth. 1986. Judging probable cause. *Psychological Bulletin* 99:3–19.

Engwall, L. 1976. Response time of organizations. *Journal of Management Studies,* 13:1–15.

Eyre, D. P., M. C. Suchman, and V. D. Alexander. 1987. The social construction of weapons procurement: proliferation as rational myth. Paper read at the annual meetings of the American Sociological Association, Chicago.

Fiol, C. M., and M. A. Lyles. 1985. Organizational learning. *Academy of Management Review,* 10:803–13.

Fischhoff, B. 1975. Hindsight or foresight: the effect of outcome knowledge on judgment under uncertainty. *Journal of Experimental Psychology: Human Perception and Performance* 1:288–99.

Fligstein, N. 1985. The spread of the mutidivisional form among large firms, 1919–1979. *American Sociological Review* 50:377–91.

Fligstein, N. 1987. The intraorganizational power struggle: rise of finance personnel to top leadership in large corporations, 1919–1979. *American Sociological Review* 52:44–58.

Gould, S. J. 1982. Darwinism and the expansion of evolutionary theory. *Science* 216:380–87.

Grandori, A. 1987. *Perspectives on Organization Theory.* Cambridge, Mass.: Ballinger.

Hägg, I. 1979. Reviews of capital investments: empirical studies. *Finnish Journal of Business Economics* 28:211–25.

Håkansson, H. 1987. *Industrial Technological Development: A Network Approach.* London: Croom Helm.

Hall, R. H. 1968. Professionalization and bureaucratization. *American Sociological Review* 33:92–104.

Hall, R. I. 1976. A system pathology of an organization: the rise and fall of the old *Saturday Evening Post. Administrative Science Quarterly* 21:185–211.

Hannan, M. T., and J. Freeman. 1977. The population ecology of organizations. *American Journal of Sociology* 82:929–64.

Hannan, M. T., and J. Freeman. 1984. Structural inertia and organizational change. *American Sociological Review* 49:149–64.

Harrison, J. R., and J. G. March. 1984. Decision making and post-decision surprises. *Administrative Science Quarterly* 29:26–42.

Hastie, R., B. Park, and R. Weber. 1984. Social memory. In *Handbook of Social Cognition,* eds. R. S. Wyer and T. K. Srull, 2:151–212. Hillsdale, N.J.: Lawrence Erlbaum Associates.

Hedberg, B. L. T. 1981. How organizations learn and unlearn. See Nystrom and Starbuck 1981, 1:3–27.

Hedberg, B. L. T., and S. Jönsson. 1978. Designing semiconfusing information systems for organizations in changing environments. *Accounting, Organizations and Society* 3:47–64.

Heimer, C. A. 1985a. *Reactive Risk and Rational Action: Managing Moral Hazard in Insurance Contracts.* Berkeley: University of California Press.

Heimer, C. A. 1985b. Allocating information costs in a negotiated information order: interorganizational constraints on decision making in Norwegian oil insurance. *Administrative Science Quarterly* 30:395–417.

Herriott, S. R., D. Levinthal, and J. G. March. 1985. Learning from experience in organizations. *American Economic Review* 75:298–302.

Hilke, J. C., and P. B. Nelson. 1987. Caveat innovator: strategic and structural characteristics of new product innovations. *Journal of Economic Behavior and Organization* 8:213–29.

Holland, J. H. 1975. *Adaptation in Natural and Artificial Systems: An Introductory Analysis with Applications to Biology, Control and Artificial Intelligence.* Ann Arbor: University of Michigan Press.

Hollander, S. 1965. *The Sources of Increased Efficiency: A Study of DuPont Rayon Manufacturing Plants*. Cambridge, Mass.: MIT Press.

House, R. J., and J. V. Singh. 1987. Organizational behavior: some new directions for I/O psychology. *Annual Review of Psychology* 38:669–718.

Imai, K., I. Nonaka, and H. Takeuchi. 1985. Managing the new product development process: how Japanese companies learn and unlearn. In *The Uneasy Alliance*, eds. K. Clark, R. Hayes, and C. Lorentz, pp. 337–75. Boston: Harvard Graduate School of Business.

Johnson, H. T., and R. S. Kaplan. 1987. *Relevance Lost: The Rise and Fall of Management Accounting*. Boston: Harvard Business School Press.

Johnson, M. K., and L. Hasher. 1987. Human learning and memory. *Annual Review of Psychology* 38:631–68.

Kahneman, D., P. Slovic, and A. Tversky, eds. 1982. *Judgment under Uncertainty: Heuristics and Biases*. Cambridge: Cambridge University Press.

Kay, N. M. 1979. *The Innovating Firm: A Behavioral Theory of Corporate R&D*. New York: St. Martin's Press.

Khandwalla, P. N. 1981. Properties of competing organizations. See Nystrom and Starbuck 1981, 1:409–32.

Kimberly, J. R. 1981. Managerial innovation. See Nystrom and Starbuck 1981, 1:84–104.

Knoke, D. 1982. The spread of municipal reform: temporal, spatial, and social dynamics. *American Journal of Sociology* 87:1314–39.

Krieger, S. 1979. *Hip Capitalism*. Beverly Hills: Sage Publications.

Lant, T. K. 1987. Goals, search, and risk taking in strategic decision making. PhD thesis, Stanford University.

Levinthal, D. A., and J. G. March. 1981. A model of adaptive organizational search. *Journal of Economic Behavior and Organization* 2:307–33.

Levinthal, D. A., and D. A. Yao. 1988. The search for excellence: organizational inertia and adaptation. Unpublished paper, Carnegie-Mellon University.

Levy, J. S. 1986. Organizational routines and the causes of war. *International Studies Quarterly* 30:193–222.

Lindblom, C. E. 1959. The "science" of muddling through. *Public Administration Review* 19:79–88.

Lounamaa, P. H., and J. G. March. 1987. Adaptive coordination of a learning team. *Management Science* 33:107–23.

Machina, M. J. 1987. Choice under uncertainty: problems solved and unsolved. *Journal of Economic Perspectives* 1:121–54.

MacCrimmon, K. R., and D. A. Wehrung. 1986. *Taking Risks: The Management of Uncertainty*. New York: Free Press.

MacRae, D. 1985. *Policy Indicators*. Chapel Hill: University of North Carolina Press.

Maidique, M. A., and B. J. Zirger. 1985. The new product learning cycle. *Research Policy* 14:299–313.

Mansfield, E. 1968. *The Economics of Technological Change*. New York: Norton.

March, J. G. 1981. Footnotes to organizational change. *Administrative Science Quarterly* 26:563–77.

March, J. G. 1987. Ambiguity and accounting: the elusive link between information and decision making. *Accounting, Organizations and Society* 12:153–68.

March, J. G. 1988. Variable risk preferences and adaptive aspirations. *Journal of Economic Behavior and Organization* 9:5–24.

March, J. G., and J. P. Olsen. 1975. The uncertainty of the past: organizational learning under ambiguity. *European Journal of Political Research* 3:147–71.

March, J. G., and Z. Shapira. 1987. Managerial perspectives on risk and risk taking. *Management Science* 33:1404–18.

Martin, J., and C. Siehl. 1983. Organizational culture and counterculture: an uneasy symbiosis. *Organizational Dynamics* (Autumn):52–64.

Martin, J., S. B. Sitkin, and M. Boehm. 1985. Founders and the elusiveness of a cultural legacy. In *Organizational Culture,* eds. P. J. Frost, L. F. Moore, M. R. Louis, C. C. Lundberg, and J. Martin, pp. 99–124. Beverly Hills: Sage Publications.

Mazmanian, D. A., and J. Nienaber. 1979. *Can Organizations Change? Environmental Protection, Citizen Participation, and the Corps of Engineers.* Washington, D.C.: The Brookings Institution.

Merton, R. K. 1940. Bureaucratic structure and personality. *Social Forces* 18:560–68.

Meyer, J. W., and B. Rowan. 1977. Institutionalized organizations: formal structure as myth and ceremony. *American Journal of Sociology* 83:340–63.

Mezias, S. J. 1987. Technical and institutional sources of organizational practices: the case of a financial reporting method. PhD thesis, Stanford University.

Miller, D. T., and M. Ross. 1975. Self-serving biases in the attribution of causality. *Psychological Bulletin* 82:213–25.

Miller, D., and P. Friesen. 1982. Structural change and performance: quantum vs. piecemeal-incremental approaches. *Academy of Management Journal* 25:867–92.

Moore, M. H., and M. J. Gates. 1986. *Inspector-General: Junkyard Dogs or Man's Best Friend?* New York: Russell Sage Foundation.

Muth, J. F. 1986. Search theory and the manufacturing progress function. *Management Science* 32:948–62.

Nelson, R. R., and S. G. Winter. 1982. *An Evolutionary Theory of Economic Change.* Cambridge, Mass.: Harvard University Press.

Neustadt, R. E., and E. R. May. 1986. *Thinking in Time: The Uses of History for Decision Makers.* New York: Free Press.

Nystrom, N. C., and W. H. Starbuck, eds. 1981. *Handbook of Organizational Design.* Oxford: Oxford University Press.

Nystrom, N. C., and W. H. Starbuck. 1984. To avoid organizational crisis, unlearn. *Organizational Dynamics* (Spring):53–65.

Olsen, J. P. 1976. The process of interpreting organizational history. In *Ambiguity and Choice in Organizations,* eds. J. G. March and J. P. Olsen, pp. 338–50. Bergen: Universitetsforlaget.

Olsen, J. P. 1983. *Organized Democracy.* Bergen: Universitetsforlaget.

Ouchi, W. G. 1980. Markets, bureaucracies and clans. *Administrative Science Quarterly* 25:129–41.

Pettigrew, A. M. 1985. *The Awakening Giant: Continuity and Change in Imperial Chemical Industries.* Oxford: Basil Blackwell.

Pfeffer, J. 1981. *Power in Organizations.* Marshfield, Mass.: Pitman Publishing.

Powell, W. W. 1986. How the past informs the present: the uses and liabilities of organizational memory. Paper read at the Conference on Communication and Collective Memory, Annenberg School, University of Southern California.

Pressman, J. L., and A. B. Wildavsky. 1973. *Implementation.* Berkeley: University of California Press.

Preston, L., and E. C. Keachie. 1964. Cost functions and progress functions: an integration. *American Economic Review* 54:100–7.

Radner, R. 1975. A behavioral model of cost reduction. *Bell Journal of Economics* 6:196–215.

Rapping, L. 1965. Learning and World War II production functions. *Review of Economics and Statistics* 47:81–86.

Rogers, E. M., and F. F. Shoemaker. 1971. *Communication of Innovations.* New York: Free Press.

Rosenberg, N. 1982. *Inside the Black Box: Technology and Economics.* Cambridge: Cambridge University Press.

Ross, J., and B. M. Staw. 1986. Expo 86: an escalation prototype. *Administrative Science Quarterly* 31:274–97.

Røvik, K.-A. 1987. Læringssystemer og Læringsatferd i Offentlig Forvaltning: En Studie av Styringens Kunnskapsgrunnlag. Universitetet i Tromsø, Norway.

Scott, W. R. 1985. Conflicting levels of rationality: regulators, managers, and professionals in the medical care sector. *Journal of Health Administration Education* 3:113–31.

Scott, W. R. 1987. *Organizations: Rational, Natural, and Open Systems,* 2d ed. Englewood Cliffs, N.J.: Prentice-Hall.

Siegel, S. 1957. Level of aspiration and decision making. *Psychological Review* 64:253–62.

Simon, H. A. 1955. A behavioral model of rational choice. *Quarterly Journal of Economics* 69:99–118.

Simon, H. A. 1971. Designing organizations for an information rich world. In *Computers, Communications and the Public Interest,* ed. M. Greenberger, pp. 37–52. Baltimore: Johns Hopkins University Press.

Sitkin, S. B. 1986. Secrecy in organizations: determinants of secrecy behavior among engineers in three Silicon Valley semiconductor firms. PhD thesis, Stanford University.

Slovic, P., B. Fischhoff, and S. Lichtenstein. 1977. Behavioral decision theory. *Annual Review of Psychology* 28:1–39.

Smith, H. T., and T. R. G. Green, 1980. *Human Interaction with Computers.* New York: Academic Press.

Sproull, L. S. 1981. Beliefs in organizations. See Nystrom and Starbuck (1981) 2:203–24.

Sproull, L. S., S. Weiner, and D. Wolf. 1978. *Organizing an Anarchy: Belief, Bureaucracy, and Politics in the National Institute of Education.* Chicago: University of Chicago Press.

Starbuck, W. H. 1983. Organizations as action generators. *American Sociological Review* 48:91–102.

Starbuck, W. H. 1976. Organizations and their environments. In *Handbook of Industrial and Organizational Psychology,* ed. M. D. Dunnette, pp. 1067–123. Chicago: Rand McNally.

Starbuck, W. H., and J. M. Dutton. 1973. Designing adaptive organizations. *Journal of Business Policy* 3:21–28.

Starbuck, W. H., and F. J. Milliken, 1988. Executives' perceptual filters: what they notice and how they make sense. In *The Executive Effect: Concepts and Methods for Studying Top Managers,* ed. D. Hambrick. Greenwich, Conn.: JAI Press.

Staw, B. M., and J. Ross. 1978. Commitment to a policy decision: a multi-theoretical perspective. *Administrative Science Quarterly* 23:40–64.

Steinbruner, J. D. 1974. *The Cybernetic Theory of Decision.* Princeton, NJ: Princeton University Press.

Stinchcombe, A. L. 1986. *Stratification and Organization.* Cambridge: Cambridge University Press.

Tamuz, M. 1987. The impact of computer surveillance on air safety reporting. *Columbia Journal of World Business* 22:69–77.

Thompson, J. D. 1967. *Organizations in Action.* New York: McGraw-Hill.

Tirole, J. 1986. Hierarchies and bureaucracies: on the role of collusion in organizations. *Journal of Law, Economics and Organization* 2:181–214.

Tolbert, P. S., and L. G. Zucker. 1983. Institutional sources of change in the formal structure of organizations: the diffusion of civil service reform, 1880–1935. *Administrative Science Quarterly* 28:22–39.

Tushman, M. L., and E. Romanelli. 1985. Organizational evolution: a metamorphosis model of convergence and reorientation. In *Research in Organizational Behavior,* eds. L. L. Cummings and B. M. Staw, 7:171–222. Greenwich, Conn.: JAI Press.

Van Maanen, J. 1973. Observations on the making of policemen. *Human Organization* 32:407–18.

Weick, K. E. 1979. *The Social Psychology of Organizing,* 2d ed. Reading, Mass.: Addison-Wesley.

Whetten, D. A. 1987. Organizational growth and decline processes. *Annual Review of Sociology* 13:335–58.

Wiewel, W., and A. Hunter. 1985. The interorganizational network as a resource: a comparative case study on organizational genesis. *Administrative Science Quarterly* 30:482–96.

Wildavsky, A. 1983. Information as an organizational problem. *Journal of Management Studies* 20:29–40.

Winter, S. G. 1986. The research program of the behavioral theory of the firm; orthodox critique and evolutionary perspective. In *Handbook of Behavioral Economics,* eds. B. Gilad and S. Kaish, 1:151–87. Greenwich, Conn.: JAI Press.

Wright, T. P. 1936. Factors affecting the cost of airplanes. *Journal of Aeonautical Sciences* 3:122–28.

Yelle, L. E. 1979. The learning curve: historical review and comprehensive survey. *Decision Sciences* 10:302–28.

Zald, M. N. 1970. *Organizational Change: The Political Economy of the YMCA.* Chicago: University of Chicago Press.

Zucker, L. G. 1977. The role of institutionalization in cultural persistence. *American Sociological Review* 42:726–43.

Zucker, L. G. 1986. Production of trust: institutional sources of economic structure, 1840 to 1920. In *Research in Organizational Behavior,* eds. L. L. Cummings and B. M. Staw, 8:55–111. Greenwich, Conn.: JAI Press.

Zucker, L. G. 1987. Institutional theories of organization. *Annual Review of Sociology,* 13:443–64.

2

Symbols and Organizations:
From Barnard to the Institutionalists

W. RICHARD SCOTT

An important benefit of receiving invitations to participate in events such as that being celebrated by the present volume is that it forces us to do what we should be doing as a matter of course: reread the classics. And Chester I. Barnard's *Functions of the Executive* is a classic! I had forgotten how many of our current ideas concerning organizations stem from his early ingenuity; and I was surprised to find, tucked in among the more familiar arguments, neglected suggestions and unexpected insights.

This chapter is organized in three parts. In the first, I discuss Barnard's impact on the development of organization theory generally. In the second, I focus attention on his contributions to our understanding of the symbolic aspects of organizations. In the third and final section, I consider some more recent lines of work that build on Barnard's foundation, but represent somewhat novel lines of investigation.

BARNARD AND THE DEVELOPMENT OF ORGANIZATION THEORY

Barnard: Rational System Theorist

Barnard provides one of the strongest and most articulate statements in the literature of a rational system conception of organizations. Rational system theorists view organizations as deliberately designed instruments for the attainment of specified goals (see Scott 1987b, pp. 31–35). His succinct definition is justly famous: "Formal organization is that kind of cooperation among men [*sic*] that is conscious, deliberate, purposeful" (Barnard 1938, p. 4).

Long before Simon, Barnard perceived that organizational systems could compensate for the cognitive limitations of individuals. By specifying ends, developing subgoals, and routing information to specialized decision makers, one could achieve consistency of purpose and attain the benefits of cooperative action. "What is important here . . . is the superlative degree to which logical processes must and can characterize organization action as contrasted with individual action, and the degree to which decision is specialized in organization. It is the deliberate adoption of means to ends which is the essence of formal organization" (Barnard 1938, p. 186).

And, as is well known, Barnard provides a lucid analysis of the "economy of incentives" required to secure contributions from individual participants to organizational purposes. This work became the basis for the Barnard–Simon theory of contributions–inducements on which organizational equilibrium is founded. Only when organizations are successful in securing incentives sufficient to motivate individuals to continue to participate (make contributions of time, energy, and resources) can the organization survive (see Barnard 1938, pp. 139ff.; Simon 1957, pp. 110–22; March and Simon 1958, pp. 83–88).

It is in this frame of mind that Barnard argued that "the functions of the executive . . . are those of control, management, supervision, administration, in formal organizations" (Barnard 1938, p. 6).

Thus, it is no mystery why sophisticated rational system theorists, from Simon to Williamson, have turned to Barnard for inspiration and guidance.

Barnard: Natural System Theorist

There is another, very different side to Barnard's theory of organization. More than most early theorists, Barnard was acutely aware that organizations were also nonrational systems. He was among the first to insist that the formal structures of organizations are supplemented and supported by informal systems. He realized that "informal organizations are necessary to the operation of formal organizations as a means of communication, of cohesion, and of protecting the integrity of the individual" (Barnard 1938, p. 123). While recognizing the importance of economic incentives to reward contributions, he stressed that the most important inducements are those of "a personal, non-materialistic character," including

> the opportunities for distinction, prestige, personal power, and the attainment of dominating position . . . [and] ideal benefactions [such as] pride of workmanship, sense of adequacy, altruistic service for family or others, loyalty to organization in patriotism, etc., aesthetic and religious feeling. . . ."
>
> The most intangible and subtle of incentives is that which I have called the condition of communion. . . . It is the feeling of personal comfort in social relations that is sometimes called solidarity, social integration, the gregarious instinct, or social security (in the original, not in its present debased economic, sense). (Barnard 1938, pp. 145–46, 148)

And, in this vein, Barnard does not stress the executive's functions of management, supervision, and administration, but instead views as the executive's principal function "to formulate and define the purposes, objectives, ends, of the organizations. . . . The function of formulating grand purposes and providing for their redefinition is one which needs sensitive systems of communication, experience in interpretation, imagination, and delegation of responsibility" (Barnard 1938, pp. 231, 233).

This is a different Barnard—one who has shifted his melody from the brass to violins. This is the Barnard followed not by Simon but by Selznick (1957); not by Williamson but by Wilson (1973) and by Peters and Waterman (1982). It is the influence of this facet of Barnard, as a natural system theorist stressing the nonrational aspects of organization, that I want to trace here, with the certainty that his rational system contributions are appropriately celebrated in the chapters contributed by Hart, Moe, and Williamson, among others.

But before proceeding with this task, I wish to comment briefly on the duality that characterizes Barnard's work.

Barnard: Rational *and* Natural System Theorist

One image that comes to mind when we encounter the two divergent perspectives that can be detected in Barnard's views is a Janus-faced visage—a two-faced image looking simultaneously in different directions, perceiving contrasting aspects of organizations. For many purposes, two faces may be superior to one. But it is better, I think, to view Barnard as a kind of Colossus: a theorist who consciously attempted to straddle two apparently different and irreconcilible views of organizations. To the question, Are organizations rational or natural systems? Barnard's response would have been, Both! And it is the foolish manager who attends to only one side while neglecting the other. More than other theorists before or since, Barnard emphasized the dual nature of organizations.[1]

Consider his views on formal and informal structure. He grants them equal importance and insists on their interdependence: "Formal organizations arise out of and are necessary to informal organizations; but when formal organizations come into operation, they create and require informal organizations" (Barnard 1938, p. 120). Similarly, he insisted that authority is both top-down and bottom-up. On the one hand, "Men impute authority to communications from superior positions. . . . This authority is to a considerable extent independent of the personal ability of the incumbent of the position. . . . This is the authority of position" (Barnard 1938, p. 173). On the other hand, the decision as to whether an order has authority or not "lies with the persons to whom it is addressed, and does not reside in 'persons of authority' or those who issue these orders" (Barnard 1938, p. 163).

In short, Barnard exhibited an extraordinary awareness of the subtlety and complexity, of the interdependence of rational and natural forces. In this respect, he was far ahead of his time—indeed, perhaps he remains ahead of our own time.

BARNARD AND THE SYMBOLIC ASPECTS OF ORGANIZATIONS

In emphasizing Barnard's influence on the development of the natural system perspective in organization theory, I focus on two clusters of work. In the first, concerned with the analysis of symbolic control systems within organizations, his influence is quite direct and palpable. In the second, dealing with the institutional aspects of organizational environments, his influence is less obvious and strong.

Symbolic Control Systems

Two strands of work dealing with symbolic control systems in organizations strongly reflect Barnard's imprint: his discussion of the symbolic functions of leaders and his analysis of corporate cultures.

Leaders as manipulators of symbols   Although he does not use these terms, Barnard clearly differentiated between two types of leadership functions: cognitive and cathectic (see Scott, 1987b, p. 268). The cognitive side emphasizes the analytic aspects of decisions: the ways in which leaders act to guide the choices of their subordinates. Barnard anticipated Simon's distinction between value and factual premises, recognizing that, although all decisions incorporate both components, decisions involving heavier value loadings are typically made higher in the hierarchy than those placing emphasis on factual components. He notes that

> Responsibility for abstract, generalizing, prospective, long-run decision is delegated *up* the line, responsibility for definition, action, remains always at the base where the authority for effort resides.

> The formulation and definition of purpose is then a widely distributed function, only the more general part of which is executive. (Barnard 1938, pp. 232–33)

Such passages emphasize the cognitive functions of purposes: guiding, directing, and constraining choices and, presumably, actions.

But other, more eloquent parts of Barnard's discourse stress the cathectic—the emotional, motivational aspects of goal setting. Individuals must be moved to act, and they must develop faith in and commitment to a larger moral purpose. Barnard emphasizes the

> great role of persuasion in securing adherence to organization and submission to its requirements . . . [Given] the limitations imposed by the physical environment and the biological constitution of human beings, the uncertainties of

the outcome of cooperation, the difficulties of common understanding of purpose . . . [and many similar factors]—all of these elements of organization
. . . spell the necessity of leadership, the power of individuals to inspire cooperative personal decision by creating faith: faith in common understanding,
faith in the probability of success, faith in the ultimate satisfaction of personal
motives . . . (Barnard 1938, p. 259)

This aspect of leadership has been pursued and elaborated by organizational theorists such as Selznick (1957), who viewed leaders as defining,
shaping, and protecting values. It is leadership that transforms a mechanistic organization into a purposive and committed institutional system,
shaped and driven by the pursuit of precious, and often precarious, values
(see Clark 1960). Managers can oversee routine decisions: decisions that
leave the structure unchanged. Only leaders can make critical decisions:
choices that select and shape the ends of organizations. Other organizational analysts, such as Chandler (1962, p. 11), have proposed a similar
distinction between entrepreneurial or strategic decisions and operating decisions.

Such views have not been without their critics. Wolin (1960) provides
an excoriating critique of organization theories such as Barnard's that attempt, in his view, to obscure the political aspects of administrative systems; and Perrow (1986, pp. 62–68) is more than usually caustic in point-
ing out the manipulative and exploitative aspects of what he terms
"Barnard's company town."

Recent theorists have developed a somewhat different version of the
symbolic functions of leaders. Following the work of Edelman (1964) on
the symbolic functions of political leadership, Pfeffer (1981) has argued
that leaders emphasize their symbolic functions because they are unable to
control the organization's actual activities or, particularly, its outcomes—
its successes and failures. In this more cynical view, leaders succeed not by
setting and achieving objectives or controlling events, but by managing the
interpretation of events. Rationality is retrospective (see Weick 1979; March
& Olsen 1976); purposes do not arise out of visions of future possibilities
but are constructed through (re)interpretations of past actions. Barnard's
conception of the role of the moral leader has, at least in some views, been
succeeded by the disparaging view of ineffectual executives who must be
rescued by the rhetorical skills of the "spin doctors."

Once again, however, we note the subtlety of Barnard's conception—
the emphasis on contrasting but not necessarily incompatible aspects of a
phenomenon. His dualistic view of leadership stressed both the cognitive
(guiding) and the cathetic (motivating) functions of the leadership role.

Corporate cultures   More than any other single theorist, Barnard is the
father of the concept of corporate culture. The entire second half of his
Functions of the Executive is one long excursus on the importance of creating
a shared vision or purpose, the necessity of generating common meanings

and enhanced commitment, and the virtues of increasing individuals' "capacity to be dominated by organizational personality" (Barnard 1938, p. 221). Along with but even more than his contemporaries, the human relations theorists, Barnard recognized that shared values and meanings, internalized by participants, could constitute a strong system of control—much more powerful than one based exclusively on material rewards or on force.[2]

For a time, Barnard's insights remained undeveloped and, to many readers, seemed quaint and old-fashioned. But a new generation of analysts, including Deal and Kennedy (1982), Ouchi (1980), and Peters and Waterman (1982), has rediscovered and reemphasized the importance of these normative and cognitive control systems. Peters and Waterman (1982, pp. 85, 117) acknowledge their indebtedness to Barnard: "We, in our comments on the excellent companies, were anticipated decades ago by both Chester Barnard . . . and Philip Selznick. . . . There's nothing new under the sun. Selznick and Barnard talked about culture and value shaping forty years ago."

Recently, students of organizations have attempted to move beyond the efforts of these prescriptive approaches, which assert the importance of culture, to begin to treat the phenomenon more analytically. Many challenges confront those who seek to study corporate culture: how best to describe and measure cultures; how to determine how widely shared and salient a set of beliefs and values are; how to deal with inconsistent and competing belief systems; how to understand the ways in which cultural elements are used—selected, reconstructed, interpreted—by individual actors; how to understand the ways in which cultural symbols can and cannot be managed. Serious efforts to answer these questions are now underway (see Frost et al. 1985; Martin & Meyerson 1986; Pondy 1982; Schein 1985; Smiricich 1983; Swidler 1986), but much remains to be learned about how cultures are created and changed and how they function as systems of motivation and control.

Unlike his more general analysis of organizational structure and of leadership, Barnard's analysis of organizational culture gave less emphasis to their more rational and cognitive aspects than to the nonrational, motivational aspects. To some extent, this deficiency has been remedied by the efforts of the ethnomethodologists, who have taken up the challenge of examining how common images, meanings, and interpretations arise in interaction, creating a shared social reality (see, for example, Bittner 1967; Cicourel 1968). Weick and his associates have also emphasized the centrality of these cognitive processes in molding and maintaining shared systems of actions (see Weick 1979; Pondy 1983).

A general deficiency in much of the recent work on organizational culture is that, unlike most important approaches to understanding organizations in recent decades, it remains within a closed system framework. Organizational cultures are viewed primarily as resulting from internal organizational forces—from shared values developed out of interactions, a common history, and critical events generating distinctive meanings and particular heros and sagas. This deficiency is at least partly addressed by recent work on institutional environments.

Institutional Environments

Barnard's direct influence on current efforts to examine institutional environments of organizations is, as noted, not strong. I had expected to be able to state that Barnard's work shunted attention away from the effects of wider environmental forces on organizations to focus attention exclusively on internal processes. However, my recent rereading of *Functions of the Executive* persuades me that such a judgment would be both unfair and inaccurate. He gave much more attention to organizational environments than I had remembered.

For example, his conceptual model of organizations as systems of consciously coordinated activities rather than persons strongly pushes in the direction of an open systems perspective, since it recognizes that individuals "stand outside all organizations and have multiple relationships with them" (Barnard 1938, p. 100). This insight has been enthusiastically embraced by such open systems theorists as Weick (1969, p. 46), who states that "It is vital to note that it is behaviors, not persons, that are interstuctured," although Weick credits Allport (1962) with the insight.[3] Pfeffer and Salancik (1978, p. 30), in their influential volume on environmental forces, stress the same concept but attribute it to Weick and Allport.

Even more directly relevant, Barnard (1938, p. 196) recognized that all organizations operate in environments, both physical and social. He recognized that the environment of an organization depends on the purposes or goals of that organization, and so anticipated the important concept of "domain." He even briefly discusses relations among organization, recognizing that many organizations are "incomplete, subordinate, and dependent" and asserting that "all organizations except the state or a church are partial systems, being parts of larger systems, and can only be regarded as in isolation and independent within special limits" (Barnard 1938, p. 98).

Although in these and other passages, Barnard did acknowledge the importance of the environment, he did not attempt to follow up these insights systematically. This pursuit, in my view, has been the most important feature of contemporary organization theory. Attaining a better understanding of the vital role environments play in creating and shaping organizational structures and activities has dominated the agenda of organization theorists since the early 1960s. Nor did Barnard perceive the important ways in which environments symbolically shape organizations.

Changing conceptions of environments   Our conception of organizational environments has been undergoing rapid and varied transformations. To begin with, analysts no longer treat the environment as a residual category, as everything that is "external to" or "not part of" the organization. Another important change involves a shift from a focus on generalized attributes of environments to more specific interorganizational connections. Early efforts were directed at identifying important features or dimensions of environments (e.g., uncertainty, complexity, munificence), which could then be used to predict the structural features or behavior of organizations. More recent work has emphasized the value of identifying salient relations and flows linking particular organizations. Thus, DiMaggio (1986, p. 337) argues as follows:

> For most organizations, the salient environment is composed of a specific set of other organizations, often identifiably members of the same organizational field. It is less useful to learn that an organization's environment is "munificient" or "turbulent" than to identify the organizational sources of such munificence or turbulence. [Moreover] . . . the effects of environmental variables may depend on the position that an organization occupies in its field. . . .

A third important change in how environments are viewed involves shifting the level of analysis upward and expanding the scope of our purview. Early models, such as those proposed by Evan (1966) focused attention on organizational *sets*—a single focal organization and its relevant exchange partners. Later models suggested the value of encompassing *populations*— all organizations of a given type, in order to examine how such distributions of organizational forms survive, reproduce, or fail over time as a function of changes in their environments (see Aldrich & Pfeffer 1976; Hannan & Freeman 1977). Other models examined the ways in which various populations of organizations, organized into *communities* made up of both supportive and competitive relations, adapted to environments employing both individual and communal strategies (see Warren 1967; Astley 1985). And still others have emphasized the extent to which organizations participate in and are shaped by wider interorganizational *fields*—systems of relations that encompass both similar and diverse organizations, both competitive and symbiotic relations, both local and nonlocal linkages, and both vertical and horizontal connections (see DiMaggio and Powell 1983; Scott & Meyer 1983).

But most relevant to the argument developed here is that conceptions or organizational environments have recently been expanded to include symbolic elements. Since the mid-1970s, analysts have increasingly employed models that shifted attention from economic to social or cultural aspects of environments, from technical to institutional facets of environments. Prior to these developments, organizations had been viewed primarily as production or exchange systems. Their structures were seen as being shaped largely by their technologies (Woodward 1965; Perrow 1967), their transactions (Williamson 1975), or power-dependence relations growing out of imbalances in their resource exchanges (Pfeffer & Salancik 1978). Environments were conceived fundamentally as "task environments" (Dill 1958; Thompson 1967); as stocks of resources or sources of technical information (Aldrich & Mindlin 1978); as foci of exchange relations (Evan 1966). Such views are not wrong, but they are clearly incomplete. No organization is just a production system and many are not primarily production systems.

Meyer and Rowan (1977) were among the first to argue that it is important to supplement views of environments as consisting of technical flows and exchanges—and the parallel view of organizations as systems for coordinating these exchanges and controlling production activities—with an awareness of the existence of institutional rules and belief systems that constitute an independent source of "rational" organizational forms. These systems are viewed as consisting of sets of *rational myths*—rational in that they specify in a rulelike way how certain activities are to be conducted to achieve a given objective; mythical in that the rules "work" because, and only to the extent that, they rest on widely shared beliefs. Organizations constructed so as to conform to—be isomorphic with—these belief systems are more likely to be regarded as legitimate, to secure necessary resources, and to survive (see also, Meyer, Scott, & Deal 1981; DiMaggio & Powell 1983).

The conception of institutional environments is not intended to supplant that of technical environments, but to complement it. Meyer and I have proposed that *technical* environments be defined as those in which "a product or service is exchanged in a market such that organizations are rewarded for effective and efficient control of the work process." Thus, technical environments exercise output controls over organizations. *Institutional* environments "are characterized by the elaboration of rules and requirements to which individual organizations must conform if they are to receive support and legitimacy from the environment" (Scott & Meyer 1983, p. 140). Institutional environments exercise process or structural controls over organizations, determining the procedures they employ, the qualifications of their staff, and the types of facilities to be employed.

Each of the two types of environments varies in its strength: technical environments range from strong to weak states, as do institutional environments. The concepts should be treated not as dichotomies, but as continuums. More important, the two types of environments tend to be negatively associated, but not strongly so: it is possible to observe all combinations, from environments that exhibit both strong technical and institutional pressures to those in which both technical and institutional pressures are weak and underdeveloped. Of course, we also observe situations in which institutional forces are strong but technical forces are weak as well as the reverse.

Examples of types of organizations that confront both strong technical and institutional controls are utilities, airline companies, and banks. Such organizations face both output and procedural controls and must be attentive to both efficiency/effectiveness demands and procedural requirements. As a result, they tend to exhibit more elaborated and complex administrative components, since they must relate to and satisfy the demands of two somewhat independent types of controlling agents—customers and regulators.

Types of organizations operating in environments characterized by high technical but moderate or minimal institutional requirements include most manufacturing organizations and many types of service units. These organizations are primarily controlled by the decisions of clients or customers who decide whether or not to continue to buy the products and services offered. Such firms are also subject to some types of institutional requirements, including conformity to auditing requirements, health and safety rules, and due process procedures in their treatment of employees; but these requirements are not as strong as the technical demands confronted.

Other types of organizations, such as schools, mental health agencies, and law firms, operate in environments characterized by strong institutional pressures and relatively weak technical controls. These organizations carry on their activity subject to a variety of rules and procedural controls—accredication and certification bodies, professional associations, and governmental rules concerning what types of personnel are to be employed or what sorts of procedures will be reimbursed. They succeed primarily by conforming to these institutional requirements; the resources they receive to operate do not usually depend heavily on the quality or quantity of their outputs. Process criteria of quality are emphasized; and competition concerns conformity to institutional forms and procedures.

When neither technical nor institutional environments are highly developed, it is difficult for organizations to flourish. Examples of organizations operating in such environments include personal service units, such as health clubs and child care services. Such organizations tend to be relatively small and weak. Strong and stable organizations can emerge in either strong technical or institutional environments, but one or the other supporting framework is required. We are now witnessing the increasing institutional development of rules and requirements governing the delivery of child care services and services to the elderly. As such institutional supports develop, we would expect to observe the simultaneous development of stronger and more stable organizational forms (see Scott 1981).

The two types of environments—technical and institutional—exemplify two contrasting meanings of rationality. Technical environments embody the connotation that "rational" structures are those that efficiently and effectively produce specified goods and services—that efficaciously accomplish specific goals. Institutional environments represent the connotation contained in the concept of "rationale": the extent to which organizational personnel are capable of rendering an account, a theory, an explanation that justifies past actions and renders them understandable and acceptable (see Scott & Lyman 1968).

These different views of rationality correspond closely with Hannan and Freeman's (1984, p. 153) discussion of the two major competences exhibited by organizational forms. They assert that one advantage organizations offer is their *reliability:* "organizations have unusual capacities to produce collective products of a given quality repeatedly." The second competence associated with organizations is their *accountability:* "organizations can make internally consistent arguments that appropriate rules and procedures existed to reproduce rational allocations of resources and appropriate organizational actions."[4]

Elaboration: Pursuing the Implications of an Institutional Perspective

An institutionalist perspective, in my view, carries much promise. In this concluding section, I want to call attention to several insights that I believe are associated with this approach and to point out some directions in which I believe further work is needed.

Institutional elements   As noted, an institutional perspective emphasizes the importance of symbolic aspects of environments. With this emphasis, organization analysts have begun to connect their efforts to work in such areas as the sociology of knowledge and the sociology of culture. The symbolic elements of interest include both normative and cognitive systems. The former have received more attention from analysts than the latter. Normative systems affecting organization include the more formal and codified approches such as legal and regulatory frameworks and professional/occupational codes, but also the more informal systems, which include mores, customs, and established practices (see, e.g., Champagne, Neef, & Nagel 1981; Moch & Seashore 1981; Noll 1985; Van Mannen & Barley, 1984).

Of equal or greater importance are the cognitive systems that define and shape social reality. Berger and Luckmann (1967) forcefully called attention to the collective definitions by which, in interactive processes, individuals shape their social reality—first creating it and then relating to it as something "objective" and external to their own actions. Among the most fundamental of these processes are those that define the basic social units. Meyer, Boli, and Thomas (1987, pp. 12, 19) stress the importance of these overlooked ontological processes that create and legitimize "the social entities that are seen as 'actors.' " They emphasize

> the extent to which organizational structures are not only influenced but internally *constituted by the wider environment.* The wider setting contains prescriptions regarding the types of organizational actors that are socially possible and how they conceivably can be structured. Collectivities are thus as much the embodiment of the prescriptions of the available cultural forms as they are the aggregation of lower-level units and interests.

Other important types of meaning systems that help define and shape organizations that have received some research attention include conceptions of domain definition and consensus (Braito, Paulson, & Klonglan 1972) and theories governing practice.

It is important to stress three distinguishing features of recent work on institutional systems. First, unlike in most work in the symbolic interaction tradition, the work of ethnomethodologists, or the recent studies of corporate culture, symbolic systems *external* to the organization are emphasized. The symbolic interaction tradition and social–psychological variants of phenomenology employ a microlevel perspective in which rules and meanings are negotiated by organizational participants. Institutional views stress the extraordinary power of exogenous definitions of reality. Connecting to other macro–micro distinctions, institutionalists stress "frames" over "situations" (see Goffman 1974; Gonos 1977); they emphasize "paradigms" rather than "schemas" (see Brown 1978; Pfeffer 1981).

Second, as Meyer and colleagues emphasize, from an institutional perspective, organizational structures are not simply "influenced" by their environments; they are *constituted* by them. Interactions with the technical environment involve exchanges in which ingredients and resources are secured, combined, and transformed by organizations; however, many transactions with the institutional environment involve acquisition of elements that are secured and incorporated without being transformed. Indeed, the organization makes great efforts to visibly display the acquired features, be they professional actors (e.g., certified public accountants), offices (e.g., affirmative action officer), or structural units (utilization review bodies in hospitals, environmental protection units in industry) (see Taylor 1984). This strong pressure toward structural isomorphism within specific institutional environments helps account for the otherwise inexplicable uniformity of organizational forms within and across societies among organizations such as state bureaucracies, hospitals and schools (see Meyer & Rowan 1977; DiMaggio and Powell 1983).

Third, the fact that the meaning systems are institutionalized belief systems—externally created and widely recognized frameworks for carrying on specified work performances—serves to legitimate the organization, supporting participants' and audiences' conceptions of it as a rational collective actor. This emphasis distinguishes the arguments of institutional theorists from those of both ethnomethodological theorists and Barnard and his followers. The ethnomethodologists, as noted, stressed the cognitive aspects of symbolic systems, emphasizing their contributions to sensemaking and the creation of meaningful work for participants. Institutionalists add that when such meanings are widely shared—by clients as well as performers and across work settings—they add immeasurably to the stability and acceptability of these systems. In stressing the motivating elements of symbolic systems, Barnard neglected their cognitive functions. He failed to observe the ways in which symbolic systems shape meanings for performers and their constituencies, providing not only internal direction but, more important, external legitimation and support.

Multiple institutional environments   Some versions of institutional theory have stressed the emergence of a general "bureaucratic" or "organizational" model that has helped shape and support the spread of rational administrative forms across numerous populations of organizations (see Berger, Berger & Kellner 1973; Meyer & Rowan 1977; Zucker 1983). While such broad templates have supported the process, it is important to emphasize that, just as technical environments vary greatly in the specifics of their supports and constraints and give rise to very different types of organizations (e.g., batch versus mass, versus process production forms, as identified by Woodward, 1965), so institutional environments vary greatly in the specifics of their rules and assumptions and may be expected to give rise to quite different types of organizational forms (for example, is legitimate decision-making power centralized in the administration, located in professionalized workers, or granted to clients as informed consumers of services). Concepts such as "organizational field" or "societal sector" are useful precisely because they point to the specificity of different organizational systems and their supporting environments and call for their detailed analysis (see Scott 1987a).

Institutional foundations of technical environments   The distinction between institutional and technical environments can mislead analysts to the extent that they mistakenly assume the presence of one excludes the other. I have tried to emphasize in this discussion that all organizations operate in both technical and institutional environments, but it is all too easy to overlook the institutional supports of even the most technical organizations. Thus, markets themselves are institutionally structured systems, supported by beliefs regarding private property, norms governing fair exchange, and related belief systems (see Stinchcombe 1983, pp. 130–44). We have just pointed out that both individual and collective actors, their rights, possibilities for action, and capacities are institutionally defined. The rise of the corporation as a corporate actor represents only one instance—a central and dramatic one, to be sure—of these institution-building processes at work (see Creighton 1988). Institutional categories and rules are also promulgated in the form of industry "standards" and specifications that attempt to impose some uniformity in size, dimensions of components, and parts (see Noble 1986). Similarly, standards are developed to guide accounting practices (see Meyer 1986; Zald 1986). Occupational systems and labor markets are, in part, institutionally structured. And the list goes on. Some work has been done, but much remains if we are to fully understand the institutional underpinnings of technical systems and production organizations.

More than most other organization theorists, Barnard provides us with a complex model of the duality of organizations, emphasizing the ways in which they combine rational and natural elements within a single system. While he recognized the importance of environments for organizations, he did not systematically pursue these interconnections. In particular, he treated the cultural and symbolic aspects of organizations as (1) primarily internal rather than external and (2) predominantly cathetic rather than cognitive in their functions.

In work carried on since his time, analysts have given increased attention to organizational–environment interrelations and, increasingly, to the structural characteristics of environments themselves. But only recently have we begun to recognize the duality of these environmental contexts and the extent to which environments are composed of both technical and institutional features. The institutional features themselves also contain both normative and cognitive aspects. Normative systems shape but cognitive systems constitute organizational forms.

Thus, in contrast to Barnard's view that symbols function in organizations primarily in a cathetic mode as a series of internal devices to elicit the cooperation and commitment of participants, institutionalists stress that symbols also function in organizations to provide an externally devised cognitive framework, allowing conforming organizations to constitute themselves as rational actors, borrowing meaning and garnering legitimacy and support from their environment.

I should like to think that Chester Barnard, wherever he is, is smiling happily over the emergence of a more complex, dualistic conception not only of organizations, which he pioneered, but of their environments.

NOTES

I am indebted to my colleague John W. Meyer for helpful comments on an earlier draft of this paper.

1. Lay persons—participants, managers—in the real world can be found to share Barnard's dualistic conception. In relaxing with *The Daily Californian* prior to my lecture, I came across an article on the sports page about the University of California at Berkeley's top-ranking tennis doubles team of Tiffiny Silveria and Alissa Finerman. Finerman was asked by the reporter to comment on theories regarding what makes a good doubles team: "There are two types of relationships in doubles. There's the business relationship—'what's your objective?' And there's the emotional relationship—'how do you feel?' We have a good combination of both" (*The Daily Californian*, April 28, 1988).

2. Barnard emphasized the positive sides of these controlling cultures. Clearly, one must also be mindful of their dark side: the extent to which organizational cultures can inappropriately dominate and exploit individual participants.

3. Weick corrects this oversight in his second edition, acknowledging the priority of Barnard's conception (see Weick 1979, pp. 94–95).
4. For a fuller discussion of these models of organization–environment connections, see Scott (1987b, pp. 119–25).

REFERENCES

Aldrich, Howard E., and Sergio Mindlin. 1978. Uncertainty and dependence: two perspectives on environment. In *Organization and Environment*, ed. Lucien Karpit, pp. 149–70. Beverly Hills, Calif.: Sage Publications.

Aldrich, Howard E., and Jeffrey Pfeffer. 1976. Environments of organizations. *Annual Review of Sociology* 2:79–105.

Allport, Floyd H. 1962. A structuronomic conception of behavior: individual and collective. *Journal of Abnormal and Social Psychology* 64:3–30.

Astley, W. Graham. 1985. The two ecologies: population and community perspectives on organizational evolution. *Administrative Science Quarterly* 30:224–41.

Barnard, Chester I. 1938. *The Functions of the Executive*. Cambridge, Mass.: Harvard University Press.

Berger, Peter L., Brigitte Berger, and Hansfried Kellner. 1973. *The Homeless Mind: Modernization and Consciousness*. New York: Random House/Vintage Books.

Berger, Peter L., and Thomas Luckmann. 1967. *The Social Construction of Reality*. New York: Doubleday.

Bittner, Egon. 1967. The police on skid row: a study of peace keeping. *American Sociological Review* 32:699–715.

Braito, Rita, Steve Paulson, and Gerald Klonglan. 1972. Domain consensus: a key variable in interorganizational analysis. In *Complex Organizations and Their Environments*, ed. Merlin B. Brinkerhoff and Phillip R. Kunz, pp. 176–92. Dubuque, Iowa: William C. Brown.

Brown, Richard Harvey. 1978. Bureaucracy as praxis: toward a political phenomenology of formal organizations. *Administrative Science Quarterly* 23:365–82.

Champagne, Anthony, Marian Neff, and Stuart Nagel. 1981. Laws, organizations, and the judiciary. In *Handbook of Organizational Design*, ed. Paul C. Nystrom and William H. Starbuck. 1:187–209. Oxford: Oxford University Press.

Chandler, Alfred D., Jr. 1962. *Strategy and Structure*. Cambridge, Mass.: The MIT Press.

Cicourel, Aaron. 1968. *The Social Organization of Juvenile Justice*. New York: Wiley.

Clark, Burton R. 1960. *The Open Door College*. New York: McGraw-Hill.

Creighton, Andrew L. (1988) The emergence of incorporation in the early nineteenth century: an overview. Presented at the Stanford Social Science History Workshop, Stanford University, Stanford, Calif.

Deal, Terrance E., and Allan A. Kennedy. 1982. *Corporate Cultures*. Reading, Mass.: Addison-Wesley.

Dill, William R. 1958. Environment as an influence on managerial autonomy. *Administrative Science Quarterly* 2:409–43.

DiMaggio, Paul. 1986. Structural analysis of organizational fields: a blockmodel approach. In *Research in Organizational Behavior,* ed. Barry M. Staw and L. L. Cummings, 8:335–70. Greenwich, Conn.: JAI Press.

DiMaggio, Paul J., and Walter W. Powell. 1983. The iron cage revisited: Institutional isomorphism and collective rationality in organizational fields, *American Sociological Review* 48:147–60.

Edelman, Murray. 1964. *The Symbolic Uses of Politics.* Urbana: University of Illinois Press.

Evan, William M. 1966. The organization set: toward a theory of interorganizational relations. In *Approaches to Organizational Design,* ed. James D. Thompson, pp. 173–88. Pittsburgh: University of Pittsburgh Press.

Frost, Peter J., Larry F. Moore, Meryl Reis Louis, Craig C. Lundberg, and Joanne Martin, eds. 1985. *Organizational Culture.* Beverly Hills, Calif.: Sage.

Goffman, Erving. 1974. *Frame Analysis.* Cambridge, Mass.: Harvard University Press.

Gonos, George. 1977. "Situation" vs. "frame": the "interactionist" and the "structuralist" analyses of everyday life. *American Sociological Review* 42:854–67.

Hannan, Michael T., and John H. Freeman. 1977. The population ecology of organizations. *American Journal of Sociology* 82:929–64.

Hannan, Michael T., and John H. Freeman. 1984. Structural inertia and organizational change. *American Sociological Review* 49:149–64.

March, James G., and Johan P. Olsen. 1976. *Ambiguity and Choice in Organizations.* Bergen: Universitetsforlaget.

March, James G., and Herbert A. Simon. 1958. *Organizations.* New York: John Wiley & Sons.

Martin, Joanne, and Debra Meyerson. 1986. Organizational cultures and the denial, channeling, and acceptance of ambiguity. Research Report No. 807R, Research Paper Series. Stanford, Calif.: Graduate School of Business, Stanford University.

Meyer, John W. 1986. Social environments and organizational accounting. *Accounting, Organizations and Society* 11:345–56.

Meyer, John W., John Boli, and George M. Thomas. 1987. Ontology and rationalization in the Western cultural account. In *Institutional Structure: Constituting State, Society and the Individual,* ed. George M. Thomas, John W. Meyer, Francisco O. Ramirez, and John Boli, pp. 12–37. Newbury Park, Calif.: Sage Publications.

Meyer, John W., and Brian Rowan 1977. Institutionalized organizations: formal structure as myth and ceremony. *American Journal of Sociology* 83:340–63.

Meyer, John W., W. Richard Scott, and Terrence E. Deal. 1981. Institutional and technical sources of organizational structure: explaining the structure of educational organizations. In *Organization and the Human Services: Cross-Disciplinary Reflections,* ed. Herman D. Stein, pp. 151–79. Philadelphia: Temple University Press.

Moch, Michael, and Stanley E. Seashore. 1981. How norms affect behaviors in and of corporations. In *Handbook of Organizational Design,* ed. Paul C. Nystrom and William H. Starbuck, 1:210–37. New York: Oxford University Press.

Noble, David F. 1986. *Forces of Production: A Social History of Industrial Automation.* New York: Oxford University Press.

Noll, Roger G., ed. 1985. *Regulatory Policy and the Social Sciences.* Berkeley: University of California Press.

Ouchi, William G. 1980. Markets, bureaucracies and clans. *Administrative Science Quarterly* 25:129–41.

Perrow, Charles. 1967. A framework for the comparative analysis of organizations. *American Sociological Review* 32:194–208.

Perrow, Charles. 1986. *Complex Organizations: A Critical Essay,* 3rd ed. New York: Random House.

Peters, Thomas J., and Robert H. Waterman, Jr. 1982. *In Search of Excellence.* New York: Harper & Row.

Pfeffer, Jeffrey. 1981. Management as symbolic action: the creation and maintenance of organizational paradigms. In *Research in Organizational Behavior,* ed. L. L. Cummings and Barry Staw, 3:1–52. Greenwich, Conn.: JAI Press.

Pfeffer, Jeffrey, and Gerald R. Salancik. 1978. *The External Control of Organizations.* New York: Harper & Row.

Pondy, Louis R., ed. 1983. *Organizational Symbolism.* Greenwich, Conn.: JAI Press.

Scott, Marvin B., and Stanford M. Lyman. 1968. Accounts. *American Sociological Review* 33:46–62.

Scott, W. Richard. 1981. Reform movements and organizations: the case of aging. In *Aging: Social Change,* ed. Sara B. Kiesler, James N. Morgan, and Valerie Kincade Oppenheimer, pp. 331–44. New York: Academic Press.

Scott, W. Richard. 1987a. The adolescence of institutional theory. *Administrative Science Quarterly* 32:493–511.

Scott, W. Richard. 1987b. *Organizations: Rational, Natural and Open Systems,* 2d ed. Englewood Cliffs, NJ: Prentice-Hall.

Scott, W. Richard, and John W. Meyer. 1983. The organization of societal sectors. In *Organizational Environments: Ritual and Rationality,* ed. John W. Meyer and W. Richard Scott, pp. 129–54. Beverly Hills, Calif.: Sage Publications.

Selznick, Philip. 1957. *Leadership in Administration: A Sociological Interpretation.* New York: Harper & Row.

Schein, Edgar H. 1985. *Organizational Culture.* San Francisco: Jossey-Bass.

Simon, Herbert A. 1957. *Adminstrative Behavior,* 2d ed. New York: Macmillan.

Smircich, Linda. 1983. Concepts of culture and organizational analysis. *Administrative Science Quarterly* 28:339–58.

Stinchcombe, Authur L. (1983). *Economic Sociology.* New York: Academic Press.

Swidler, Ann. 1986. Culture in action: symbols and strategies. *American Sociological Review* 51:273–86.

Taylor, Serge. 1984. *Making Bureaucracies Think: The Environmental Impact Statement Strategy of Administrative Reform.* Stanford, Calif.: Stanford University Press.

Van Mannen, John and Stephen R. Barley. 1984. Occupational communities: culture and control in organizations. In *Research in Organizational Behavior,* ed. Barry M. Staw and L. L. cummings. 6. Greenwich, Conn.: JAI Press.

Warren, Roland L. 1967. The interorganizational field as a focus for investigation. *Administrative Science Quarterly* 12:396–419.

Weick, Karl E. 1969; 1979. *The Social Psychology of Organizing.* Reading, Mass.: Addison-Wesley.

Williamson, Oliver E. 1975. *Markets and Hierarchies: Analysis and Antitrust Implications.* New York: Free Press.

Wilson, James Q. 1973. *Political Organizations*. New York: Basic Books.

Wolin, Sheldon S. 1960. *Politics and Vision*. Boston: Little, Brown.

Woodward, Joan. 1965. *Industrial Organization: Theory and Practice*. New York: Oxford University Press.

Zald, Meyer N. 1984. The sociology of enterprise, accounting and budget rules. *Accounting, Organizations and Society*. 11:327–40.

Zucker, Lynne G. 1983. Organizations as institutions. In *Research in the Sociology of Organizations*, ed. Samuel B. Bacharach, 2:1–47. Greenwich, Conn.: JAI Press.

3

On the Organizational Ecology of Chester I. Barnard

GLENN R. CARROLL

On first thought, little current work in organizational theory seems further afield of Barnard's *Functions of the Executive* than that of organizational ecology. After all, Barnard's efforts highlight the role of the chief executive officer (CEO) and the dynamics of internal organizational cooperation. By contrast, organizational ecology emphasizes environmental selection, a process that assumes limits on CEO capabilities. The ecological line of theory also emanates from a different and distinct tradition. Early human ecologists drew on biological theory and applied it to the human condition. The focus was on macrosociological adjustments to the environment. Accordingly, early ecologists studied whole societies (Lenski & Lenski 1974), urban communities (Burgess 1925; Park 1926; McKenzie 1924, 1926), and ethnic groups (Park 1929). Occasionally, there were attempts to study institutions (Hughes 1936) and specific cultural objects such as newspapers (Park 1923). However, a theory of formal organizations qua organizations never developed. The closest effort was Hawley's (1950) widely hailed theory of social organization in general.[1]

Despite this separate tradition, and despite the apparent differences in orientation, Barnard's book shows many conceptual affinities with current organizational ecology. Although many of these points of intersection are not features for which *Functions of the Executive* has been well remembered, they were also not trivial matters to Barnard. Indeed, I believe they are the cornerstones of his work, for they represent an important part of the orienting metatheory on which he built his more detailed theory of cooperation and executive action. For this reason, I think that if Chester Barnard were alive today, he would be sympathetic toward organizational ecology. Perhaps he would even be an advocate.

ORGANIZATIONAL ECOLOGY

Much like neoclassical microeconomics, organizational ecology assumes a selection model.[2] In economics, the competitive market is the selection mechanism, and technical efficiency is usually taken to be the selection criterion. In organizational ecology, the environment is assumed to optimize on criteria other than just technical efficiency. Social and political factors can drive the selection process as well.

The selection models of organizational ecology use the same logic as biological models of selection. Individual social units, in this case organizations, are assumed to have some characteristics that do not change rapidly and vary across space. Selection enters through the interaction of organizational and environmental characteristics. When the environment and the organizational form match, selection is positive and enhances survival. When they do not, selection acts against the organizational form. A system with finite resources operating under these principles may require a long time to reach equilibrium (and indeed organizational ecology is notable for assuming nonequilibrium). But if it does, the negatively selected forms will not be present—they are outcompeted by the organizational forms which more closely match the prevailing environmental conditions.

The most important differences between previous organizational sociology and organizational ecology concern levels of analysis and mechanisms of change. The common assumption of other sociological theories of organization is that change in the distributions of organizational structures arises mainly by adaptive change in individual organizations. Ecological theory assumes that individual organizations have modest capacities to make major changes in structure and that change in the distributions of organizational structures comes about mainly through the entry of new organizations and the demise or merger of old ones. Usually this process is characterized by some systematic correspondence between the forms of old and new organizations, on the one hand, and the states of the environment at the two points in time on the other hand. Since populations are defined by organizational forms, ecological theory thus posits a model of selective change of populations of organizations. So the two bodies of theory operate at different levels of analysis, organizational and populational, and rely on different mechanisms of change, adaptation and selection.

Underlying the selection mechanism of organizational ecology are two other assumptions: first, that resources are finite, and second, that competition is the motor of selection. Hannan and Freeman (1977, p. 940) explain the logic of the model succinctly: "Organizational forms presumably fail to flourish in certain environmental circumstances because other forms successfully compete with them for essential resources. As long as the resources which sustain organizations are finite and populations have unlimited capacity to expand, competition must ensue." As noted earlier, such a view does not imply that technical efficiency will be the selection criterion of the competitive process.

Empirical research within organizational ecology has focused primarily on the correspondence between environmental characteristics and organizational founding and failure rates.[3] One stream of this research is very akin to industrial organization economics. It studies environmental variables such as variability of demand (Freeman & Hannan 1983), level of concentration (Carroll 1985), and technological innovation (Brittain & Wholey 1988). A second stream of empirical research looks at social and political factors that economists seldom consider. These include political turmoil (Carroll, 1987), regime change (Amburgey et al. 1988), electoral results (Carroll & Huo 1988), institutional legitimacy (Hannan and Freeman 1987, 1988), community endorsement (Singh et al. 1986), and lifestyles of members (McPherson 1983).

Irrespective of the environmental conditions examined, the range of empirical applications across organizational forms is very wide. At present writing these include the following types of organizations: restaurants (Freeman & Hannan 1983), labor unions (Hannan & Freeman 1987, 1988 Carroll & Huo 1988), social service providers (Singh et al. 1986), newspaper publishers (Carroll 1987, Amburgey et al. 1988), voluntary associations (McPherson 1983; McPherson & Smith-Lovin 1988), semiconductor manufacturers (Brittain & Wholey 1988; Bocker 1988), wineries (Delacroix et al. 1989), trade associations (Aldrich & Staber 1988), and others (see Carroll 1984, for a review).

The wide range of empirical applications is possible only because of the generality of certain ecological conceptions. The one that deserves emphasis here, because of its affinity with Barnard's views in *Functions of the Executive,* is the claim that organizational survival is the primary outcome of theoretical interest. Concepts such as efficiency and effectiveness have few if any implications for the theory unless they can be shown to affect this outcome.

BARNARD'S *FUNCTIONS OF THE EXECUTIVE*

Although most organizational ecologists have probably read Barnard's book at one time or another, it seems to have had virtually no direct influence on ecological theory. Undoubtedly this is because Barnard's book emphasized cooperation within organizations and the role of executives in securing it. Barnard's impact in organizational theory was especially strong in the early days of its development, when what Scott (1987) has called the rational system model of organizations held sway. Organizational ecology, by contrast, subscribes to the open system model of organizations, a more recent view that emphasizes environmental factors.

Upon rereading *Functions of the Executive,* the labeling of Barnard as a closed system theorist seems incomplete and possibly even unfair. For although he does dwell at length on the internal aspects of organizations and the executive's ability to manage them, Barnard also shows a keen sensitivity to the broader underlying social and political environmental conditions necessary to sustain formal organization. In fact, in the Introduction to *Functions of the Executive,* Barnard qualifies his entire effort by taking into accounting environmental forces. After noting that "successful cooperation in or by formal organization is the abnormal, not the normal, condition," and that "most cooperation fails in the attempt, or dies in infancy, or is short-lived," he dismisses as superficial the common explanations for this phenomenon—poor leadership or management. Instead, Barnard argues that "at root the cause of the instability and limited duration of formal organizations lies in the forces outside. These forces both furnish the material which are used by organizations and limit their action. The survival of an organization depends upon the maintenance of an equilibrium of complex character in a continuously fluctuating environment of physical, biological, and social materials, elements, and forces, which calls for readjustment of processes internal to the organization" (p. 6).

Of course, even such explicit open-system theorizing does not imply that Chester Barnard was an organizational ecologist. However, many other passages in *Functions of the Executive* show clearly that fifty years ago Barnard grappled with many of the issues that concern organizational ecologists today. Although many of these were minor topics in Barnard's book and do not deserve more than a simple mention, the list as a whole is impressive in its range and breadth: (1) a recognition of the highly *inertial* nature of organizations (pp. 15, 60); (2) the use of a *population* metaphor to discuss the emergence and spread of formal organization (p. 5); (3) a discussion of the conceptual problems of *identifying the date of establishment* of an organization, especially when the new organization results from a schism within an existing organization (pp. 103–4); (4) great concern with organizational *founding and survival* (pp. 44, 82–83, 101–3, 240–44, 251–53); (5) a recognition of the strong *liability of newness* in organizations (pp. 5–6); (6) a hierarchical conceptualization of *organizational communities,* with some forms (church and state in particular) viewed as superordinate to others (pp. 96–99); (7) a view of *competition* among organizations that relies on resource overlaps, not actions or conflicts (p. 100); and (8) the argument that survival is the only meaningful measure of an organization's *efficiency* and that it depends on many non-economic factors (pp. 44, 92–93, 244, 251–53).

This last point is particularly important because it is found repeatedly throughout *Functions of the Executive* and because it is the strongest ecological statement in the book. By efficiency, Barnard does not mean practical or technical efficiency as is commonly meant even today. Rather he refers to an "efficiency of effort in the fundamental sense," which he takes

to be "efficiency relative to the securing of necessary personal contributions to the cooperative system" (p. 92)—in other words, the ability of the
organization to offer inducements strong enough to elicit the continued
contribution of its members. The reasoning behind the definition goes as
follows:

> The life of an organization depends on its ability to secure and maintain the
> personal contributions of energy (including the transfer of control of materials
> or money equivalent) necessary to effect its purposes. This ability is a com-
> posite of perhaps many efficiencies and inefficiencies in the narrow senses of
> these words, and it is often the case that inefficiency in some respect can be
> treated as the cause of total failure, in the sense that if corrected success would
> then be possible. But certainly in most organizations—social, political, na-
> tional, religious—nothing but the absolute test of survival is significant objec-
> tively; there is no basis for comparison of the efficiencies of separate aspects.
> (pp. 92–93)

The argument that survival is the only appropriate measure of efficiency
of an organizational economy is repeated at least five times in the book
(pp. 44, 57, 93, 244, 261). It is closely linked to the understanding that
personal contributions depend on much more than monetary inducement.
Consider the following statement:

> It is said that a commercial organization cannot survive unless its income ex-
> ceeds its outgo, a statement that begs the point. It is only true if no one will
> contribute the deficit in commercial goods for non-commercial reasons. But
> this not infrequently occurs. Family pride, philanthropic motives, etc., often
> induce economic contributions for non-commercial motives that enable an or-
> ganization that is economic in character to survive. And the fact is plain that
> organizations in large numbers that are unsuccessful economically nevertheless
> continue to exist, whatever may be the motives. (p. 25)

The paragraph following this one extends the argument to noncommercial
organizations (see also p. 44).

From this highly selective review, we can reconstruct "the organizational
ecology" of Chester I. Barnard. It goes somewhat as follows. Organizations have strong inertial forces and these limit the ability of individuals—
even executives—to change them. Competition with other organizations
occurs over the loyalties of individuals and their services. Organizations
that succeed in attracting and sustaining contributions of individuals sufficient to allow survival are successful. No other comparative measure of
success exists, and the conditions that lead to this one are psychological,
sociological, and political as well as economic.

The genius of Barnard's vision is its broad scope. His conceptualization
allows for meaningful comparative analysis across all types of formal organizations. It also makes sense when applied over very long periods of
time. As with organizational ecology, such an orientation forces one to
consider only fundamental differences in environments, across both organizational forms and time.

Where this reconstruction of Barnard seems weak is in its ability to account for short-term performance changes among fairly similar types of organizations. However, Barnard did not attempt to use his ecologically inclined formulation in that problem context. Rather, this is where he typically used his arguments about cooperation and executive action. Because these arguments constitute the greater part of his book, it is easy to understand why Barnard has been remembered as a closed-system theorist. It is also true that the bulk of his efforts assume an adaptationist posture theoretically. Nonetheless, these general labels should not obscure the fact that *Functions of the Executive* synthesizes adaptational and selectional ideas with more success than many contemporary attempts.

BARNARD'S ECOLOGY AND THE CRITICS

Critics of organizational ecology have argued that the perspective is environmentally deterministic (Astley & Van de Ven 1983), that it ignores power (Perrow 1979), and that any important role or managerial discretion is denied (Hrebeniak & Joyce 1985). To the extent that *Functions of the Executive* and organizational ecology share the same metatheoretical assumptions—and I have argued that in many instances this is the case—what holds for one should hold for the other. That is, when it comes to the topics that fall within organizational ecology's domain, Barnard's views do not differ fundamentally from those of most ecologists. Thus, it seems useful to consider how valid these same criticisms seem when applied to Barnard's book.

We need not think very deeply or very long to realize that most of these criticisms seem way off target when directed at Barnard. *Functions of the Executive* is, after all, a widely recognized cornerstone of classical management theory. It seems imperative to ask, then, why criticisms that would never be brought up in the context of Barnard are used repeatedly in the analysis of organizational ecology.

The answer lies not in real theoretical disagreements, but instead in the confusion created by a failure to recognize differences in (1) the levels of analysis used and (2) the substantive emphases of the two works. Barnard proceeds by introducing a few assumptions about the matters that concern ecologists and then spends most of his time developing ideas about executive action in individual organizations. Conversely, Hannan and Freeman (1977) begin by stating a set of assumptions about individual organizations, and then spend most of their energies developing theory about organizational forms and populations. The explicit differences are in levels of analysis—organizational versus populational. The implicit differences are in the presumptions about causal importance assigned to topics of emphasis and neglect.

When theories are cast at the same level of analysis, it makes a great deal of sense to assume that when a theorist emphasizes some particular variable and ignores another that some sort of causal priority underlies the different treatments. Likewise, when a theory postulates an aggregation rule that leads to predictions at a higher level of analysis, it makes sense to treat that theory as an alternative explanation to another theory cast at the higher level. And it would seem that one could safely assume the failure of such a theory to mention the higher-level cause implies that the theorist believes it is not as important as the lower-level one being advanced. However, neither of these situations is the same as when two theories are cast at different levels of analysis and there are no rules of aggregation or transformation. In this case, a comparison of explanations across levels of analysis makes sense only in conjunction with some (perhaps implicit) argument about the aggregation of phenomena.

Let me illustrate this point with a model from organizational ecology. As noted elsewhere (Carroll 1984; Hannan & Freeman, 1989), ecologists have identified what appears to be a common pattern in the evolution of diverse organizational populations over time. Railroads, labor unions, banks, and newspapers each emerge as organizations in small numbers, increase rapidly in population size, and then stabilize or decline in numbers. Although several processes might explain this common pattern, the most novel argument has been proposed by Hannan (1986). He argues that the characteristic growth trajectory reflects the operation of opposing processes in legitimation and competition. At low density, growth in numbers mainly legitimates a population and the organizational form it uses. But when density is high in relation to resources, increases in density mainly strengthen processes of competition.

How does the legitimacy of an organizational population vary with its numbers? Institutional theory in sociology stresses legitimacy as taken-for-grantedness rather than legality or official approval (Meyer & Rowan 1977; Meyer & Scott 1983). That is, an organizational form is legitimate to the extent that relevant actors regard it as the "natural" way to organize for some purpose. From this perspective, rarity of a form poses serious problems of legitimacy. When few instances of a form exist, it can hardly be the "natural" way to achieve some collective end. On the other hand, once a form becomes prevalent, further proliferation is unlikely to have much effect on its taken-for-grantedness. Legitimacy thus grows monotonically with density, but at a decreasing rate.

In the case of competition, effects of variation in the upper range are especially strong. When numbers are few, adding an organization to the population increases the frequency and strength of competitive interactions only slightly if at all. But when density is high, further growth exacerbates competition (adjusting for availability of resources). In other words, growing density increases competition at an increasing rate.

The model proposed by Hannan (1986) implies that growth in organizational populations is more complicated than the commonly used logistic model. Instead of linear dependence on density, this model posits that density dependence in rates of founding and mortality is *nonmonotonic*. The model builds on the assumption that processes of legitimation and competition for limited resources shape rates of founding and failure and that these processes are sensitive to density. In particular, the instantaneous rate of organizational founding, $\lambda(t)$, is specified as

$$\lambda(t) = \exp\left[a_1 N + a_2 N^2 \right] \tag{1a}$$

where N is density, and the hypotheses predict that

$$a_1 > 0; \ a_2 < 0; \ |a_1| > |a_2|. \tag{1b}$$

For mortality, the instantaneous rate of organizational death, $u(t)$, is specified as

$$u(t) = \exp\left[b_1 N + b_2 N^2 \right] \tag{2a}$$

where N is again density, and the hypotheses are that

$$b_1 < 0; \ b_2 > 0; \ |b_1| > |b_2|. \tag{2b}$$

So far the model has been upheld, at least partially, in empirical studies of national labor unions (Hannan & Freeman 1987, 1988), newspapers (Carroll & Hannan 1989), semiconductor manufacturers (Hannan & Freeman 1989), local telephone companies (Barnett & Carroll 1987), and medical diagnostic imaging companies (Mitchell 1987).

Returning to the question of levels of analysis in theory, it should be obvious that it is one thing to say, as Hannan does, that when organizational density is low, increases in density will legitimate the organizational form and legitimation increases founding rates and depresses mortality rates. It is quite another thing to say that individual entrepreneurs found a particular type of organization in order to assist in the legitimation of a particular organizational form. Of course, they might do that—but the odds are that they opened the business for less lofty reasons, such as the desire to make money. The point is that the two explanations of the same phenomena, because they operate at different levels of analysis, do not have to be the same. Nor are they necessarily rivals. The acceptance of one does not disprove the other; neither does the rejection of one lead to the acceptance of the other.

I think this point is well understood and accepted. However, in the slippery trenches of theoretical warfare, it is often either forgotten or abused. Thus, I would argue that organizational ecology's emphasis on environment and organizational form at the population level in no way implies its guilt in the many sins that have been attributed to it at the individual or organizational level. In fact, much of the criticism has been directed not toward the essential features of organizational ecology but instead toward Hannan and Freeman's (1977) strong assumption of inertia. Oddly enough, this is an organizational level assumption that the theory could do without in its strictest form, and one that was much more relaxed in their earlier formulation (see Hannan & Freeman 1974).

Indeed, Hannan and Freeman (1984) themselves have recently backed off from the strong version of this assumption, arguing that inertia is an outcome variable that pertains primarily to the core rather than to peripheral features of organizations. This reformulation allows for much rational fine-grained adaptation. It even allows for the possibility of major structural reorganization guided by executive officers, although such events are thought to be extremely precarious.

STRATEGY THEORY AND ORGANIZATIONAL ECOLOGY

The group of researchers who appear to be most offended by organizational ecology are those who study strategic management. Because these researchers spend their time studying how executive decisions transform organizations, they emphasize the changes that can be made and the ways in which they can be used to overcome environmental threats. Thus, strategy researchers are usually loathe even to consider the strong assumption of inertia.

In the strategy research context, rejection of the strong version of this assumption makes a great deal of sense. But it is essential to recognize that this assumption was never intended to apply in that context. As noted, it was formulated to facilitate the development of a macrosociological theory of organization which attempts to explain long-term change in the organizational world. Because individual organizations rarely maintain dominant positions over long periods, the theory necessarily downplays individual organizational change. Instead, it jumps to the population level of analysis, and emphasizes the selective change that occurs there.

It is entirely possible, as I believe Barnard hints, to have it both ways. Short-term change among individual organizations can be primarily adaptive while long-term change in populations of organizations can be through selection. The different units of analysis and the different time frames can explain the need for different goals. Nor do the two views necessarily contradict each other.[4]

Such a synthesis gets into trouble unless some limits are placed on adaptation. Otherwise, organizations could change forms entirely whenever selection pressures start operating against them (something that is implausible, given the high observed rates of organizational failure). As noted earlier, the limits to adaptation needed do not have to be severe. Furthermore, they can be effective conceptually when placed on (1) the speed of adaptation, (2) the prevalence of successful adaptation, or (3) the extent of adaptation possible for a given organization (e.g., core or peripheral features of organizations).

In general, strategy researchers have few problems in accepting weak assumptions of organizational inertia. In fact, in reading the literature on strategic management, it seems as though when one studies intentional organizational change, the thing that strikes one most is the limited range of possibilities. Statements to this effect are found throughout *Functions of the Executive*. Assumptions about the limits to change are also implicit in the common strategy dictums about protecting and leveraging an organization's "distinctive competencies." Thus, it is not very controversial to claim that strategy formulation involves a process of limited choice, with the limits imposed in part by the existing organization.

There are, I presume, many examples in the strategy literature of analyses that start from this basic position. Most of these deal primarily with internal organizational affairs under the control of executives (although the goal of the analysis may be to redirect a firm's environmental posture). What is potentially interesting about an ecological slant on the inertia question are the new research problems it opens up. To begin with, the ecological frame provides reference points for measuring inertia, namely the competing organizational forms. To what extent do organizational adaptations involve transformations across the strategic postures implied by different forms? Which transitions are most frequently completed and which are most likely to enhance success? The ecological perspective also drives strategic thinking to a higher level of analysis, the population level.

Such a conceptualization of organizational strategy has been prefigured, in many ways, by Caves and Porter's (1977) formulation of strategic groups. They begin with the observation that industries are typically characterized by heterogeneous firms but that these firms frequently show certain structural similarities with some though not all firms in the industry. When the structural features in question are not easily acquired by other firms (e.g., a distribution channel), they can be seen as obstacles to adopting a given strategy. To the extent that these obstacles pose real "barriers to entry" to a given strategy, those firms with similar structural features constitute a strategic group. Any given industry might be composed of a set of such strategic groups.

In the initial formulation, firms within a strategic group were thought to be mutualistically interdependent with other firms in their group. Strategic groups were also expected to generate performance effects, both across groups and for the industry as a whole. Caves and Porter (1977) argued that

> because of their structural similarity, group members are likely to respond in the same way to disturbances from inside or outside the group, recognizing their interdependence closely and anticipating their reactions to one another's moves quite accurately. Profit rates may differ systematically among the groups making up an industry, the differences stemming from competitive advantages that a group may possess against others. The industry's profits and (perforce) the average level of its group's profits depend on the general structural traits

of the industry and also the internal heterogeneities that demarcate its groups. (pp. 92–93)

Recent research seems to have tempered these claims. While numerous studies have shown the existence of strategic groups (Porter 1979; Newman 1978; Oster 1982), and some evidence suggests that group structure affects industry performance (see McGee & Thomas 1986, for a review), the most important hypothesis of the theory—that positing performance differences across groups—has not had much empirical support. In fact, several leading researchers (Cool & Schendel 1987, 1988) have now apparently given up on this argument, suggesting instead that the strategic group formulation only explains differences in firm conduct. Their position is bolstered by the apparently large performance differences among firms within the same strategic group.

These conclusions could be the result of questionable methodological procedures. There seems to be little agreement about how to operationalize the strategic group concept and thus how to investigate the effects of group membership. The brewing industry, which has been the subject of much empirical research on the topic, has been found to have as few as two groups (Tremblay 1985) and as many as six groups (Hatten & Schendel 1977) over the same period of history. Even the same researchers have waffled in their assessments of this industry, sometimes claiming that thirteen brewing companies sort out into six groups, and at other times seeing only three groups even when analyzing the same outcome variables (compare Hatten & Schendel 1977; Hatten, Schendel, & Cooper 1978). Other applications (e.g., Cool & Schendel 1987, 1988, to the pharmaceutical industry) have used statistical procedures that allow so much movement by firms across groups that the defining criterion of mobility barriers is called into question.

Although important, these methodological issues will not necessarily resolve the current impasse in the group–performance link. However, this is one problem for which the insight of Barnard and the tools of organizational ecology might help considerably. To this point, the only performance variables used in the strategic group research are the usual short-run financial measures such as return on equity. For many well-known reasons, there are technical problems of comparability in these measures. However, as we have seen earlier, there is also the larger conceptual problem, which Barnard dealt with at length: only survival can measure organizational efficiency and utility in a general sense. Organizational ecologists would agree that survival is the relevant outcome variable. They would add further that strategic group differences in survival should be analyzed only in conjunction with environmental conditions. In other words, the ecological prediction is that the interaction between strategic group membership and environmental condition should affect rates of organizational mortality.

Recasting the problem in such terms permits use of methods developed in organizational ecology. It also suggests new ways to investigate many of the central ideas in the strategic group literature. For instance, the rate of firm mobility across strategic groups can be modeled directly, using hazard function models. Likewise, the troubling question about within-group interdependence among firms—is it mutualistic or competitive?—can be modeled as a density issue, following the lead of Hannan (1986). Competitive intragroup relations among firms would show a positive effect of group density on mortality rates, mutualistic relations a negative effect (see Barnett & Carroll 1987; Brittain & Wholey 1988).

Perhaps the most interesting possibility would be to model all strategic groups simultaneously within the density framework. That is, one could specify the mortality rate for organization i in strategic group j as

$$u_{ij}(t) = \exp\left[\beta_{1j}N_j + \beta_{2j}N_j^2 + \sum_{j \neq k}^{k} \alpha_{1k}N_k + \alpha_{2k}N_k^2\right]$$

where N_j is the density of group j and N_k is the set of density variables for all other strategic groups. The matrix of parameters β and α can then be used to assess the group structure of the population (see May 1973).[5] Among other things, the matrix gives information pertinent to (1) Hannan's (1986) model of legitimation and competition, (2) interdependencies across strategic groups, (3) the hierarchical structure among the strategic groups, and (4) the equilibrium group structure, including the possible competitive exclusion of certain groups. All of these would add significantly to our ability to analyze and understand strategic groups.

In conclusion, I argue that, despite numerous criticisms to the contrary, organizational ecology is not antithetical to the study of strategy. In fact, once the strong assumption of inertia is relaxed, conventional strategic theory can be applied within the ecological perspective quite easily. In many ways this is exactly what Chester Barnard did. Perhaps the greater potential contribution of organizational ecology to strategy, however, comes through the new questions and concepts it prompts. Foremost among these are issues concerning strategic groups. The ecological framework provides the tools and tradition for studying mobility across strategic groups and the interdependencies among groups. Both problems are pivotal to the further development of research on strategic groups of firms.

NOTES

This chapter was prepared for presentation at the Transamerica seminar on organization theory, convened by Oliver E. Williamson at the Berkeley Business School in celebration of the fiftieth anniversary of the publication of Chester I. Barnard's *Functions of the Executive*. The chapter was written at the Center for Advanced Study in the Behavioral Sciences in Palo Alto, California. The financial support of the Institute of Industrial Relations at the University of California, Berkeley, and the National Science Foundation (grant BNS-8700864) is gratefully acknowledged. I am indebted to the following persons for helpful comments on earlier drafts: Homa Bahrami, William Barnett, Warren Boeker, Robert Burgelman, Will Mitchell, and Anand Swaminathan.

1. Although it was never considered an integral part of human ecology, much of open system theory in organizational sociology owes a great debt to Hawley and others. This can be seen most clearly in the resource dependence theory of Pfeffer (1972), which draws explicitly on ecological theory to characterize organization–environment relations.

2. The seminal theoretical statement of organizational ecology was advanced by Hannnan and Freeman (1977). Later extensions and discussion of this line of thought include Aldrich (1979), Carroll (1984), and Hannan and Freeman (1984).

3. An earlier stage of empirical research consisted of the development of baseline stochastic models for the founding and mortality processes. See Carroll and Delacroix (1982), Carroll (1983), Freeman et al. (1983), Delacroix and Carroll (1983), and Hannan and Freeman (1987).

4. The possibility of such a synthesis is readily apparent when one uses bioecology as an analogy. Individual organisms are often adaptive in ways that species are not.

5. One would, of course, want to estimate the corresponding group-specific founding rates as well.

REFERENCES

Aldrich, Howard E. 1979. *Organizations and Environments.* Englewood Cliffs, N.J.: Prentice-Hall.

Aldrich, Howard E., and Udo Staber. 1988. Organizing business interests. In *Ecological Models of Organizations,* ed. Glenn R. Carroll, pp. 127–52. Cambridge, Mass.: Ballinger.

Amburgey, Terry L., Marjo-Ritta Lehisalo, and Dawn Kelly. 1988. Suppression and failure in the political press: government control, party affiliation and organizational life chances. In *Ecological Models of Organizations,* ed. Glenn R. Carroll, pp. 153–74. Cambridge, Mass.: Ballinger.

Astley, W. Graham, and Andrew H. Van de Ven. 1983. Central perspectives and debates in organization theory. *Administrative Science Quarterly* 28:245–73.

Barnard, Chester I. 1947. (1938) *Functions of the Executive.* Cambridge, Mass.: Harvard University Press.

Barnett, William P., and Glenn R. Carroll. 1987. Competition and mutualism among early telephone companies. *Administrative Science Quarterly* 32:400–421.

Boeker, Warren P. 1987. Ecological models of strategy and competition in the U.S. brewing industry. Paper presented at the meetings of the Academy of Management, New Orleans.

Boeker, Warren P. 1988. Organizational origins: entrepreneurial and environmental imprinting at the time of founding. In *Ecological Models of Organizations,* ed. Glenn R. Carroll, pp. 33–52. Cambridge, Mass.: Ballinger.

Brittain, Jack N., and Douglas R. Wholey. 1988. Competition and coexistence in organizational communities: population dynamics in electronics component manufacturing. In *Ecological Models of Organizations*, ed. Glenn R. Carroll, pp. 195–222. Cambridge, Mass.: Ballinger.

Burgess, E. W. 1925. The growth of the city: an introduction to a research project. In *The City*, eds. R. E. Park, E. W. Burgess, and R. D. McKenzie, pp. 47–62. Chicago: University of Chicago Press.

Carroll, Glenn R. 1983. A stochastic model of organizational mortality: review and reanalysis. *Social Science Research* 12:303–29.

Carroll, Glenn R. 1984. Organizational ecology. *Annual Review of Sociology* 10:72–93.

Carroll, Glenn R. 1985. Concentration and specialization: dynamics of niche width in populations of organizations. *American Journal of Sociology* 90:1262–83.

Carroll, Glenn R. 1987. *Publish and Perish: The Organizational Ecology of Newspaper Industries*. Greenwich, Conn.: JAI Press.

Carroll, Glenn R., and Jacques Delacroix. 1982. Organizational mortality in the newspaper industries of Argentina and Ireland: an ecological approach. *Administrative Science Quarterly* 27:169–98.

Carroll, Glenn R., and Y. Paul Huo. 1988. Organizational and electoral paradoxes of the Knights of Labor. In *Ecological Models of Organizations*, ed. Glenn R. Carroll, pp. 175–94. Cambridge, Mass.: Ballinger.

Carroll, Glenn R., and Michael T. Hannan. 1989. Density dependence in the evolution of populations of newspaper organizations. *American Sociological Review* 54:524–41.

Caves, Richard E., and Michael E. Porter. 1977. From entry barriers to mobility barriers. *Quarterly Journal of Economics* 91:241–62.

Cool, Karel O., and Dan Schendel. 1987. Strategic group formation and performance: the case of the U.S. pharmaceutical industry, 1963–1982. *Management Science* 33:1102–24.

Cool, Karel O., and Dan Schendel. 1988. Performance differences among strategic group members. *Strategic Management Journal* 9:207–23.

Delacroix, Jacques, and Glenn R. Carroll. 1983. Organizational foundings: an ecological study of the newspaper industries of Argentina and Ireland. *Administrative Science Quarterly* 28:274–91.

Delacroix, Jacques, Anand Swaminathan, and Michael E. Solt, 1989. Density dependence vs. population dynamics: an ecological study of failings in the California wine industry. *American Sociological Review* 54:245–62.

Freeman, John, and Michael T. Hannan. 1983. Niche width and the dynamics of organizational populations. *American Journal of Sociology* 88:1116–45.

Freeman, John, Glenn R. Carroll, and Michael T. Hannan. 1983. The liability of newness: age dependence in organizational death rates. *American Sociological Review* 48:692–710.

Hannan, Michael T. 1986. Competitive and institutional processes in organizational ecology. Technical Report, 86–13, Department of Sociology, Cornell University.

Hannan, Michael T., and John Freeman. 1974. Environment and the structure of organizations. Presented at annual meetings of the American Sociological Association, Montreal.

Hannan, Michael T., and John Freeman. 1977. The population ecology of organizations. *American Journal of Sociology* 82:929–64.

Hannan, Michael T., and John Freeman. 1984. Structural inertia and organizational change. *American Sociological Review* 49:149–64.

Hannan, Michael T., and John Freeman. 1987. The ecology of organizational founding: American labor unions, 1836–1885. *American Journal of Sociology* 92:910–43.

Hannan, Michael T., and John Freeman. 1988. The ecology of organizational mortality: American labor unions, 1836–1885. *American Journal of Sociology* 94:25–42.

Hannan, Michael T., and John Freeman. 1989. *Organizational Ecology*. Cambridge, Mass.: Harvard University Press.

Hatten Kenneth, and Mary L. Hatten. 1985. Some empirical insights for strategic marketers: the case of beer. In *Strategic Marketing and Management*, eds. H. Thomas and D. Gardner, pp. 275–92. New York: John Wiley.

Hatten, Kenneth, and Dan Schendel. 1977. Heterogeneity within an industry: firm conduct in the U.S. brewing industry. *Journal of Industrial Economics* 26:97–113.

Hatten, Kenneth, Dan Schendel, and Arnold C. Cooper. 1978. A strategic model of the U.S. brewing industry. *Academy of Management Journal* 21:592–610.

Hawley, Amos. 1950. *Human Ecology*. New York: Ronald.

Hrebeniak, Lawrence, and William F. Joyce. 1985. Organizational adaptation: strategic choice and environmental determinism. *Administrative Science Quarterly* 30:336–49.

Hughes, Everett C. 1936. The ecological aspect of institutions. *American Sociological Review* 1:180–84.

Lenski, Gerhard, and E. Lenski. 1974. *Human Societies*. New York: McGraw-Hill.

May, Robert. 1973. *Stability and Complexity in Model Ecosystems*. Princeton, N.J.: Princeton University Press.

McGee, John, and Howard Thomas. 1986. Strategic groups: theory, research and taxonomy. *Strategic Management Journal* 7:141–60.

McKenzie, Roderick D. 1924. The ecological approach to the study of the human community. *American Journal of Sociology* 30:287–301.

McKenzie, Roderick D. 1926. The scope of human ecology. *American Journal of Sociology* 32:141–54.

McPherson, J. Miller. 1983. An ecology of affiliation. *American Sociological Review* 48:519–35.

McPherson, J. Miller, and Lynn Smith-Lovin. 1988. A comparative ecology of five nations: testing a model of competition among voluntary organizations. In *Ecological Models of Organizations*, ed. Glenn R. Carroll, pp. 85–110. Cambridge, Mass.: Ballinger.

Meyer, John W., and Brian Rowan. 1977. Institutionalized organizations: Formal structure as myth and ceremony. *American Journal of Sociology* 83:340–63.

Meyer, John W., and W. Richard Scott. 1983. *Organizational Environments: Ritual and Rationality*. Beverly Hills: Sage.

Mitchell, Will. 1987. Dynamic tension: Theoretical and empirical analyses of entry into emerging industries. Paper presented at Stanford Asilomar Conference on Organizations.

Newman, Howard H. 1978. Strategic groups and the structure-performance relationship. *Review of Economics and Statistics* 60:417–27.

Oster, Sharon. 1982. Intraindustry structure and the ease of strategic change. *Review of Economics and Statistics* 64:376–83.

Park, Robert E. 1923. The natural history of the newspaper. *American Journal of Sociology* 29:273–89.

Park, Robert E. 1926. The urban community as a spatial pattern and a moral order. In *The Urban Community*, eds. R. E. Park, E. W. Burgess and R. D. McKenzie. Chicago: University of Chicago Press.

Park, Robert E. 1929. *The Immigrant Press and Its Control*. New York: Harper.

Perrow, Charles. 1979. *Complex Organizations*. Glenview, Ill.: Scott Foresman.

Pfeffer, Jeffrey. 1972. Merger as a response to organizational interdependence. *Administrative Science Quarterly* 17:382–94.

Porter, Michael E. 1979. The structure within industries and companies performance. *Review of Economics and Statistics*, 61:214–27.

Schendel, Dan, and G. R. Patton. 1978. A simultaneous equation model of corporate strategy. *Management Science* 24:1611–21.

Scott, W. Richard. 1987. *Organizations: Rational, Natural and Open Systems*, 2d. Englewood Cliffs, N.J.: Prentice-Hall.

Singh, Jitendra, David J. Tucker, and Robert J. House. 1986. Organizational legitimacy and the liability of newness. *Administrative Science Quarterly* 31:171–93.

Tremblay, Victor J. 1985. Strategic groups and the demand for beer. *Journal of Industrial Economics* 34:183–98.

4

Incentives in Organizations: The Importance of Social Relations

JEFFREY PFEFFER

When I was invited to participate in the Barnard Series Lectures, I suspect many thought I would consider resource dependence and its connection to the work of Barnard. Resource dependence (Pfeffer & Salancik 1978) certainly has many points of connection with Barnard's (1938) work, and, its concepts have much to say about incentives and wage structures in organizations (Pfeffer & Davis-Blake 1987; Pfeffer 1989). However, this chapter is not about resource dependence.

For me, resource dependence represented the development of a set of ideas that come from a somewhat more fundamental theoretical perspective. I have tried to develop this perspective in several distinct lines of inquiry, including my work with Salancik on social information processing (Salancik & Pfeffer 1978b) and with O'Reilly on organizational demography (McCain, O'Reilly, & Pfeffer 1983; Wagner, Pfeffer, & O'Reilly 1984; Pfeffer & O'Reilly 1987), and my work on power in organizations (Pfeffer 1981). This perspective proceeds from two underlying assumptions: (1) that organizations and people in them are interdependent with other organizations and with other individuals, and (2) that as a consequence of this interdependence—this social relationship—we are much better served in our attempts to understand either individual or organizational behavior by investigating the effects and constraints of social context (see, e.g., Granovetter 1985; Baron 1988). The specifics of what this means and

This paper is a revised and expanded version of a presentation made on March 24, 1988, at the University of California, Berkeley, as part of a series of lectures celebrating the fiftieth year of the publication of Chester Barnard's *The Functions of the Executive*. My thinking about incentives and inequality in organizations has been profoundly influenced by my work with James N. Baron, Alison Davis-Blake, Alison Konrad, and Nancy Langton. I also appreciate the commnets of Charles O'Reilly, who has been a continuing source of motivation to explore these issues. The support of the Graduate School of Business and the Robert M. and Anne T. Bass Faculty Fellowship is gratefully acknowledged.

how it is operationalized varies, of course, depending on whether we are talking about the effects of demography (Pfeffer 1983), physical setting (Pfeffer 1982), or resource constraints (Pfeffer & Salancik 1978). But the general principle has guided my research and, I believe, provides an important heuristic for our understanding of organizations and the actions and feelings of individuals who work in organizations.

SOCIAL RELATIONS AND INCENTIVES

Barnard recognized both the fundamental importance of incentives in organizations and the social character of cooperative systems. On the importance of incentives, he wrote, "The contributions of personal efforts which constitute the energies of organizations are yielded by individuals because of incentives. . . . the subject of incentives is fundamental in formal organizations and in conscious efforts to organize . . . in all sorts of organizations the afforrding of adequate incentives becomes the most definitely emphasized task in their existence" (1938, p. 139). And, in writing about cooperative systems, he noted that "When the individual has become associated with a cooperative enterprise he has accepted a position of contact with others similarly associated. From this contact there must arise social interactions between these persons individually, and these interactions are social . . . cooperation compels changes in the motives of individuals which otherwise would not take place" (1938, pp. 40–41).

Barnard recognized that inducements and incentives were both monetary and nonmonetary. He argued (1938, p. 143) that "the unaided power of material incentives . . . is exceedingly limited." Others have developed his idea of the balance between inducements and contributions (e.g., March & Simon 1958), and most treatments of motivation in organizations recognize both monetary and nonmonetary sources or determinants of motivated behavior (e.g., Lawler 1973). Nonetheless, because of the orientation implied by thinking about inducements and contributions, costs and benefits, money has come to play an overly important role in our thinking about causes of behavior. The modal prescription to almost any organizational situation that requires some specified behavior or behavior change is to measure it and compensate it. Although a large body of research deals with the potentially dysfunctional aspects of using extrinsic rewards (Deci 1971, 1972; Lepper & Greene 1978; Staw 1977), we still need to be reminded that the connection between incentive or reward systems and performance is often nonexistent (Deutsch 1985).

Barnard also recognized the inherently social, relational nature even of monetary incentives. He wrote that "the real value of differences of money rewards lies in the recognition or distinction assumed to be conferred thereby, or to be procured therewith—one of the reasons why differentials either in money income or in material possessions are a source of jealousy and disruption if not accompanied by other factors of distinction" (1938, pp. 145–46).

Money is important not only for what it can purchase, but because a given level of monetary incentive signifies status. But this signaling of status is only in relation to the monetary incentives provided to others with whom the individual compares himself. Festinger (1954) long ago recognized the importance of social comparison processes, and the literature on feelings of deprivation and justice (e.g., Deutsch 1985; Greenberg 1982) emphasizes the importance of the relative standing of the reward or allocation, not just its absolute amount (Alwin 1987).

Unfortunately, much of the subsequent development of the literature on incentives in organizations has not been sensitive to these issues. Pay is an increasing focus of attention (e.g., Kanter 1987). And because much analysis of social organization proceeds from a framework best characterized as methodological individualism (Homans 1961; Baysinger & Mobley 1983), the tendency has been to analyze individual pay in isolation. Data on individual pay are difficult enough to come by, particularly when one wants a large sample and some information that helps us understand how individual income is determined or what the effects of pay are on attitudes and behavior. The idea of understanding pay in a distributional sense, in its relation to the pay of others in the social system, imposes substantially higher data requirements, particularly if we want to move beyond experiments (Leventhal 1976; Martin 1982) to examine actual pay allocations and their causes and effects. Thus, we persist in studying incentives and compensation, motivation, attitudes and performance as inherently individual and individualized processes, even though ample theoretical and empirical evidence tells us otherwise (Granovetter 1985; Salancik & Pfeffer 1978b; O'Reilly & Caldwell 1979). Just as the study of job design dimensions benefitted from an expansion of concern to consider the social context in which attributes are experienced (Griffen et al. 1987; Thomas & Griffen 1983), so, too, should the examination of incentives in organizations be expanded to consider, as Barnard indicated, both the social and status differentiating elements of compensation systems.

DIMENSIONS OF ORGANIZATIONAL INCENTIVE SYSTEMS

A number of dimensions of organizational incentive systems are both important and theoretically interesting. One fundamental property of incentives is the general level of reward offered. Different amounts of rewards are offered to people working in the core and the periphery sectors of the economy (e.g., Bibb & Form 1977), in concentrated and less concentrated industries (Dalton & Ford 1977), in union and nonunion establishments (Freeman & Medoff 1984), in larger and smaller firms (Stolzenberg 1978), in public and private sector organizations (Smith 1976; Asher & Popkin 1984), in more powerful and less powerful departments (Moore & Pfeffer 1980), and in volatile and stable industries. We know comparatively more about how the level of rewards varies over contexts than we do about the consequences of this variation in reward level. Some have argued that organizations that are shielded from market pressures because of monopoly product market positions or for other reasons will use their market power to offer higher wages and thereby attract a higher quality work force (Alchian & Kessel 1962). Others argue that higher rewards are seen as a "gift," and employees reciprocate with greater effort (Akerlof 1984). But whether the level of pay obtains more skilled or more motivated employees has been more often assumed than examined (e.g., Ehrenberg & Milkovich 1987). Leonard (1987) found that higher wages were not related to supervisory intensity, and although they reduced turnover, it was not enough to justify the wage bonuses. An important research issue is the consequences of higher levels of rewards for subsequent performance.

The level of reward, although important, may not be the most significant dimension of organizational incentive systems. In the first place, people are, on occasion, embedded in internal labor markets (Doeringer & Piore 1971; Pfeffer & Cohen 1984). As a consequence of this, the individuals develop both firm-specific skills and firm-specific attachments. This firm-specificity of skill and commitment, of necessity, limits the ability or even the desire to engage in comparisons with outside job alternatives that would make the organizational level of rewards important. Second, the literature on social comparison processes (Smith 1973) tells us that people are more likely to compare themselves and their situations to others who are both similar and close by, so that the comparison process is readily accomplished. This suggests that social evaluations are often likely to be undertaken with respect to one's organizational colleagues, who are at once more likely to be similar and also more accessible for information. For instance, Subbarao and deCarufel (1983) reported that, even for a sample of academics in one university in Canada, perceptions of pay equity were based more on internal than on external comparisons. This does not mean that all comparisons are necessarily internal, and indeed, the issue of who to choose for comparisons remains an important focus of research (e.g., Martin 1982; Stouffer et al. 1949; Runciman 1966).

If people do engage in comparisons that are primarily internal, it is the relative position in the hierarchy of rewards, as well as the absolute amount, that becomes important (Alwin 1987). This suggests that some fundamental issues in reward systems are (1) the level of differentiation, and (2) the allocation of people to the differentiated positions in the reward structure. The first dimension asks how much differentiation there is among positions or individuals in the organization. The second dimension asks along what basis (e.g., ability, race, gender, age) individuals are sorted into those differentiated positions.

Forms of Differentiation

Rewards may be allocated differentially and dispersion in reward allocations assessed along several dimensions, each of which can be important.
One dimension is the amount of vertical differentiation, or the degree of
wage inequality across hierarchical levels in the organization. Abegglen
and Stalk (1985) have noted that the difference in salary between the highest and lowest paid manager in the typical large Japanese organization is
much smaller than that in similar firms in the United States. Moreover,
Abegglen and Stalk reported that while this vertical differentiation has been
decreasing in Japan, it has been increasing in the United States. Simon
(1957) noted that because of the norm that supervisors must be paid more
than those they supervise, the more levels in the organization, the more
unequal salaries are because of vertical differentiation in rewards. Mahoney (1979) investigated the norms about appropriate differences in wages
across adjacent levels. But clearly the extent to which wages across adjacent levels or ranks vary differs, even within the United States, and even
more so across cultures.

Abrahamson (1973) studied differences in salary between the rank of
full professor and associate professor and between associate professor and
assistant professor in a sample of universities. He found a greater difference between adjacent ranks in research than in teaching universities.
Abrahamson argued that in research universities activities were talent complementary (Stinchcombe 1963), so that a single person could have a disproportionate impact on the total organization's performance. In teaching
institutions, contributions are more talent additive, with each individual
contributing only proportionately to the total result, and the technology
precluding disproportionate effects. Abrahamson proposed that in talent-
complementary settings, reward dispersion was greater. A similar argument has been pursued by Jacobs (1981), in a theoretical model seeking to
understand both vertical and horizontal inequality.

Another model explaining why vertical inequality might vary has been
proposed by Lazear and Rosen (1981). Their tournament model suggests
that effort, particularly at the highest executive ranks, is fostered not only
by current compensation but also by an opportunity to compete for the
top job in the organization. However, with many competitors, the odds of
any given individual "winning" are less than when there are fewer competitors. Since competitors are already fairly evenly matched at this level,
who wins is really a matter of luck (March & March 1977). Thus, to
motivate continued effort, their model suggests that the greater the number
of vice presidents, and thus the lower the probability of any given individual being promoted to the top job, the higher should be the difference in
salary between the top position and that earned by the vice presidents. In
other words, the diminished probability of winning is balanced by a larger
prize.

Differences across salary levels may vary for other reasons, as well. Different amounts of competition for and supply of labor for positions at different ranks lead to demographic effects on interlevel differences in salary. The salary determination process may differ in terms of the basis on which wages are set and the relative power of those affected. It seems clear that the two models described earlier at best provide only partial answers to why salaries vary across levels in different organizations. The effect of norms, institutional arrangements, power, and competition and labor market factors all need to be explored systematically.

The degree of horizontal differentiation in salaries also differs across organizational settings. Not only do presidents make more than vice presidents, but vice presidents of some functions and divisions make more than those in others, and this horizontal wage dispersion also varies over contexts. In a university setting, we can ask not only what causes varying degrees of difference across academic ranks in different institutions, but also why salaries within rank but across departments are more dispersed in some settings than in others. My subjective impression is that there is less variation by field or academic specialty at the University of California at Berkeley than at Stanford, for instance. In other words, full professors' salaries (or associate or assistant professors, for that matter) are more equal across departments at Berkeley than they are at Stanford. This difference may be attributable to Berkeley's particular history, institutional politics and power distribution, the fact that it is a public organization, or because of the process by which salaries are set at the two places. Given the fact that different academic disciplines have very different labor market conditions, that salaries do not vary as much as is suggested by considering supply–demand balance is itself worthy of note because it suggests administrative intervention, which mitigates the operation of market forces in determining wage dispersion.

One of the major factors that may determine the degree of wage dispersion across departments or divisions is the extent to which the organization, its dominant coalition, or its history and tradition dictates a policy of promoting interdependence and cooperation and a feeling of common fate by reducing differences across subunits. One of the reasons why Japanese firms, for instance, can more readily transfer people across departments and divisions as part of a training and socialization process (Ouchi & Jaeger 1978) is that there are fewer department or division-specific wage differences. To transfer from marketing to human resources within many U.S. firms means either taking a cut in pay or slowing one's salary progression. Transfers, then, are evaluated in terms of their effect on the individual's salary and career. This is less true in organizations in which subunit differentiation is diminished and people are paid more equally across subunits.

Not only does vertical and horizontal differentiation occur, but for jobs in which there is more than a single incumbent, the degree of dispersion in the rewards and incentives offered to those incumbents can also differ. So, to continue with our academic example, we can ask not only (1) why is there more or less dispersion across ranks (levels) in different contexts, and (2) why is there more or less dispersion within ranks across academic disciplines in different settings, but also (3) why is there more or less dispersion within rank and within field in different organizations? This last question asks why pay is not more directly related to performance, to the extent that such performance differs for people doing the same job in the same place (Frank 1984; Bishop 1987).

Each of these dimensions of inequality within organizations warrants examination. In the first place, we need to understand the relative contribution of each form of differentiation in producing some overall level of wage inequality. Using a national sample of Swedish blue-collar workers, Hedstrom (1988) reported that of the total wage inequality in the sample, 21 percent came from differences across organizations and 79 percent from within organization differences in wages. Of this latter wage inequality, Hedstrom reported that 60 percent was attributable to differences in salaries across levels, and 40 percent was from differences in salaries paid to people working at the same level. Freeman (1982), using data from nine industries and a narrow range of occupations available from the Department of Labor's Industry Wage Surveys, reported that 40 percent of the variation in wages of production workers was due to within-establishment differentials, with 60 percent from between-establishment differences. He further noted that of the within-establishment wage variation, "on average, 66 percent is due to within-establishment differences in occupational means" (1982, p. 7). Freeman (1982, p. 8) provided results indicating that these averages mask a tremendous amount of interindustry variation in the sources of wage dispersion. For instance, in the wool textiles industry, 48 percent of the variation in earnings is due to between-establishment differences, while 76 percent of the variation in wages is attributable to between-establishment differences in the paints and varnishes industry. Freeman's results also indicate that, on average, a much greater proportion of earnings inequality in the United States is from between-establishment differences than Hedstrom's data suggest is the case in Sweden. This finding is expected because of national bargaining over wages and a solidaristic wage policy in Sweden. It is important to extend this line of inquiry to other countries, industries, and a broader range of occupations, and to ask under what circumstances wage dispersion originates in differences between organizations or organizational subunits, across levels, or within levels in organizations.

In addition to understanding where wage inequality originates, we also need to understand how it is differentially produced in different organizations and different labor markets. Some theoretical ideas are available for starting such an inquiry, but much theoretical and empirical work remains to be accomplished.

Allocation Regimes

A given level of differentiation describes a system of rewards and incentives. That system can be further analyzed by asking the basis by which people are allocated to the various positions in the system. Several such allocation principles or regimes suggest themselves from the literature on hiring and careers.

Seniority is an important avenue for mobility in many organizational settings. Seniority has been shown to be more highly related to wages, even within levels, than performance (Medoff & Abraham 1980, 1981). Economists have developed a number of rationales for rewarding on the basis of seniority (Rosen 1985), many of them emphasizing the importance of seniority-based rewards as a form of deferred compensation. Such deferred compensation is important to ensure continuity in employment in settings with a lot of on-the-job learning and development of firm-specific human capital (e.g., Williamson 1975; Goldberg 1980). The returns to seniority differentiate wage structures in the United States and Japan (Kalleberg & Lincoln 1988).

Performance is obviously another way of allocating rewards (Leventhal 1976). There is evidence that performance does account for a substantial amount of the variation in salaries in professional sports and that, furthermore, after changes in the baseball labor market that made it more competitive, performance increased in importance compared with seniority as a determinant of salaries (Hill & Spellman 1983). Of course, professional sports are unique in that there are comparatively few people to be monitored and, in many instances, performance can be both precisely assessed and the criteria for its evaluation clearly established (Abrahamson 1979). Performance, as noted earlier, is used less in other settings. But it still has an effect on determining the allocation of people to positions in the salary structure (Konrad & Pfeffer in press).

Ascriptive characteristics, such as social background, race, and gender, constitute another set of allocative principles for sorting people into positions. Kanter (1977) has provided an excellent description of the pressures for homosocial reproduction in organizations facing uncertainty and a need for trust and effective interpersonal communication. There is ample evidence of the effect of gender on salaries, even in situations such as academia where performance is at once more variable and more measurable (Ferber & Loeb 1974; Ferber & Kordick 1978; Ferber & Green 1982; Tuckman 1979).

Understanding which sorting rule is used under what circumstances remains an important research task. Pfeffer (1977), Granovetter (1974), Kanter (1977), and others have emphasized the critical role that uncertainty plays in affecting the use of social similarity or more objective characteristics related to performance or ability (Salancik & Pfeffer 1978a). But task interdependence, organizational size (Pfeffer 1977; Stolzenberg 1978), the nature of the technology, and the organization's demography may all play a role, also.

The questions just posed are important for those who want to understand the basis of social stratification. Research on stratification has progressed from analyses focusing on strictly individual attributes such as age, work experience, education, and social background (e.g., Jencks et al. 1977) to analyses that have considered the position of individuals in the macroeconomy (Beck et al. 1978; Tolbert et al. 1980). However, as many authors have recognized (Pfeffer 1977; Baron & Bielby 1980; Baron 1984; Tolbert 1986), wages are determined by and in organizations. Understanding stratification therefore necessarily involves understanding the processes through which organizations create positions and job titles (Baron & Bielby 1986), assign wages to positions, and select people to staff those positions (Cohen & Pfeffer 1986; Collins 1979).

But as Barnard (1938) and others have noted, incentives and mobility structures are consequential for organizations as well (Kanter 1977; Halaby & Sobel 1979). Incentives can affect motivation and performance, turnover and absenteeism, and cooperation among employees (Lawler 1973). Understanding the consequences of incentives for organizations is important but requires that we pay attention to the social nature of incentives and their structure. This focus has received much less emphasis so far. Our discussion of incentive structures has focused heavily on dispersion or inequality. Given the social nature of organizations and the potency of social comparison processes, it seems that wage differentiation, along all of its possible dimensions, is critical for understanding how incentives operate.

ANALYTICAL ISSUES

Two analytical or methodological issues warrant some discussion when considering the social nature of incentives and, in particular, their degree of dispersion. The first is how to measure or assess dispersion, and the second is how to analyze the degree of dispersion present in some social organization net of compositional or demographic factors. We consider each issue, albeit briefly, in turn.

The Measurement of Inequality

Inequality is, first of all, an aggregate-level of property of an organization (Lazersfeld & Menzel 1980). Although derived by combining individual-level data, where available, it is, like the demographic composition of an organization (Pfeffer 1983), a structural feature of the social system and not reducible to analysis at the individual level (Blau 1977). Estimating individual-level wage regressions cannot help us understand, except indirectly, how organization-level wage inequality is produced or what its consequences are. This point is implicitly recognized in that all studies examining the consequences or determinants of wage dispersion use aggregate measures at the organizational or industry level of analysis.

An empirical example makes this point and helps illustrate why it is true. Using data from the 1969 Carnegie Commission Survey of college and university faculty (Trow 1975; Szafran 1984), Konrad and Pfeffer (in press) reported an individual-level wage regression in which research productivity was significantly related to salary, even after experience, gender, and organizational attributes such as size, type (university, four-year college, or two-year college), and level of resources were taken into account. This is not surprising, as other studies of faculty salaries have also found effects of individual productivity (e.g., Tuckman 1979). Using the same data, and aggregating to the departmental level of analysis, Pfeffer and Langton (1988) reported that there was no net relationship between the coefficient of variation in productivity within departments and the coefficient of variation of salaries, the dependent variable of interest, in those departments. In other words, although productivity apparently helped account for the variation in salaries at the individual level of analysis, variation in productivity within departments did not help explain different variations in salaries within academic departments.

This seeming anomaly is resolved quickly as soon as we recognize that the variation in salaries investigated in the individual-level wage regressions reported by Konrad and Pfeffer has both a between-organization and a within-organization component. Pfeffer and Langton were interested in understanding causes of wage variation within departments (within organizations), and thus employed measures and a formulation that restricted attention to that aspect of organizational wages. This latter focus is consistent with the earlier discussion about the importance of within-organization comparisons. Readers can think of their own organizations to see that, in many cases, there is not a very strong relationship between productivity and salary *within* departments, once experience or seniority is taken into account. What productivity in academia does is primarily to enable people to find jobs in higher-paying settings. Within those settings, productivity effects are much reduced. If we want to explore wage variation within organizations, individual-level regressions that cross organizations do not by themselves provide information sufficient for the inquiry. The estimates so derived, unless controls for the mean organizational salary or dummy variables for each organization are included, combine within-organization and between-organization sources of income dispersion.

A tremendous amount of research attention has been given to the measurement of income inequality. That discussion is summarized in Allison (1978) and Schwartz and Winship (1979), and need not be repeated here. The good news is that for income distributions such as those most often encountered in organizational research, with few outliers at either tail of the distribution, the correlations among the measures are quite high. The preferred measure, according to Allison (1978), is the coefficient of variation, or the standard deviation divided by the mean. A second preferred measure is the Gini index, a traditional measure of inequality (Blau 1977; Blau & Schwartz 1984), calculated as the area under the Lorenz curve obtained by plotting the percentage of the population, on one axis, and the percentage of income or some other resource obtained by the corresponding percentage of the population, on the other.

Economists typically have measured income inequality by computing the variance in the natural logarithm of earnings for the sample being studied. Thus, for instance, Harrison, Tilly, and Bluestone (1986, p. 28), studying societal-level income inequality in the United States and its change over time, wrote: "There are any number of ways to characterize 'inequality.' We employ the economist's standard indicator: the variance of the natural logarithm." Freeman (1982, p. 6) measured wage dispersion by the variance and the standard deviation in both the natural logarithm of earnings and natural dollar units. Hirsch (1982) measured earnings inequality by calculating the variance of the natural logarithm of earnings and also by computing a Gini coefficient. He reported a correlation of .93 between the two indicators. Pfeffer and Davis-Blake (in press) reported a correlation of .95 between the Gini index and the coefficient of variation, computed for a sample of academic administrators in more than eight hundred colleges and universities. Blau and Schwartz (1984, p. 16) reported correlations ranging from .85 to 1.00 between the Gini index and the coefficient of variation for a number of variables ranging from income to education. And Schwartz and Winship (1979) reported a correlation of about .7 between those same two indicators of inequality.

Since the standard deviation of a distribution of wages is likely to be larger the larger the mean, it seems to be useful to divide by the mean to produce a normalized measure of wage dispersion—the coefficient of variation. This normalization is not necessarily a concern in many of the economists' studies, as they compare either wages over time (in constant dollars) or wages across industries or establishments, in which the mean undoubtedly is fairly constant. The high correlation among the various measures of wage dispersion, however, means that the choice of a particular measure is probably not too consequential for the results obtained.

Analyzing Dispersion

Common to many theories of income determination, ranging from human capital economics (Becker 1962, 1964; Mincer 1970) to equity theory (Adams 1965), is the idea that incomes vary according to variation in either the inputs, such as education or experience, of the employees or in their performance or output. Consequently, the questions inevitably posed in wage dispersion research ask about the effects of other variables such as establishment size, form of control, or unionization (net of these compositional or demographic effects). This leads to the question of how to control for differences in composition or productivity in the analyses, so that wage dispersion can be analyzed controlling for the effects of variation in education, job tenure, and so forth.

The simplest way of controlling for demographic or compositional differences is to include indicators of these compositional factors in the equations predicting wage dispersion. Thus, for instance, Pfeffer and Langton (1988), examining variation in wage dispersion in a sample of academic departments, included in the equation measures of heterogeneity in gender, the coefficient of variation in years of experience and academic publication, and heterogeneity in academic rank. With these measures included in the equation, any remaining effects were presumably attributable to factors other than diversity in experience or performance in the departments. It is interesting to note that, although these demographic effects were statistically significant, together the indicators of variation in both research productivity and rank and experience accounted for less than 20 percent of the variation in the degree of wage dispersion across departments.

One objection to this simple procedure is that it confounds two possible demographic effects—demographic effects due solely to composition and demographic effects that may result from the operation of social comparison processes. For instance, we know that salary is related to tenure in the job (Medoff & Abraham 1980, 1981). Thus, it would not be surprising to find that in organizations in which everyone had been in his or her job about the same amount of time, wages were more equal than in places where people had occupied their positions for very different tenures.

However, demographic factors are also related to the perceptions of social similarity and, potentially, to social integration and cohesion (Wagner et al. 1984). Social comparison processes may work with more potency in more demographically homogeneous subunits (Kanter 1977; Pfeffer 1983).* This effect of social comparison may also be to reduce wage dispersion. Thus, James Baron has argued for use of an alternative procedure involving computing a dependent measure of wage dispersion that already controls for the effects of simple demography. This is done by first estimating a multiple regression using the entire sample in which the dependent variable is wages (or the natural logarithm of wages, if one prefers the logarithmic transformation) and the independent variables are individual factors expected to affect wages such as age, work experience, education, tenure in the job or the organization, additional skills or training, and gender and race. In addition to these variables, a dummy variable for each department, organization, or subunit (whatever level of analysis is being used) is included to capture differences in mean wages across units. This

---

* The following discussion is based on my collaborative work with James Baron, James Lincoln, and Arne Kalleberg on inequality in U.S. and Japanese establishments. Baron and I have had particularly long discussions and debates about the issue of how to control for demographic composition.

estimated equation is then used to construct a predicted wage for each individual in the entire sample. Then, each person's actual wage is subtracted from that predicted, and this result is squared (so that all deviations are positive). For each subunit or organization in the sample, the sum of the squared deviations for individuals in the organization is computed and divided by n, the number of cases in each organization or subunit. Either this number or its square root serves as the dependent variable in subsequent analyses. This number is conceptually the average amount of deviation in an organization's wage distribution from that predicted by its demographic composition.

This measure also has its problems. In the first place, one needs a comparatively large number of cases per organization for the procedure to tolerate a dummy variable for each separate organization in the sample. Second, it is never entirely clear what to include in the original equation computing the predicted wage regression. In the former procedure, compositional variables can be entered or omitted from the equation and their net effects computed directly. In this latter procedure, once the dependent variable is created, the entire process must be redone to eliminate or add individual-level factors. For instance, one would want to account for dispersion in wages that derives from lower compensation of women and nonwhites. But including gender, for instance, in the original predictive equation means that the estimate of wage dispersion produced is net of any linear effect of gender-based wage inequality.

In current research using the data for manufacturing establishments in Japan and the United States (Kalleberg & Lincoln 1988), both the coefficient of variation and the estimated wage deviation measures are being used. The correlation between the two measures is .67.

Conceptually, wage dispersion across organizations may vary because (1) the organizations differ in their composition, (2) the organizations provide different returns to the same variables, such as education or performance, (3) the organizations use different factors in their wage determination practices, or (4) because of some combination of these factors. Sorting out these varying sources of differences in wage dispersion requires substantial empirical research.

WHY DOES WAGE DISPERSION VARY?

Wage dispersion varies across organizational contexts because the social relations that derive from conditions of the task, governance, and the nature of the institution vary in ways that predictably affect it. Because incentive systems and organizations are both inherently social, it is to the social and political nature of organizations that we should look to understand wage structures. Although efficiency considerations may govern wage systems, they do so only insofar as they are embedded in a set of social relations and institutional norms and practices that affect the wage-setting process. By themselves, efficiency concerns are not proximately related to wage distributions in organizations, if for no other reason than there seems to be only a tenuous connection between allocation regimes and performance, measured at the individual, group, or organizational level (Leventhal 1976; Deutsch 1985; Bishop 1987).

By social relations, we mean the degree of contact and interdependence that characterize organizations or subunits, as well as the norms and governance structures that affect the distribution of power and control and the values that are central to the organization. Social contact, interdependence, and other factors affecting the operation of social comparison processes have direct but at times potentially complex effects on wage dispersion. Norms, political interests, and governance systems have similarly complex effects. We consider each set of factors in turn.

Social Comparison Processes

The evidence generally supports the idea that individuals prefer more equal distributions of wages or other organizational rewards than a principle of equity or proportionality implies, in which individuals are compensated strictly in proportion to their performance or to the inputs such as education and experience they bring to the job. Individuals may prefer more equal allocations because equality reduces interpersonal conflict and enhances the quality of interpersonal relations in the workplace (Lazear 1989). For instance, Deutsch (1985, p. 158) reported "Even when the groups were nominal rather than interacting groups . . . there were some significant effects of the distributive system on attitudes toward other group members. The subjects in the equality and need conditions reported having cooperative feelings toward one another; those in the winner-takes-all and proportionality conditions reported having competitive feelings toward one another." Deutsch (1985, p. 159) also reported that people working under more equal reward allocation rules found the task more pleasant and interesting.

Social rewards from organizational participation are important (Hackman 1976). There is evidence that these social rewards are enjoyed more by those working in more equal reward allocation conditions. Thus, it is only logical that existing evidence suggests people tend to prefer more equal reward allocations (Leventhal 1976; Cook & Hegtvedt 1983).

Equal reward allocations, or at least allocations more equal than those implied by a proportionality or equity rule, enhance the quality of social relations in work groups. Consequently, it follows that there will be more pressure for more equal reward allocations and less dispersion of rewards in situations in which social relations are important to work group members and social comparison processes are facilitated.

Several factors associated with the organization of work increase the importance of social relations and affect the ease with which social comparison processes are accomplished. The size of the work group, department, or organization is one factor. Baker (1984) found that in larger commodities trading networks, information was less well diffused. In larger networks generally, social relations are more diffuse, information less completely shared, and thus, social comparison processes inhibited and social relations less close. In a study of wage dispersion in college and university academic departments, Pfeffer and Langton (1988) found that departmental size was positively related to the amount of wage dispersion. However, examining the amount of wage dispersion for a set of high-level academic administrator positions, Pfeffer and Davis-Blake (in press) found no effect of size on the degree of wage dispersion once other factors, including the degree of specialization, were controlled.

Task interdependence and having many friends in one's own department should both enhance the ease with which social comparison and social information exchange are accomplished and place a premium on smooth relations in the workplace. Pfeffer and Langton (1988) found that the percentage of the department working alone on research was positively associated with the degree of wage dispersion; the more social contact reported among departmental members, the lower the degree of wage dispersion is.

Social comparison processes, and certainly information about wages, are affected by whether salaries are public or private. Tolbert (1986) reported that the male–female wage differential was smaller in public than private colleges and universities, an effect she attributed to the openness of salaries in public organizations. Pfeffer and Langton (1988) found that wage dispersion was greater in private colleges and universities, a finding also reported by Pfeffer and Davis-Blake (in press). Indeed, private control was the major predictor of the amount of wage dispersion of administrator salaries found by Pfeffer and Davis-Blake.

Social contact is an important factor affecting social relations at work. Frank (1984) reported much greater wage dispersion among real estate agents than among automobile salespeople in Ithaca, New York, even though the performances of both could be unambiguously measured. He argued that the difference was that automobile salespeople worked together in one location whereas the real estate people worked outside the office with clients, making social relations and comparisons more intense among the former.

Governance

Wage dispersion is affected by the relative power of various interests in organizations and how workplaces are governed. Pfeffer and Langton (1988) reported that in departments in which there was more equality of decision making on nonpersonnel matters, wage dispersion was less. Conversely, departments that reported a more autocratic governance structure had greater wage dispersion. These findings are consistent with Freeman's (1982) results on the effect of unionization on wage variation—he reported that unionization reduced the degree of wage variation in establishments. Hirsch (1982), using an industry level of analysis, reported a similar finding. The power of lower-level participants, increased through collective bargaining or certain governance arrangements in departments, tends to reduce the amount of wage variation observed.

The Division of Labor

Inequality is also produced, in part, through the division of labor in the workplace. Braverman (1974), for instance, argued that increasing levels of technological development did not lead to a deskilling of all workers but rather to a bipolarization of skill levels. Task specialization means that jobs require different skills and are differentially critical for organizational functioning. Thus, these differentiated positions should be compensated unequally. Pfeffer and Davis-Blake (in press) reported that position proliferation in administrative activities resulted in greater wage inequality. Although it does not treat wages directly, the work of Baron and Bielby (1986) on the proliferation of job titles strongly implies that one reason titles proliferate is to segregate the work force by gender, so that men and women can be paid unequally.

The way work is organized and the social relations that emerge in the workplace, as well as the power relations that characterize work organizations, are important factors in understanding why wages vary more in some settings than in others. There is, of course, a component of technical rationality to these explanations of wage variation. But we lodge the primary explanation for wage dispersion in the social relations that emerge—in part because of technical constraints and in part for other reasons—in the workplace. The pattern of results is to suggest that wage dispersion varies less when more information exists about wages inside the organization, produced through public control, task interdependence, or social contact (see also, Langton & Pfeffer 1989). And wage dispersion varies less when more power is possessed by the work force and less task specialization exists.

CONSEQUENCES OF WAGE DISPERSION

Much of the literature on the causes of wage dispersion in organizations is motivated by implicit, if not explicit, beliefs about the consequences of such inequality in organizations. Thus, for instance, Abegglen and Stalk (1985) argued that the greater salary differentiation in U.S. than in Japanese firms causes goal incongruence and forestalls the development of as much common culture and orientation. By contrast, Frank (1984), Bishop (1987), and other economists, as well as organization theorists (Lawler

1971, 1973; Luthans & Kreitner 1975) worry that not rewarding people on the basis of their performance diminishes the incentive effects of compensation and diminishes organizational performance. This latter concern is a prominent theme in the recent literature on pay in organizations (e.g., Kanter 1987) and in recent discussions on pay for performance.

Some effects of wage dispersion may be positive, particularly if the dispersion is produced by paying people on the basis of their productivity or performance. Bishop (1987, p. S37) argued that "Adjusting relative wage rates to reflect relative productivity produces three kinds of benefits for the firm. First, it serves as an incentive for greater effort. Second, it tends to attract to the firm more able workers and those who like to work hard. . . . Third, it reduces the probability of losing the best performers to other firms and raises the probability that the least productive workers will leave." Leventhal (1976) made many of the same arguments, relying on the literature in social psychology.

The potentially positive incentive and selection effects are balanced by the negative effects of wage dispersion on social relations in the workplace. The experimental literature reviewed by Deutsch (1985) and cited previously in this article speaks to these negative consequences. One issue is whether or not these consequences are evident in the field as well as in experimental settings. And a second issue is the conditions under which negative effects of wage inequality are experienced.

Limited field evidence indicates that wage inequality has negative consequences. Hirsch (1982) and Dickens et al. (1987) both reported evidence that wage dispersion, measured at the industry level of analysis, was positively associated with unionization and with union success in representation elections. Although unionization, itself, is not necessarily a negative outcome (see, e.g., Freeman & Medoff 1979, for a discussion of the positive effects of unionization), the fact that union success in representation elections increases with wage dispersion does suggest that wage dispersion is not perceived as a positive property of the workplace.

Pfeffer and Langton (1989) reported that wage inequality was negatively associated with satisfaction with one's employing organization, as measured by a five-item scale. Moreover, Pfeffer and Langton reported that this negative effect of wage inequality on satisfaction was stronger in public colleges and universities, where salaries are more likely to be public, and thus available for social comparison. They also reported that the negative effect on satisfaction was greater for persons with lower salaries. Not surprisingly, people at the upper end of the distribution of wages are not bothered by more wage dispersion. Faculty working in fields that were paradigmatically more developed (Lodahl & Gordon 1972) were less affected in their job satisfaction by wage dispersion. This result is also sensible in that fields with more highly developed paradigms are characterized by more consensus on standards of evaluation (Hargens 1988). Consequently, wage dispersion should be more legitimate and comprehensible in fields with shared views of teaching, research, and the nature of the discipline.

As theories of psychological commitment suggest (Salancik 1977; Staw 1980; Pfeffer & Lawler 1980), there was evidence that wage dispersion affected satisfaction more for persons who had spent less time in their employing organizations and were therefore less committed to them. And there was evidence that being a departmental chairperson, another measure of commitment and investment in the organization, diminished the effect of wage dispersion on job satisfaction. Contrary to expectations, women's attitudes were not less affected by wage dispersion than those of men.

Social contact had no net effect on the relationship between wage dispersion and job satisfaction. On the one hand, social contact increases the ease with which social comparison processes operate and the flow of information between departmental members. On the other hand, social contact—and for that matter working together—provides more trust and more interpersonal attraction within the department. It may be that wage dispersion is less disliked if the people benefiting from the inequality are better known and closer friends.

Pfeffer and Davis-Blake (1988) have examined the effect of wage dispersion on turnover for a set of high-level college and university administrators in more than eight hundred colleges and universities. Unlike Pfeffer and Langton (1989), they found no main effect of wage dispersion on satisfaction. However, they did find a significant interaction between wage dispersion and salary level; for low-salary people, greater wage dispersion was significantly associated with increased turnover. Moreover, Pfeffer and Davis-Blake reported that this effect was stronger for people in public than in private colleges and universities and for people in jobs with a better developed external labor market. They found no interaction with tenure in the job, however. Thus, when wages are known because of the public setting, and there are external market opportunities, people who earn less in highly dispersed wage distributions are more likely to leave their positions.

These studies provide some evidence of wage dispersion effects on individuals within organizations. It is desirable to investigate whether this effect of wage inequality was affected by the basis of the inequality, as well as by the process by which wages are determined. It is possible, for instance, that inequality based on differences in performance is less disliked than inequality based on personal favoritism or ascriptive characteristics such as gender or race. And Greenberg (1987) has reviewed evidence indicating that the process by which allocations are made, as well as the actual outcomes, affects reactions to decisions. Specifically, procedures that involve participants more in the process appear to be preferred. However,

Deutsch's (1985) review indicates that inequality may be disliked regardless of its basis. In any event, the basis of wage regimes and the consequent effect on organizations remains to be empirically examined.

Organizations are social entities, and the employment relation is, fundamentally, a social one (Baron 1988). In spite of these obvious facts, much of the literature continues to explore rewards in organizations from an overly economic and excessively individualized perspective. Indeed, even this chapter has focused primarily on the distribution of wages in organizations. We could also have examined the dispersion or inequality in nonmonetary rewards such as job autonomy, status, power and authority, and interesting work. People work for rewards other than money, as Barnard (1938) noted, and the allocation and distribution of these nonmonetary rewards needs to be better understood.

For both monetary and nonmonetary rewards, it may be the distribution, rather than the absolute amount, that is most consequential for understanding the effects of rewards on behavior. Theories of social comparison (Festinger 1954) tell us that we judge our well-being in relation to those around us (Stouffer et al. 1949; Martin 1981, 1982). This means that we cannot understand the effect of money, or for that matter, other dimensions of work such as status, power, and autonomy, on reactions to work without considering the distributional aspects of reward and work systems. Indeed, Pfeffer and Davis-Blake (1988), in their study of the determinants of turnover among high-level college administrators, reported that salary has no significant main effect on the propensity to leave the position. Salary did have an effect compared with that paid to people doing the same job elsewhere; a higher comparative salary diminished the probability of turnover. And, as already noted, a significant interaction occurred between salary level and the degree of wage dispersion in the organization. But salary, by itself, accounted for no variation in the likelihood of turnover.

It is important to investigate the extent to which other aspects of organizational rewards such as status, power, and autonomy and freedom on the job are also valued in a comparative frame. If we included information on the distribution, both within and across organizations, on these job dimensions, we might enhance our ability to understand and predict reactions to workplace characteristics. This social, comparative, fundamentally relational aspect of organizations remains largely unexplored in both our theories and our empirical research on organizations.

The very concept of incentives and rewards is, to some extent, challenged by a concern with the social and distributional aspects of organizations. An incentive provided to one individual but not to others, whether it is based on superior performance, productivity, or qualifications, enriches that individual at the expense of others in the organization. The earlier literature in organizational sociology and social psychology dealt with issues of restriction of output (Roy 1952, 1953; Seashore 1954) and social pressures on individuals to not be rate busters. Much of this behavior was, presumably, motivated by a desire not to have management change piece rates or work standards to make the job more onerous or less well-compensated per unit of effort. But the discussion in this chapter suggests another reason for this pattern of behavior: to maintain comparative equality in rewards and, by so doing, preserve harmony and the quality of social relationships at work. It seems that taking this early research seriously, rediscovering the social and relational character of organizations and life in organizations, can help us understand why experiments in pay for performance and other such systems have not always been successful (e.g., Dolan 1985). This emphasis can also help us devise both theories and practice more closely attuned to the social realities of organizations and the social relations that inevitably arise in them and affect how they function.

REFERENCES

Abegglen, James C., and George Stalk, Jr. 1985. *Kaisha: The Japanese Corporation*. New York: Basic Books.

Abrahamson, Mark. 1973. Talent complementarity and organizational stratification. *Administrative Science Quarterly* 18:186–93.

Abrahamson, Mark. 1979. A functional theory of organizational stratification. *Social Forces* 58:128–45.

Akerlof, George A. 1984. Gift exchange and efficiency wages: four views. *American Economic Review* 74:79–83.

Adams, J. S. 1965. Inequity in social exchange. In *Advances in Experimental Social Psychology, Vol. 2*. ed. L. Berkowitz, 267–99. New York: Academic Press.

Alchian, Armen A., and Reuben A. Kessel. 1962. Competition, monopoly, and the pursuit of money. In *Aspects of Labor Economics:* 157–75. Princeton, N.J.: Princeton University Press.

Allison, Paul D. 1978. Measures of inequality. *American Sociological Review* 43:865–80.

Alwin, Duane F. 1987. Distributive justice and satisfaction with material well-being. *American Sociological Review* 52:83–95.

Asher, Martin, and Joel Popkin. 1984. The effect of gender and race differentials on public-private wage comparisons: A study of postal workers. *Industrial and Labor Relations Review* 38:16–25.

Baker, Wayne E. 1984. The social structure of a national securities market. *American Journal of Sociology* 89:775–811.

Barnard, Chester I. 1938. *Functions of the Executive*. Cambridge, Mass.: Harvard University Press.

Baron, James N. 1984. Organizational perspectives on stratification. In *Annual Review of Sociology*, ed. Ralph Turner, 10:37–69. Palo Alto, Calif.: Annual Reviews.

Baron, James N. 1988. The employment relation as a social relation. *Journal of the Japanese and International Economies* 2:492–525.

Baron, James N., and William T. Bielby. 1980. Bringing the firm back in: stratification, segmentation, and the organization of work. *American Sociological Review* 45:737–65.

Baron, James N., and William T. Bielby. 1986. The proliferation of job titles in organizations. *Administrative Science Quarterly* 31:561–86.

Baysinger, B. D., and W. H. Mobley. 1983. Employee turnover: individual and organizational analysis. In *Research in Personnel and Human Resources Management,* ed. K. Rowland and G. Ferris, 269–320. Greenwich, Conn.: JAI Press.

Beck, E. M., Patrick M. Horan, and Charles M. Tolbert III. 1978. Stratification in a dual economy: a sectoral model of earnings determination. *American Sociological Review* 43:704–20.

Becker, Gary. 1962. Investment in human capital: a theoretical analysis. *Journal of Political Economy* Suppl. 70:9–44.

Becker, Gary. 1964. *Human Capital: A Theoretical and Empirical Analysis with Special Reference to Education.* New York: Columbia University Press.

Bibb, Robert, and William H. Form. 1977. The effects of industrial, occupational, and sex stratification on wages in blue-collar markets. *Social Forces* 55:974–96.

Bishop, John. 1987. The recognition and reward of employee performance. *Journal of Labor Economics* 5:S36–S56.

Blau, Peter M. 1977. *Inequality and Heterogeneity.* New York: Free Press.

Blau, Peter M., and Joseph E. Schwartz. 1984. *Crosscutting Social Circles: Testing a Macrostructural Theory of Intergroup Relations.* New York: Academic Press.

Braverman, Harry. 1974. *Labor and Monopoly Capital: The Degradation of Work in the Twentieth Century.* New York: Montly Review Press.

Cohen, Yinon, and Jeffrey Pfeffer. 1986. Organizational hiring standards. *Administrative Science Quarterly* 31:1–24.

Collins, Randall. 1979. *The Credential Society.* New York: Academic Press.

Cook, Karen S., and Karen A. Hegtvedt. 1983. Distributive justice, equity, and equality. *Annual Review of Sociology* 9:217–41.

Dalton, James A., and E. J. Ford, Jr. 1977. Concentration and labor earnings in manufacturing and utilities. *Industrial and Labor Relations Review* 31:45–60.

Deci, Edward L. 1971. Effects of externally mediated rewards on intrinsic motivation. *Journal of Personality and Social Psychology* 18:105–15.

Deci, Edward L. 1972. The effects of contingent and noncontingent rewards and controls on intrinsic motivation. *Organizational Behavior and Human Performance* 8:217–29.

Deutsch, Morton. 1985. *Distributive Justice: A Social Psychological Perspective.* New Haven, Conn.: Yale University Press.

Dickens, William T., Douglas R. Wholey, and James C. Robinson. 1987. Correlates of union support in NLRB elections. *Industrial Relations* 26:240–52.

Doeringer, Peter B., and Michael J. Piore. 1971. *Internal Labor Markets and Manpower Analysis.* Lexington, Mass.: Lexington.

Dolan, Carrie. 1985. Back to piecework: many companies now base workers' raises on their productivity. *Wall Street Journal* November 15:1.

Ehrenberg, R., and G. Milkovich. 1987. Compensation and firm performance. In *Human Resources and the Performance of the Firm*, ed. M. Kleiner et al., pp. 87–122. Madison, Wis.: Industrial Relations Research Association.

Ferber, Marianne A., and Carole A. Green. 1982. Traditional or reverse sex discrimination? A case study of a large public university. *Industrial and Labor Relations Review* 35:550–64.

Ferber, Marianne A., and Betty Kordick. 1978. Sex differentials in the earnings of Ph.D.s. *Industrial and Labor Relations Review* 31:227–38.

Ferber, Marianne A., and Jane W. Loeb. 1974. Professors, performance and rewards. *Industrial Relations* 13:69–77.

Festinger, Leon. 1954. A theory of social comparison processes. *Human Relations* 7:117–40.

Frank, Robert H. 1984. Are workers paid their marginal products? *American Economic Review* 74:549–71.

Freeman, Richard B. 1982. Union wage practices and wage dispersion within establishments. *Industrial and Labor Relations Review* 36:3–21.

Freeman, Richard B., and James L. Medoff. 1979. The two faces of unionism. *The Public Interest* 57:69–93.

Freeman, Richard B., and James L. Medoff. 1984. *What Do Unions Do?* New York: Basic Books.

Goldberg, Victor P. 1980. Bridges over contested terrain: exploring the radical account of the employment relationship. *Journal of Economic Behavior and Organization* 1:249–74.

Granovetter, Mark S. 1974. *Getting a Job: A Study of Contacts and Careers*. Cambridge, Mass.: Harvard University Press.

Granovetter, Mark. 1985. Economic action and social structure: the problem of embeddedness. *American Journal of Sociology* 91:481–510.

Greenberg, Jerald. 1982. Approaching equity and avoiding inequity in groups and organizations. In *Equity and Justice in Social Behavior,* eds. J. Greenberg and R. L. Cohen, pp. 389–435. New York: Academic Press.

Greenberg, Jerald. 1987. A taxonomy of organizational justice theories. *Academy of Management Review* 12:9–22.

Griffin, Ricky W., Thomas S. Bateman, Sandy J. Wayne, and Thomas C. Head. 1987. Objective and social factors as determinants of task perceptions and responses: an integrated perspective and empirical investigation. *Academy of Management Journal* 30:501–23.

Hackman, J. Richard. 1976. Group influences on individuals. In *Handbook of Industrial and Organizational Psychology,* ed. Marvin Dunette, pp. 1455–1525. Chicago: Rand McNally.

Halaby, Charles N., and Michael E. Sobel. 1979. Mobility effects in the workplace. *American Journal of Sociology* 85:385–416.

Hargens, Lowell L. 1988. Scholarly consensus and journal rejection rates. *American Sociological Review* 53:139–51.

Harrison, Bennett, Chris Tilly, and Barry Bluestone. 1986. Wage inequality takes a great U-turn. *Challenge* 29:26–32.

Hedstrom, Peter. 1988. *Structures of Inequality: A Study of Stratification within Work Organizations*. Stockholm, Sweden: Almquist and Wiksell.

Hill, James Richard, and William Spellman. 1983. Professional baseball: the reserve clause and salary structure. *Industrial Relations* 22:1–19.

Hirsch, Barry T. 1982. The interindustry structure of unionism, earnings, and earnings dispersion. *Industrial and Labor Relations Review* 36:22–39.

Homans, George C. 1961. *Social Behavior: Its Elementary Forms*. New York: Harcourt, Brace and World.

Jacobs, David. 1981. Toward a theory of mobility and behavior in organizations: an inquiry into the consequences of some relationships between individual performance and organizational success. *American Journal of Sociology* 87:684–707.

Jencks, Christopher, Susan Bartlett, Mary Corcoran, James Crouse, David Eaglesfield, Gregory Jackson, Kent McClelland, Peter Mueser, Michael Olneck, Joseph Schwartz, Sherry Ward, and Jill Williams. 1977. *Who Gets Ahead?* New York: Basic Books.

Kalleberg, Arne L., and James R. Lincoln. 1988. The structure of earnings inequality in the United States and Japan. *American Journal of Sociology* 94:S121–S153.

Kanter, Rosabeth Moss. 1977. *Men and Women of the Corporation*. New York: Basic Books.

Kanter, Rosabeth Moss. 1987. From status to contribution: some organizational implications of the changing basis for pay. *Personnel* 64:12–37.

Konrad, Alison M., and Jeffrey Pfeffer. In press. Do you get what you deserve? Factors affecting the relationship between productivity and pay. *Administreative Science Quarterly*.

Langton, Nancy, and Jeffrey Pfeffer. 1989. Labor market dimensions and salary variation within markets. Unpublished ms., Graduate School of Business, Stanford University, Palo Alto, Calif.

Lawler, Edward E. 1971. *Pay and Organizational Effectiveness: A Psychological View*. New York: McGraw-Hill.

Lawler, Edward E. 1973. *Motivation in Work Organizations*. Monterey, Calif.: Brooks/Cole.

Lazear, Edward P. 1989. Pay equality and industrial politics. *Journal of Political Economy* 97:561–80.

Lazear, Edward P., and Sherwin Rosen. 1981. Rank-order tournaments as optimum labor contracts. *Journal of Political Economy* 89:841–64.

Lazersfeld, Paul F., and Herbert Menzel. 1980. On the relation between individual and collective properties. In *A Sociological Reader on Complex Organizations*, 3d ed., eds. Amitai Etzioni and Edward W. Lehman, pp. 508–21. New York: Holt, Rinehart, and Winston.

Leonard, Jonathan S. 1987. Carrots and sticks: pay, supervision, and turnover. *Journal of Labor Economics* 5:S136–S152.

Lepper, M. R., and D. Greene. 1978. *The Hidden Costs of Reward: New Perspectives on the Psychology of Human Motivation*, Hillsdale, N.J.: Lawrence Erlbaum.

Leventhal, G. S. 1976. The distribution of rewards and resources in groups and organizations. In *Advances in Experimental Social Psychology*, Vol. 9. ed. Leonard Berkowitz. New York: Academic Press.

Lodahl, Janice, and Gerald Gordon. 1972. The structure of scientific fields and the functioning of university graduate departments. *American Sociological Review* 37:57–72.

Luthans, Fred, and Robert Kreitner. 1975. *Organizational Behavior Modification.* Glenview, Ill.: Scott, Foresman and Company.

Mahoney, Thomas A. 1979. Organizational hierarchy and position worth. *Academy of Management Journal* 22:726–37.

March, James C., and James G. March. 1977. Almost random careers: the Wisconsin school superintendency, 1940–1972. *Administrative Science Quarterly* 22:377–409.

March, James G., and Herbert A. Simon. 1958. *Organizations.* New York: John Wiley.

Martin, Joanne. 1981. Relative deprivation: a theory of distributive injustice for an era of shrinking resources. In *Research in Organizational Behavior,* ed. L. L. Cummings and Barry M. Staw, 3:53–107. Greenwich, Conn.: JAI Press.

Martin, Joanne. 1982. The fairness of earnings differentials: an experimental study of the perceptions of blue-collar workers. *Journal of Human Resources* 17:110–22.

McCain, Bruce E., Charles O'Reilly, and Jeffrey Pfeffer. 1983. The effects of departmental demography on turnover: the case of a university. *Academy of Management Journal* 26:626–41.

Medoff, James L., and Katherine G. Abraham. 1980. Experience, performance, and earnings. *Quarterly Journal of Economics* 95:703–36.

Medoff, James L., and Katherine G. Abraham. 1981. Are those paid more really more productive? The case of experience. *Journal of Human Resources* 16:186–216.

Mincer, Jacob. 1970. The distribution of labor incomes: a survey. *Journal of Economic Literature* 8:1–26.

Moore, William L., and Jeffrey Pfeffer. 1980. The relationship between departmental power and faculty careers on two campuses: the case for structural effects on faculty salaries. *Research in Higher Education* 13:291–306.

O'Reilly, Charles A., and David Caldwell. 1979. Informational influence as a determinant of perceived task characteristics and job satisfaction. *Journal of Applied Psychology* 64:157–65.

Ouchi, William G., and Alfred M. Jaeger. 1978. Type Z organization: stability in the midst of mobility. *Academy of Management Review* 3:305–14.

Pfeffer, Jeffrey. 1977. Toward an examination of stratification in organizations. *Administrative Science Quarterly* 22:553–67.

Pfeffer, Jeffrey. 1981. *Power in Organizations.* Marshfield, Mass.: Pitman Publishing.

Pfeffer, Jeffrey. 1982. *Organizations and Organization Theory.* Marshfield, Mass.: Pitman.

Pfeffer, Jeffrey. 1983. Organizational demography. In *Research in Organizational Behavior, Vol. 5,* ed. L. L. Cummings and Barry M. Staw. Greenwich, Conn.: JAI Press.

Pfeffer, Jeffrey. 1989. A political perspective on careers: interests, networks, and environments. In *Handbook of Career Theory.* ed. Michael B. Arthur, Douglas T. Hall, and Barbara S. Lawrence. New York: Cambridge University Press.

Pfeffer, Jeffrey, and Yinon Cohen. 1984. Determinants of internal labor markets in organizations. *Administrative Science Quarterly* 29:550–72.

Pfeffer, Jeffrey, and Alison Davis-Blake. 1987. Understanding organizational wage structures: a resource dependence approach. *Academy of Management Journal* 30:437–55.

Pfeffer, Jeffrey, and Alison Davis-Blake. In press. Determinants of salary dispersion in organizations. In *Industrial Relations*.

Pfeffer, Jeffrey, and Alison Davis-Blake. 1988. Salary dispersion and turnover among college administrators. Unpublished ms. Graduate School of Business, Stanford University, Palo Alto, Calif.

Pfeffer, Jeffrey, and Nancy Langton. 1988. Wage organization of work: inequality and the case of academic departments. *Administrative Science Quarterly* 33:588–606.

Pfeffer, Jeffrey, and Nancy Langton. 1989. Wage dispersion, satisfaction, and performance: evidence from college faculty. Unpublished ms. Graduate School of Business, Stanford University, Palo Alto, Calif.

Pfeffer, Jeffrey, and John Lawler. 1980. Effects of job alternatives, extrinsic rewards, and behavioral commitment on attitude toward the organization: a field test of the insufficient justification paradigm. *Administrative Science Quarterly* 25:38–56.

Pfeffer, Jeffrey, and Charles A. O'Reilly III. 1987. Hospital demography and turnover among nurses. *Industrial Relations* 26:158–73.

Pfeffer, Jeffrey, and Gerald R. Salancik. 1978. *The External Control of Organizations: A Resource Dependence Perspective.* New York: Harper & Row.

Rosen, Sherwin. 1985. Implicit contracts—a survey. *Journal of Economic Literature* 23:1144–75.

Roy, Donald. 1952. Quota restriction and goldbricking in a piecework machine shop. *American Journal of Sociology* 57:427–42.

Roy, Donald. 1953. Work satisfaction and social reward in quota achievement. *American Sociological Review* 18:507–14.

Runciman, W. G. 1966. *Relative Deprivation and Social Justice: A Study of Attitudes to Social Inequality in Twentieth Century England.* Berkeley: University of California Press.

Salancik, Gerald R. 1977. Commitment and the control of organizational behavior and belief. In *New Directions in Organizational Behavior,* ed. Barry M. Staw and Gerald R. Salancik, pp. 1–54. Chicago: St. Clair Press.

Salancik, Gerald R., and Jeffrey Pfeffer. 1978a. Uncertainty, secrecy, and the choice of similar others. *Social Psychology* 41:246–55.

Salancik, Gerald R., and Jeffrey Pfeffer. 1978b. A social information processing approach to job attitudes and task design. *Administrative Science Quarterly* 23:224–53.

Schwartz, Joseph, and Christopher Winship. 1979. The welfare approach to measuring inequality. In *Sociological Methodology, 1980,* ed. Karl F. Schuessler. San Francisco: Jossey-Bass.

Seashore, Stanley E. 1954. *Group Cohesiveness in the Industrial Work Group.* Ann Arbor, Mich.: Institute for Social Research.

Simon, Herbert A. 1957. The compensation of executives. *Sociometry* 20:32–35.

Smith, Peter. 1973. *Groups Within Organizations.* New York: Harper & Row.

Smith, Sharon P. 1976. Pay differentials between federal government and private sector workers. *Industrial and Labor Relations Review* 29:179–97.

Staw, Barry M. 1977. Motivation in organizations: toward synthesis and redirection. In *New Directions in Organizational Behavior,* ed. Barry M. Staw and Gerald R. Salancik, pp. 55–95. Chicago: St. Clair Press.

Staw, Barry M. 1980. Rationality and justification in organizational life. In *Research in Organizational Behavior,* eds. B. M. Staw and L. L. Cummings, 2:45–80. Greenwich, Conn.: JAI Press.

Stinchcombe, Arthur L. 1963. Some empirical consequences of the Davis-Moore theory of stratification. *American Sociological Review* 38:805–8.

Stolzenberg, Ross M. 1978. Bringing the boss back in: employer size, employee schooling, and socioeconomic achievement. *American Sociological Review* 43:813–28.

Stouffer, S. A., E. A. Suchman, L. C. Devinney, S. A. Star, and R. M. Williams. 1949. *The American Soldier, Vol. 1: Adjustment During Army Life.* Princeton, N.J.: Princeton University Press.

Subbarao, A. V., and A. deCarufel. 1983. Pay secrecy and perceptions of fairness in a university environment. In *Proceedings of the Administrative Science Association of Canada,* ed. G. Johns, 4:173–81.

Szafran, Robert F. 1984. *Universities and Women Faculty: Why Some Organizations Discriminate More than Others.* New York: Praeger.

Thomas, Joe, and Ricky Griffin. 1983. The social information processing model of task design: a review of the literature. *Academy of Management Review* 8:672–82.

Tolbert, Charles, Patrick M. Horan, and E. M. Beck. 1980. The structure of economic segmentation: a dual economy approach. *American Journal of Sociology* 85:1095–1116.

Tolbert, Pamela S. 1986. Organizations and inequality: sources of earnings differences between male and female faculty. *Sociology of Education* 59:227–36.

Trow, Martin, ed. 1975. *Teachers and Students: Aspects of American Higher Education.* New York: McGraw-Hill.

Tuckman, Barbara Hauben. 1979. Salary differences among university faculty and their implications for the future. In *Salary Equity: Detecting Sex Bias in Salaries Among College and University Professors,* eds. Thomas R. Pezzullo and Barbara E. Brittingham, pp. 19–36. Lexington, Mass.: D. C. Heath.

Wagner, W. Gary, Jeffrey Pfeffer, and Charles A. O'Reilly III. 1984. Organizational demography and turnover in top management groups. *Administrative Science Quarterly* 29:74–92.

Williamson, Oliver E. 1975. *Markets and Hierarchies: Analysis and Antitrust Implications.* New York: Free Press.

5
Converging on Autonomy: Anthropology and Institutional Economics

MARY DOUGLAS

This chapter is concerned with a convergence of interest from two directions on the topic of individual autonomy. On the one hand, transaction costs theory focuses on the cost to the individual of preserving autonomy in the marketplace. It pays special attention to the causes of asymmetry among dealers, to classifying different kinds of asymmetry, and to assessing their respective effects on market structures. Its concern with individual reactions to constraints on autonomy has made it necessary to rewrite the economist's conception of the rational being.

On the other hand, the cultural theory, which has its roots in anthropology, classifies different types of cultures according to the amount of autonomy enjoyed by individuals. Taking patterns of autonomy as a key to cultural bias, cultural theory considers the different kinds of constraints and how to measure them. The way persons justify, to themselves and to others, the limitations that their society places on autonomy is central to the idea of cultural bias. The theory uses a typology that contrasts group membership (as one kind of restriction on autonomy) with restrictions on individual freedom to negotiate and choose among options. This produces something parallel to the contrast between markets and hierarchies which is prominent in transaction costs economics.

I use Chester Barnard's *Functions of the Executive* to show the difficulties of making good organizational theory without a systematic approach to culture. This famous book is particularly apt for the exposition because Chester Barnard was trying to formulate a theory of the interaction of individuals with the organization they work in. Some of what he tried to do has been achieved. Some of the difficulties that he could not surmount remain as stumbling blocks to this day. Reading a formative book fifty years after it was published is like entering an echoing cave backwards. Modern concepts bounce anachronistically off the pages of Barnard's book.

CHESTER BARNARD

Barnard's theory depends on the connection between the purposes of members of organizations and the purposes of their organizations. The connection is still missing. There are gestures toward the relationship, good arm waving, but in general the two kinds of purposes are treated separately: social psychology and personnel management attend to the individual person, and organization theory attends to the organization. The failure to coordinate the two parts of a single field is not trivial, as Barnard knew well. He assumed (plausibly) that an organization cannot succeed unless it satisfies the goals of its members. But to go any distance from that starting point he would need to know how their goals are formed. For this, I submit, he would need a cultural theory.

Barnard's thinking made liberal use of metaphors from economic theory. Most would agree that for any organization two levels of needs must be satisfied: the needs of the whole and those of its constituent parts. In his day, and since, this problem is often discussed with biological metaphors. Barnard's originality was to express it within utilitarian theory as a problem of rational choice. He tried to deal with it as an equilibrium problem. Borrowing the metaphor of international trade according to the theory of his day, he regarded any organization as the result of exchanges between various contributors; he expected that in a successful organization the exchanges would generate a surplus of satisfactions for all contributors; if not, the individuals would be contributing more than they were giving and would tend to withdraw their contributions, resulting in failure of the enterprise.

One can be impressed with the presence of this, written before exchange theory and game theory—a precursor of Mancur Olson's theory of collective action. Barnard's conception of an organization rendered ineffective by weak incentives corresponds to Mancur Olson's concept of a latent organization. But more than the prophetic vein in *The Functions of the Executive* of a man writing before his time, one catches echoes of eighteenth-century system building on the idea of individual rationality, of Ricardo, and of Bentham's greatest happiness principle and hedonic calculus.

There is an advantage in using Barnard's work to introduce cultural theory, because of the common interest in the relation between individuals and their social environment. The same methodological individualism that blocked his efforts in that direction seems to spoil the social theory of our day. It also provides a telling case against the argument that modern people autonomously choose their ideas, unlike culture-ridden primitives. Barnard exemplifies the opposite point, namely, that some modern individuals are very culture-ridden.

PROBLEMS WITH METHODOLOGICAL INDIVIDUALISM

Methodological individualism starts with an ultimate unanalyzable factor, the rational being sovereign over his own choices. This starting point gets in the way of any attempt to relate the structure of individual goals to the goals of an organized social environment. This is largely because it is not possible to say what the individual desires. The one interaction that seems to be theoretically acceptable (perhaps because it does not imply any sociological determinism) is the calculus of costs. Excessive costs for a particular choice will make a rational being change his mind about the ordering of his goals. This theorizing puts no intervening social influence between an individual and his preferences. The social environment is differentiated only by costs. Preferences arise mysteriously from within the individual (Wildavsky 1987). Theoretically costs are determined by individual preferences, but in practice economic analysis has to proceed on the basis that rational preferences are known.

Chester Barnard attempted to work out an equilibrium model to describe the balance achieved between the contributions of the members of an organization to its functioning and the return contributions made by the organization to the fulfilment of its members' private goals. As Herbert Simon says (1945) this is the start of a theory of public goods. Barnard allowed that the return to the individual would not only be in terms of remuneration and pension but also of various fringe benefits, esteem, and so forth. The attempt to work out this equilibrium theory foundered (but in very good company) on the relation of the individual to the organization.

FOUR PROBLEMS

Barnard confronted four problems in his attempt to link the rational choices of individuals to the survival of organizations.

First, he shirked making a theory-driven categorization of organizations. His classifications came from the world in which the organizations themselves function. This is using what anthropologists call actors' categories. In other words, he started with and stayed with the agents' own functioning classifications. These classifications impede theorizing: the anthropologist only ends up saying what the agents under study had been saying all along. At least it ensures that the people he is writing about will understand the book. From their comments on their own budgetary processes Barnard could make the distinction between failed and successful, complete and incomplete, and dependent and independent organizations; from their legal processes he could make the distinction between formal and informal, superordinate and subordinate organizations. In fact, he was not very concerned with making an independent classification of organizations. He certainly did not perceive the need for a categorization that would calibrate his own theory of authority, or even the need for a theory that might not be the same as that of a successful president of an organization. Sometimes he wrote as if the main objective was to distill the wisdom of successful directors.

Oliver Williamson helps Barnard's project on this first shortcoming. He, too, takes the usual administrative categories—markets and hierarchies— or the usual economists' categories—the extremes on the dimension between perfect and imperfect competition. But he defines these according to criteria that work in his theory—that is, in terms of contractual features, of which communication (one of Barnard's interests) is a major part.

Second, though Barnard talked about the environment of the organization and though he said a lot about mutual adjustment, he only described one blanket kind of environment. He shirked making a typology of the different external conditions to which the organization must adapt and which it is in a continual process of modifying. It is almost as though he chose not to typologize in order to keep to an appropriately vague level of generalization.

Williamson again helps to overcome this weakness. He identifies a set of critical dimensions for describing transactions, within which the ease of mutual adjustment varies systematically, and also the organizational structure within which a transaction is embedded. Thus, he has a theory-driven categorization of both the internal structure of firms and surrounding conditions, which enables him to develop a theory of the influence of transaction costs on market structures. (That he thinks about a dynamic interaction between kinds of organizations operating in different kinds of environments endears him to anthropologists.)

Third, Chester Barnard taught that satisfactions for the individual members need to be sufficient to compensate contributors for what they give. But he never showed any reason to expect this could happen. Far from having a theory about how firms ought to behave, he left firms crossing their fingers and just hoping that they have the right lines of communication, and that their leaders are competent (for what certainly sounds like an impossible job). This is not an equilibrium model; such a model must postulate some process that brings opposing forces into repose. Otherwise the mention of equilibrium is just interior decoration. Barnard needed something equivalent to the concept of diminishing marginal utility in economics. Without this concept in economic theory, demand and supply could never settle at a market price and the whole theory would collapse. I propose that the missing mechanism is described in cultural theory.

Williamson's model of the market is set in motion and comes to rest because he postulates that individuals rationally choose to shoulder trans-action costs when they are small and move into hierarchies when the costs become too high to be borne profitably. He escapes my rebuke to Barnard by finding a mechanism to justify the oscillations and the equilibrium; here again he has helped to achieve what Barnard was aiming at.

However, on the fourth point, I do not think Williamson rescues Barnard from his dilemma. As is usual in rational choice analysis, Barnard treated individuals' objectives as independent of those of other people or the organization. He allowed that, after a minimum subsistence level is satisfied, their principal concern is for esteem. This was not original at the time, and it has been richly elaborated since. While the desire for esteem (a cultural concept) is the linchpin of the connection that Barnard made between the organization and the individual member, he did practically nothing with the idea. Esteem is a static and empty notion in his book. He had no sense of any ongoing dialectical transformation between the goals of the individual and those of the organization. He did not conceive of a process by which the purposes of the one might interpenetrate the pur-poses of the other, and still less of how they tend to drift apart. Yet an interaction affecting their private goals and generating common ones is the cultural mechanism that would have helped his theory.

Williamson also adopts methodological individualism. He has a theory of firms, but his theory of the relationship between individuals and firms could be better. He believes firms vary, but not individuals. He has the same representative rational individual marching into one kind of contract or refusing to renew it and entering another kind for the same set of rea-sons, namely, the cost of transactions in a given economic environment. He might claim, in rebuttal, that he does not need a less impoverished concept of the individual person, since his theory is not about the relation-ship of individuals to their organization.

My argument is precisely that it does matter to the economist that ideas of esteemed behavior are generated collectively (see Douglas 1987). Bar-nard would have been helped by a theory of how individuals negotiate with one another over what kinds of esteem their organization will provide (a gold watch at the end of a lifetime of service, a place at High Table, a medal, an obituary notice, a memorial plaque) and the sources of dises-teem that they will not tolerate (South African investments, dirty wash-room, no parking, insult from employers).

The anthropologists are interested in how standards of what counts as estimable vary. We find that the different standards come out of different kinds of organization. What the individual is going to want is not entirely his own idea, but consists largely of a set of desires that the social environ-ment inspires in him. For example, in a commando unit or the fire brigade, opportunity for heroic deeds is the means of achieving esteem; elsewhere longevity rather than heroism may bring esteem; in some communities es-teem is more directly connected to wealth than Barnard reckoned. In some, jealousy is under control while in others it cuts destructive swathes. A cultural theory of variation in ideas of esteem and variations in the scope for blaming and responsibility (Wildavsky 1987, pp. 283–93) would supply some of the mechanism that Barnard lacked for explaining the success of organizations.

COMMUNICATION

What can we say about Barnard's theory of communication? It is a kind of primitive telegraph system; its elementary signals, like the morse code, need to be clear and unambiguous and their origin authenticated. The simplicity of Barnard's conception of communication becomes more painful when we see it amplified in Herbert Simon's *Administrative Behavior* (1945, chap. 8). For both, the system of communication is always external to the communicators; the code is established independently; someone (at the center?) thinks it up and the others use it as it comes. This discourse about communication allows no scope to consider how the communication categories are constructed, or how the members of an organization may adapt the categories. The communication is treated as one thing and the organization as quite another. The idea that organizations are kinds of message-coders is quite alien.

To an anthropologist in this day and age Herbert Simon's description of what he calls the presentation of a problem reads very strangely. He says that decision making cannot begin until the right way to present the problem has been found. Finding how to present it is described as a deliberate cognitive effort. If only that were the case! Problems are presented according to the way that the institution's culture has set up the categories, and it is very difficult (though not impossible) for members to rethink them. All they can do in the way of radical rethinking is to revise the institution itself. The difficulty of explaining cultural bias to economists is an uncomforting case in point.

Even in 1938 the continental insulation that rejected any notion of the shared construction of concepts is worth noting. Durkheim's *Primitive Classification* (with Marcel Mauss) came out in 1902, and his *Elementary Forms of the Religious Life* in 1912. But these books were not translated till later. Simon's footnotes in the 1945 edition (p. 24) show that he considered this teaching to partake of the fallacy of "group mind." The fallacy is to attribute organic unity to collective action. Because individuals can act together to produce a collective language and shared culture, this does not mean that they have mysteriously become welded into one thinking machine or "group mind." Durkheim's discussion of what he called collective representations has frequently been interpreted by Anglo-Saxon critics to mean that a society is one big thinking animal, a misrepresentation that allows them to dismiss the whole subject as absurd.

The heritage of ideas about collective construction of categories comes from Hegel and Marx. It is understandable that writing about the organization of capitalist industry would not put one in a milieu susceptible to Marxist ideas about categorization. Furthermore, the idea that clarity in coding messages may not be just a technical matter but involves shared second-order preferences is also incompatible with methodological individualism; each individual thinker is supposed to come freely to his own ideas. Nearly the whole effort of British social anthropology (without being under Marxist influence) was developed under the assumption that organization results from the process of adapting categories of thought. When I write that common categories are the basis of the social bond, reviewing anthropologists castigate me for stating the obvious. Considering the fact that Michel Foucault has lived, and written so effectively about the relation between power and knowledge (1977), and that he has died already, and that much water has gone under the bridge in the intervening fifty years since 1938, we can hope that ideas which were unacceptable before may be less threatening now.

THE PERSON

Focusing on the relationship of the individual to the organization, Barnard faced a problem that many have pointed out to me. It is all very well for individuals in primitive tribes to think and act in unison; the simplicity and uniformity of their experience makes that understandable. But for us today, social experience is utterly heterogeneous. There is no reason to expect coherent forms of culture to emerge. As Barnard said, a person belongs to many organizations—a golf club, a rotary club, a church—but in each he experiences a different culture. In defining the individual in an organization Barnard decided to strip him of antecedent associations. His idea of the individual was bare of history and attachments. Hirschman has pointed out that this is usually the case in theories of rational behavior (see Hirschman 1982). Barnard wrote only about the part of the individual's purposes that was related to the organization. Such a person as he postulated, whose identity could change from scene to scene and whose purposes were equally labile, might conceivably exist. But if you assume that such a person, far from being exceptional, is the best model for thinking about how human individuals behave in organizations, you have to accommodate an impossibly splintered and spineless creature within your general theory of society. This creature would be useless to a theory of rational choice because it is defined as incapable of choosing.

If you have written some capacity to choose into the makeup of your rational agent, you would want to allow him to choose which church, which sports club, which voluntary service he joins and which kind of work he does. Even the most restricted circumstances usually offer some minor choices of workplace, work friends, religious worship or not worshiping, and leisure time. In making these, as one choice affects another, we can perhaps be allowed the minimal assumption that the person is trying to arrive eventually at some manageable environment. From that assumption results a unitary person trying to fullfil a set of feasible purposes. On this assumption the various associations that constitute a person's social environment may well have some degree of homogeneity, resulting from personal proclivities. When we find an organization of a particular type rewarding behavior of a certain kind and penalizing other kinds of behavior, it is not unreasonable to assume that it is inhabited by persons of a certain type who have been attracted to it, and also that its environment has transformed others who did not choose it but found themselves in its ambit.

To sum up at this point, although Barnard does not fare very well under scrutiny, succeeding generations of economists and organization theorists have not done better on the problem he made his own. Most of his troubles come from his fidelity to the economist's conception of the ultimate rational being, which is inherently unanalyzable. Since he wants to say something about how organizations relate to their contributors, Barnard's theory needs to consider further why different individuals desire different goals, how their goals change, or how these goals mesh with the purposes of an organization. He does not try to categorize organizations into their kinds, nor to divide the kinds of environments; so he does not have a model of organizations interacting with and adjusting to their environments. His idea of an equilibrium of contributions from the organization to the members and from the members to the organization is the kind of easygoing, optimistic functionalism that has attracted the derision of Jon Elster (1983). He can only say that the equilibrium works because and when the firm is seen to work. Post facto, he can indicate which organizations have evidently achieved the right balance, because their members stay with them and they stay in business, but he has no theory to explain why many organizations fail: all he can say is that they must have got the balance wrong or had faulty communications. His references to equilibrium are more a matter of exhortation (a sermon about caring for the interests of members) than a basis for analysis.

INDIFFERENCE

Barnard's idea of equilibrium between contributions has been less fruitful than his idea about the zone of indifference within which authority is unquestioned. This is a significant enrichment of the concept of the individual, since it differentiates between preferences. Each person has some strong preferences, others more weakly adhered to, and a whole zone of not caring. Barnard taught that a leader is followed easily if his commands fall within the zone of indifference, where the members of the organization do not mind what he asks them to do. Naturally his problems arise when he asks them to follow him against their inclinations.

Where did Barnard get the idea of a zone of indifference? It is reasonable to see his usage as another metaphor borrowed from economic theory. It sounds like an adaptation of Edgeworth's technical solution to the problem of measuring utility, but Barnard's use of the term is very different from Edgeworth's. Barnard's idea may seem only a small step from saying that, for each item acquired, diminishing marginal utility produces a point at which the consumer is indifferent to the prospect of acquiring an additional increment. The step is, in fact, a big shift. The focus, which was originally on the relation of the individual to some desirable class of objects, has been shifted to a graduated nimbus of desires surrounding each individual. Desires for everything are graded into zones of intensity, the more intense fanning out gradually to a zone of indifference in which authority is easily acceptable. The idea is a prototype for the origin of conventions, as used by Thomas Schelling (1960) and David Lewis (1969). In their work some zone of indifference is the starting point of coordination; it indicates a limit to individual aims, a neutral area in which conflict is in abeyance because no one cares enough.

Herbert Simon took up the idea more exactly in Barnard's sense, in Chapter 7 of *Administrative Behavior* (1945), where he discusses the problem of achieving coordination. In this book he is a docile follower of Barnard, repeating the account of a zone of indifference as the area in which authority has no problems. However, when he (Simon 1955) writes about rational choices, what seems to be the same idea about a zone of indifference gets quite another twist. Here the question is about the grotesque optimizing calculus that economic theory expects the rational being to perform on all choices. Through a brilliant leap, the zone of indifference around each person's wishes has been transformed into the zone within which his desires can be satisfied without optimization, and therefore without the calculus. It introduces the new concept of satisficing and of bounded rationality.

In Simon's original version the boundedness of rationality appears to be a useful, necessary contrivance by which rational beings let decisions beyond a certain range of interest take care of themselves, or rather be taken care of by relying on organizational and environmental cues. The scope of the wording suggested that bounded rationality is an aid to competent decision, since without being bounded rationality cannot work at all. The discovery of this advantage to humans hinted at a new approach to thinking in general.

However, bounded rationality has come to mean merely the limits on cognitive competence. Whereas Simon treated it as a good thing because it is a form of economizing on cognitive energy, Williamson actually started to count the value of the saving. Considering that the limits on rationality take energy to overcome, Williamson regards institutional solutions to decision problems as savings in energy that would otherwise be dispersed because of boundedness (1985, p. 46). He treats boundedness as a weakness, a source of incompetence.

COGNITIVE INCOMPETENCE AND MORAL TURPITUDE

Williamson gives his own turn to the concepts of rational behavior and opportunism: "By opportunism I mean self-seeking with guile. This includes but is scarcely limited to more blatant forms, such as lying, stealing, and cheating. Opportunism more often involves subtle forms of deceit. . . . More generally, opportunism refers to the incomplete or distorted disclosure of information, especially to calculated efforts to mislead, distort, disguise, obfuscate, or otherwise confuse . . ." (1985, p. 47). Williamson regards cognitive incompetence and opportunism as indispensable assumptions for correct analysis of asymmetries in economic relations. On both issues he is picking up and altering an idea espoused by Barnard. Bounded rationality (at least in Simon's first formulation and in Barnard's concept of a zone of indifference), was an unfocused area of ideas and purposes. For each individual it indicated a horizon, appropriate relief from vigilance, and respite from choosing, without implying anything about incompetence. As to opportunism, in Barnard's 1938 version, and in Simon's of 1945, the word has no moral implications whatever.

Transaction costs theory characterizes individuals in the marketplace as weakly rational and weakly moral. This is because it focuses on uncertainty and difficulties in getting parties to stand by their contracts. Corporations consisting of formerly autonomous individuals provide a system of governance. By monitoring, penalties, and rewards, the hierarchy can make assets flow that would otherwise be blocked.

This approach removes a large element of physical automatism that was implicit in the description of market behavior. The classical idea of monopoly starts with the case of natural monopolies, advantages of location, or natural control of a physically locked-in resource; it then describes artificial monopolies made by collusion; in this view, collusion is exceptional. I have no grievance against the heavy dose of original sin in Williamson's account of human behavior. It is a distinct improvement to have shifted attention away from a price and costs system that was thought to function automatically because of natural conditions of supply and demand. The shift to all-too human interaction is a shift toward cultural factors. It opens the door for cultural analysis to enter the account of economic behavior.

The first wedge to put into this welcome opening is the structuring of knowledge and morals. First, we should observe that opportunism is rarely unlimited. Nor is the boundedness of rationality random. The zone of indifference is not entirely a private matter. What one can safely ignore is largely contained within a boundary etched by a collective process. Regarding opportunism, what counts as responsible initiative is culturally defined. What looks to the outsider like resort to low cunning, lying, stealing, and cheating may be highly prescribed. Moral attributes are really irrelevant.

AUTONOMY

The concept of autonomy will be plainer if I can illustrate the cultural structuring of opportunism. Fortunately a superb example is at hand in Gerald Mars' book on occupational crime (1984). This focuses on opportunism in the full sense. It starts with considering the scope for autonomous action in different types of organizations. It expects that wherever a chink of freedom appears for appropriating resources or for witholding information, it will be exploited. The industrial pattern of autonomy is the structure of the alternative economy.

The workplace provides asymmetries; complex arrays of advantages and disadvantages can be charted in terms of degrees and kinds of autonomy. Mars starts with a careful classification of occupations in modern industrial society. His angle on opportunism is congenial to Williamson's since he is interested in the forms of predation that each work system permits. The classification includes three types of predator, which Mars calls "hawks," "vultures," and "wolves."

Hawks are those lone operators who make their killing without needing any collaborators. They are employed taxicab drivers whose accounts the owner of the vehicle cannot check. They are the entrepreneurs who work in the interstices of Soviet bureaucracy, performing an invaluable task by knowing just where to lay their hands on a load of missing supplies, and who make a good unaccounted profit on every kind deed.

Vulture jobs are unranked, unspecialized, but some solidarity is enjoined. These jobs offer considerable autonomy and freedom to contract, but the freedom is subject to bureaucratic control. The workers are treated by the employer as a collectivity, which encourages some solidarity. "Like vultures, they need the support of a group to exploit their terrain, but when they find their opportunity, they are on their own" (Mars 1984, p. 33). They include sales representatives, travelers, and semiskilled craftsmen. Each has his semiautonomous field, his scam territory, or his "fiddle-fief" as Mars calls it, which the individual exploits to the best of his or her ability. The bureaucracy cannot impose changes that disturb the "fiddle earnings" of all members of a group. For example, if the organization starts to monitor and control all the sales representatives in a neighborhood, it provokes a collective reaction: the reps will focus on some faked excuse for blocking the reorganization. If the managerial changes affect only one individual member, the group will not react on his behalf. But when the whole staff of a restaurant or a nursing home fleece a client, it will be no good complaining to the maître d' or the doctor.

Wolves hunt in packs. They are ranked and get their biggest spoils when they work in a stratified team or gang, keeping to their ranks and specialized work roles. Wolves attack any unguarded supply line. They might typically be miners, longshoremen, long-distance truck drivers, garbage collection crews, airline crews. Every individual's skill is needed as much to organize pillage as to organize the legitimate work. And they have no place for the individual working on his own.

These are classes of workplace opportunists. Mars's system also includes one type of absolute victim in the workplace, the employee who has no autonomy whatever and so no option but to bear all the burdens assigned. These victims of opportunism he calls donkeys. Prototypical positions of minimum autonomy are the cashier in a cafeteria and the worker on the factory assembly line. Donkeys combine the extremes of powerlessness and power, because sabotage is always possible. When driven to the limits of endurance the donkey throws off his load: the cashier jams the cash register, the worker crashes the assembly line and walks away, but only to find another donkey job.

The animal names are not offensive since the writer's sympathies are with the opportunists. His informants have gleefully told him how they beat the system. Nobody recognizing themselves as running in a wolf pack, descending like vultures on a carcass, or profiting from the stupidity of others would be uncomfortable at reading how his autonomy has been asserted.

CULTURAL ANALYSIS

Mars has used for his classification of organizational environments the two dimensions developed in cultural theory, which are designed to capture as much as possible of the social environment that affects persons' relations with one another. One is the dimension of structure; the other is the dimension of boundary. Structure and boundary represent two kinds of social restriction on autonomy.

In Figure 5.1 the horizontal (group) axis presents the insulating boundary around a group; the vertical (grid) axis presents the degree to which the individual is personally insulated from the rest of society. This is a map of possible social environments, varying in the degrees and kinds of autonomy permitted to individuals. Any one social environment can be compared with any other for its structuredness. The more structure it has (i.e., the further up the grid dimension), the narrower the scope for negotiating individual options. At the theoretical limit, a person can be in such a constricted social space (in corner B) that no options are available. The less

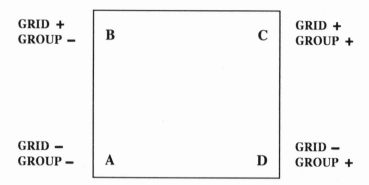

Figure 5.1

the environment is structured, the more of life would seem to be open to negotiation.

The criteria for group inclusiveness depend on the field of interaction. How does one become a member of the group? How much does it absorb its members' time and energies or give them their life support? The golf club may be an all-embracing circle of devotees whose lives revolve around its tournaments, or so might be a church or a commune. Or these groups might only meet on weekends monthly, or irregularly.

How does the group regulate its boundary against the outside world? What is involved in being admitted to the club or the fellowship, and what breaches will provoke blackballing or "disfellowshipping"? We have given a lot of thought to how this concept of relative group strength can be made operational. (By "we" I mean about twelve colleagues who are working together on developing a theory of cultural variation, and about thirty who have been applying it to various questions.) If the social unit is a firm or a college, the question is how to assess the relative strength of its group boundary compared with that of another firm or college. The investigator has to discover the relevant distinctions, say among permanent members on the payroll, *ad hoc* consultants, and boards of advisers or trustees. An Oxford college would score more for group than an American university because its trustees and the faculty are the same, and the interwar Oxbridge college would score more than the postwar one because before the war its fellows normally expected to spend their whole lives there.

It is not too difficult to create a dimension of more or less strength in the group boundary. Structure is indicated by degrees of restricting individual interactions. The idea that insulation is a key indicator of the social environment and its culture comes from Basil Bernstein's insight into educational sociology (1970, 1973, 1975). In 1970 James Hampton started to compare variations in the degree of social insulation (1980). It turns out that insulation is a very rich idea, concealing various possible implications, as we found in trying it out. More structure does not necessarily mean less

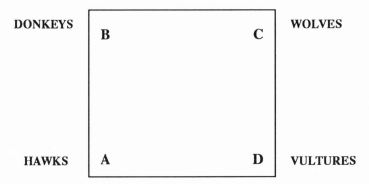

Figure 5.2

scope for opportunism (as Mars shows with his example of the Soviet bureaucracy). More structure does not necessarily imply less autonomy for the individual. The brahmin who restricts the range of his preferences so as to be content with a bowl of rice has increased his autonomy by reducing his options. Developing an all-purpose dimension of grid turns out to be more taxing than we expected. Various experiments are being made, in various contexts, to develop a model of the social environment that explains how cultural values cluster.

This background may help explain why Mars's classification of industrial opportunism does not always mesh with Williamson's account, though there is a fair amount of overlap. Mars has neatly mapped his zoo as in Figure 5.2. The line from A to B measures lessening degrees of autonomy. The donkeys are shown at B as the extreme case of reduced autonomy. Thus, he shows only one set of victims. He could easily make cells for victims of each type of predation, or otherwise enrich his model.

OPPORTUNISM

To examine Mars's account side by side with Williamson's would be a rewarding exercise. Here I can only make a few points. First, both accounts focus on the asymmetries in exchanges, and both expect the rational agent to exploit whatever specificity his or her own resources possess. Mars's account of the unwary diner being fleeced by the colluding members of a restaurant staff exactly corresponds to Williamson's account of locked assets; once he has taken off coat and hat and looked at the menu it is too late; the diner is already locked into the exploitative situation (see Mars & Nicod 1984), and this applies even more to the patient who has undressed and got into bed in the nursing home; exit is practically impossible.

Transaction costs theory says little about opportunism within a centralized system partly because it assumes that centralizing is a way of bringing opportunism under control. Nor does Mars say much about it. He is more intent on describing the bonding process that commits each member of the wolf pack to the system, much as in Fagin's kitchen the child is enrolled after he has proved himself as a pickpocket. However, if we were to take Williamson's invitation to be systematically cynical, we would look at the diagram to see what kind of predation each place is best organized for. Then the opportunism of the lone operator, which is the type Williamson starts from, preys indiscriminately against any likely victim. The hierarchy is organized to exploit its own lowest orders, as the case of the hotels and restaurants illustrate, since the best pickings go to the top ranks, and the lowest have the least autonomy. The vultures are organized for sharing loot equally; the weakness of their team organization itself ensures that they can only make short forays for big loot and must content themselves most of the time with small regular pilferings.

CATEGORIES

A brief glance at opportunism has shown the convergence on autonomy. With some idea of the technique of cultural analysis in hand, we can now return to Barnard's (and Simon's) ideas about communication. I maintained earlier that it is important to take into account the joint construction of categories, instead of treating them as neutral vehicles of things called messages, symbols, or meanings. Before any message is sent out by a would-be leader to his muster of followers, the scope for leadership has been determined by the shape of their organization. The style of the organization itself suggests how problems should be presented. There is no one right way of communicating. The method of communication is part of the style of its organization. Each type of organization perceives its problems differently.

David Bloor illustrates this with the history of a theorem in mathematics, which has received much attention from philosophers of science (Lakatos 1976). Before the bureaucratic reform of the German universities, Euler's theorem (1758) was carefully hammered out with mathematical experiment and debate so that it applied satisfactorily to polyhedra of any number of sides or edges, cubes, pyramids, and tetrahedra. Then, in the second half of the nineteenth century, the theorem was confronted with new shapes—cut out, flattened, and reformed—that still conformed to the theorem but were unlike anything that the theorem had been devised for. The reactions of mathematicians (as sketched by Lakatos) to these new attempts to stretch the concept were mapped by Bloor on the grid–group diagram as prototypical responses to anomaly. Departments that can, by their organization, be located in quadrant D (small, isolated groups, resistant to the larger outside world of maths) regarded the new shapes presented as polyhedron as abominable monsters, to be barred from the scope of the theorem. Larger, better established departments in larger, better established universities (i.e., hierarchical communities) merely created a separate compartment of theory within which the new shapes could be accommodated without disturbing Euler's theorem. This is what Bloor calls the monster-adjustment process. Smaller, more routinized, less autonomous institutions saw no need to adjust any theories or to make exceptions in the reigning theorem. He plots them as follows:

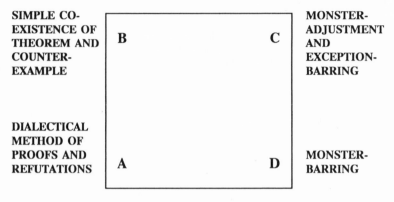

SIMPLE CO-EXISTENCE OF THEOREM AND COUNTER-EXAMPLE

B

C

MONSTER-ADJUSTMENT AND EXCEPTION-BARRING

DIALECTICAL METHOD OF PROOFS AND REFUTATIONS

A

D

MONSTER-BARRING

Figure 5.3

The explanation of the varieties of response is in the history of the organization of the German universities, following the Prussian defeat by Napoleon in 1806. The bureaucracy transformed cliquish, self-absorbed, and faction-ridden groups (D) and large, smugly entrenched hierarchical citadels of privilege (C) into competitive fields working for international acclaim (A). By opening up the university system to foreign appraisal and making personal scholarly achievement a prime reason for advancement, they installed the kind of science institutions Robert Merton (1957) has described, in which only individual invention gives individual honor. The more the organization approaches A, the more it treats the apparent anomaly as a challenge and opportunity.

David Bloor shows that the changes in the institutional structure change the way problems appear to members. He makes the attitude toward anomaly a critical test of institutional style. In one case anomaly is a threatening abomination; in another the institution has enough autonomy to sweep the anomaly quietly under the carpet, leaving everything unchanged. In one case the scope for interaction is so restricted that the members of the institution hardly know what all the fuss was about. In the competitive case, in which individual autonomy is highest, discovering an anomaly is an opportunity for an individual to make his name by refuting an accepted theorem.

Two different disciplines converge on restrictions on individual autonomy. That this is a curious coincidence should not end the matter. This convergence enables a well-defined dimension of culture to be incorporated into the concept of the rational agent, and thus gives a clearer picture of organizations and of the functions of the executive.

REFERENCES

Barnard, Chester. 1938. *The Functions of the Executive*. Cambridge, Mass.: Harvard University Press.

Bernstein, Basil. 1970, 1973, 1975. *Class, Codes, and Control*. 3 vols. London: Routledge, Kegan and Paul.

Bloor, David. 1982. Polyhedra and the abominations of Leviticus: cognitive styles in mathematics. In *Essays in the Sociology of Perception*, ed. Mary Douglas. London: Routledge, Kegan and Paul, 191–218.

Bloor, David. 1984. *Wittgenstein: A Social Theory of Knowledge*. New York: Macmillan.

Douglas, Mary, ed. 1982. *Essays in the Sociology of Perception*. London: Routledge, Kegan and Paul.

Douglas, Mary. 1987. Wants. In *The New Palgrave Dictionary of Economic Theory*. London: Macmillan.

Durkheim, Emile. 1956. *The Elementary Forms of the Religious Live*. New York: Macmillan (Orig. published in French in 1912).

Durkheim, Emile, and M. Mauss. 1963. *Primitive Classification*, ed. Rodney Needham. London: Cohen and West (Orig. published in French in 1903 in *L'Année Sociologique*).

Elster, Jon. 1983. *Explaining Technological Change: A Case Study in the Philosophy of Science*. Cambridge: Cambridge University Press.

Foucault, Michel. 1977. Knowledge and power. In *Language, Counter-Memory and Practice*. ed. D. F. Bonchard. Ithaca, N.Y.: Cornell University Press.

Gouldner, Alvin. 1970. *The Coming Crisis of Western Sociology*. London: Heinemann.

Hampton, James. 1982. Making grid and group operational. In *Essays in the Sociology of Perception*, ed. Mary Douglas, London: Routledge, Kegan and Paul, 64–82.

Hirschman, A. O. 1982. *Shifting Involvements, Private Interest and Public Action*. Princeton, N.J.: Princeton University Press.

Lakatos, Imre. 1976. *Proofs and Refutations: The Logic of Mathematical Discovery*. Cambridge: Cambridge University Press.

Lewis, David. 1969. *Convention: A Philosophical Study*. Cambridge, Mass.: Harvard University Press.

Mars, Gerald. 1984. *Cheats at Work: An Anthropology of Occupational Crime*. London: Allen and Unwin.

Mars, Gerald and Michael Nicod. 1984. *The World of Waiters*. London: Allen and Unwin.

Merton, Robert. 1957. Priorities in scientific discovery: a chapter in the sociology of science. *American Sociological Review* 22, no. 6:635–59.

Olson, Mancur. 1965. *The Logic of Collective Action*. Cambridge, Mass. Harvard University Press.

Schelling, Thomas. 1960. *The Strategy of Conflict*. New York: Oxford University Press.

Simon, Herbert. 1945. *Administrative Behavior: A Study of Decision-Making Processes in Administrative Organization*. 3rd ed. 1976. New York: The Free Press.

Simon, Herbert. 1955. A behavioral model of rational choice. *Quarterly Journal of Economics* 69:99–118.

Wildavsky, Aaron. 1987. A cultural theory of responsibility. In *Bureaucracy and Public Choice*, ed. Jan-Erik Lane. Beverly Hills: Sage Publications, 283–93.

Williamson, O. E. 1975. *Markets and Hierarchies, Analysis and Anti-Trust Implications*. New York: The Free Press.

Williamson, O. E., 1985. *The Economic Institutions of Capitalism*. New York: The Free Press.

6

The Politics of Structural Choice:
Toward a Theory of Public Bureaucracy

TERRY M. MOE

Political scientists have long relied on organization theory as their foundation for understanding public bureaucracy. This approach makes good sense, but so far the payoffs have been rather limited. The surface problem is that organization theory, as the creature of sociologists, social psychologists, and, in more recent years, economists, has developed around explanatory concerns having little or nothing to do with government. The more fundamental problem is that political scientists have allowed this to happen by largely abandoning the field of organizations.[1]

Years ago, public administration and organization theory developed in tandem, their leading figures often shared (Shafritz & Hyde 1987). But as classical theory fell into disrepute and as Chester Barnard's pioneering theoretical statement, *The Functions of the Executive* (1938), stimulated diverse new schools of thought on organizations generally, the two fields began to develop very differently. Organization theory blossomed, becoming far more heterogeneous, broadly based, and scientific. Public administration faltered as a theoretical enterprise, unable to produce an intellectual structure that could integrate politics and organization.

As a matter of principle, political scientists embraced the inherently political nature of administration. But in practice they focused their theoretical energies on bureaucratic politics—and away from bureaucratic organization. They generated their own theories of capture, subgovernments, budgeting, and the like—and virtually nothing of their own on the organizational foundations of public bureaucracy.[2] For the latter, they relied by default on mainstream theories of organization, now developed according to the concerns of other disciplines and connected only tenuously, if at all, to their own theories of bureaucratic politics.[3] Public administration thus grew into an oddly bifurcated area of study, with bureaucratic politics understood in one way and bureaucratic organization in another.

This separation is destined to continue until political scientists reassume their role as active contributors to organization theory, and, in particular, until they begin to assemble the building blocks of a genuinely political theory of public bureaucracy. As to just how they ought to proceed in building such a theory, there are no easy answers. The basic issues relating politics to organization have yet to attract the kind of systematic attention and debate they deserve, so it is difficult to say with much confidence what the right building blocks are or how they should be put together.

In this chapter, I hope to lay some groundwork that may prove useful. My point of departure is the "new economics of organization," a school of organization theory that, by virtue of its anchoring in rational choice and its attention to the logic of governance and control, seems especially promising for the study of public bureaucracy (Moe 1984).[4] I am not interested here in arguing its superiority to other organization theories. Rather, I want to use it to help illustrate more concretely why existing theories— even the best of them—tend to miss the essentials of public bureaucracy, and how a genuinely political theory of organization might emerge once these essentials are accommodated.

The analysis is organized in three parts. The first suggests why the "new economics," designed by economists to explain economic organization, is not built to capture the distinctive features of politics that shape public bureaucracy, and thus why a successful political theory is likely to be different in its fundamentals rather than a simple extension of the economic theory. The second suggests how political scientists have tried to put the new economics to use in explaining political institutions and argues that they have been more concerned with extensions than with innovations. The third sketches out a theory of public bureaucracy that, although inspired by aspects of the new economics, owes its logic and substance to the fundamentals of politics.

THE POLITICAL FOUNDATIONS OF PUBLIC BUREAUCRACY

Economists have long made intellectual sport of wandering into political science and making seminal contributions to political theory. In past decades, they have revolutionized the way we think about voting (Arrow 1963), party competition (Downs 1957), collective action (Olson 1971), local government (Tiebout 1956), and agenda setting (Niskanen 1971; Romer & Rosenthal 1978), among other things. Now they claim to have laid the foundation for a theory of organizations and institutions (Williamson 1975, 1985; Jenson 1983).

This body of work includes several related lines of economic theory, notably transaction cost economics, agency theory, and the theory of repeated games. To the extent that it addresses actual organizations, its focus is almost entirely on business firms. Economists themselves have rarely sought to extend their analyses to other types of social organization, but their claim is that these theories are broadly relevant to organizations generally.

They are undoubtedly right about this. Their concern, most abstractly, is with hierarchy, control, authority, coordination, cooperation, and efficiency—the same theoretical issues that organization theorists have been concerned with from the beginning. What they offer is a new approach, anchored in rational choice and empowered by the rigor and analytical tools of microeconomics. They urge us to understand organization by reference to individual self-interest and the pursuit of efficiency.

With some exceptions (Ouchi 1980), this has not gone over especially well in sociology, where it quickly provoked a defensive response from organization theorists (Perrow 1981; Granovetter 1985). This is understandable. Sociologists have much broader and richer explanatory concerns than economists. Marxist theory and general issues of power, status, and inequality play a much more central role in sociological analysis. And their perspective on human motivation derives from social psychological models that flatly contradict the assumptions on which most economic models are based. Although the economists are gaining converts all the time, they are likely to succeed only in contributing yet another school of thought for sociologists to attend to in their effort to understand virtually everything about organizations and society.

Political science is more fertile territory. By almost any account, it has long been shaped in pervasive ways by developments within rational choice theory. The study of public administration stands out as something of an exception. Theories of public bureaucracy have traditionally been borrowed from sociology and social psychology, and they have never done an especially good job of explaining politics. Even the dominant March–Simon tradition, whether in its earlier decision-making form (Simon 1947; March & Simon 1958; Cyert & March 1963) or its more recent "garbage can" incarnation (Cohen, March, & Olsen 1972), is not developed around explicitly political concerns. So political scientists are on the lookout for something new. As they turn their attention to the study of political institutions, which they have increasingly been prone to do in recent years— everyone, it seems, has joined the ranks of the "new institutionalism" (March & Olsen 1984)—the notion that rational choice might offer a coherent theory of organization has stirred a great deal of interest and excitement.

Devising a corresponding theory of politics, however, has not proved an especially easy task. One indicator—perhaps the best one, to judge from history—is that economists seem to be dumbfounded about how to pull this seminal contribution off. The foundations of the new economics of organization have been in place for more than ten years now, and no economist has yet been able to do the trick. In the absence of a big bang, theory building has generally taken the form of incremental applications of the new economics to various political topics—almost all of them, for reasons

I will explain later, having to do with legislatures rather than public bureaucracy. These efforts bring fresh analytical perspectives to familiar political subjects, but at this point it is not clear where they are headed.

Putting the new economics to use in understanding political organization is not simply a technical exercise. And precisely because it is not, I suspect the key to progress does not rest with the proliferation of applications, however successful they might appear in their specialized domains. It rests instead with our ability to gain perspective on our difficulties and failures. We need to understand why politics has been such a tough nut to crack. Is there something distinctively different about politics? If so, does this mean that the new economics will have to be modified in essential ways if it is to generate a theory of political organization? In my view, the answer to both questions is yes.

The most instructive way to make the case is to focus on the type of political organization most directly analogous to the business firm—public bureaucracy. Both are the quintessential producers of goods and services in their respective sectors. And not coincidentally, theories of public administration have traditionally derived from sociological and social psychological theories of business organization. If the new economics seems to have great promise as a theory of the firm, then the most immediate application in the political realm would appear to be to public administration. What happens when we try to make the transition from business firms to political firms?

Many differences between economics and politics could be brought into play here. Take a simple example. The standard new-economics explanation for the emergence of firms is that they substantially reduce transaction costs under many circumstances and are therefore more efficient than free-market exchange. The fundamental contrast is between markets and hierarchies. For most goods and services provided by government, however, there are no markets. While one could tell a story about market failure creating political demands for public bureaucracy, the usual "markets versus hierarchies" perspective is not especially helpful.

Consider another simple example. Economic actors seek to structure their relationships—their firms—as efficiently as possible, and the economic system as a whole operates to weed out those that fail. Political actors, on the other hand, are typically not concerned with efficiency in the usual economic sense, and the political system clearly does not weed out the inefficient. The actors and the systems are very different; presumably, their organizations are very different, too.

Listing these sorts of things is easy. The real problem is to try to identify those essential features of politics that might serve as a foundation for theory, a foundation that can take advantage of the new economics without being overwhelmed or misdirected by it. The four discussed here strike me as particularly important.[5]

Public Authority

Economic analysis takes a number of things as given, among them the legal setting of economic exchange. Laws delineate property rights, and rights and contracts are enforced by the courts. The economic action of theoretical interest takes place within this fixed legal structure. Most important for our purposes, the firm is understood to arise from contractual agreements among economic actors. In the classic case, actor A agrees to allow actor B to direct his behavior within rather broad limits, B agrees to compensate him, and both agree to a set of rules governing their future interaction. To put it still more simply: A and B enter into an authority relationship.

In the new economics, then, authority is a focus of explanation and endogenous to the theory. It emerges from self-interested exchange as an efficient arrangement for superior and subordinate alike, one that they voluntarily enter into and can exit at any time (subject to the terms of the contract). This is essentially the same concept of authority, by the way, that has long been central to organization theory as a whole. Its roots are in the classic works of Barnard (1938) and Simon (1951) as well as in Coase's (1937) early statement on transaction cost economics.

In politics, the kind of authority we are most concerned with does not arise out of relationships among the relevant actors. Under the Constitution and the laws made pursuant to it, there is at any given time an existing hierarchy that attaches public authority to certain political roles (public offices) and gives the occupants of those roles (politicians) the right to impose decisions on everyone else. These decisions are enforced by courts and backed by the police powers of the state.

Public authority is not voluntarily entered into or avoided, at least not in any meaningful sense. At the extreme, citizens can leave the country; but this is an extraordinarily costly alternative, and in some countries it is prohibited anyway. In general, citizens have to take the existence of public authority as given and do their best to influence how it is exercised. In democratic societies, they can do this by participating in the selection of politicians and by forming interest groups to influence the decisions politicians make in office. But the brute fact remains: authority is "out there," attached to public roles, and the individuals who occupy these roles have the right to exercise it. Everyone else is legally bound to comply with their decisions.

In economics, the type of authority holding greatest theoretical interest is an outgrowth of economic exchange. In politics, theoretical interest centers on public authority, which exists from the outset. It literally defines a crucial set of political actors—politicians—who will participate in political exchange with others, and who have rights to do things that these others cannot do on their own. One way to put it is that politicians have unique and enormously valuable property rights by virtue of their occupation of official positions. Unlike economic property rights, as we normally think of them, politicians cannot sell their rights to exercise public authority, and they can be dispossessed of them at the next election. But while their terms of office last, they are granted the rights to a very valuable set of resources. These rights and resources put them at the center of politics.

Unless we go back to a Hobbesian state of nature, in which public authority is created de novo, a theory of political organization must be built around existing public authority. The essence of politics is the struggle to control how this authority will be exercised. Public bureaucracy emerges out of this struggle. It is an instance of the exercise of public authority. Our job is less to explain where authority comes from than how existing authority is put to use in the politics of structural choice.

Political Firms

The simplest explanation of the business firm is that it arises out of contractual agreements among individuals. They agree to a set of rules, typically including a set of authority relationships, to impose a mutually beneficial order on their future exchanges with one another. They are motivated to reduce transaction costs (as well as production costs), and the structure they create is designed accordingly—introducing rules and procedures, incentive plans, mechanisms for monitoring and enforcement, and like means of facilitating cooperation and compliance among them. The firm is understood as a governance structure.

What is the analogous entity in the public sector? It is natural to think that the public analogy to the business firm is the public agency—the Occupational Safety and Health Administration, for instance, or the Food and Drug Administration. These appear to be the political firms. They are hierarchical organizations that produce goods and services for the government, just as business firms are hierarchical organizations that produce goods and services for the economy. But the analogy is not quite right.

Consider how a public agency emerges. It is created by an authoritative act on the part of politicians, who are typically responding to the demands of various social actors with stakes in what the agency is set up to do. For now, let's simply refer to these social actors as interest groups. (I'll justify this later.) The relevant partners to the "political contract," then, are politicians and interest groups. What their contract creates is a new organization, the public agency, that they will not be a part of. The agency consists of a new set of participants, public bureaucrats, and a set of rules and authority relationships to govern relationships among them.

A new public agency is literally a new actor on the political scene. It has its own interests, which may diverge from those of its creators, and it typically has resources—expertise, delegated authority—to strike out on its own should the opportunities arise. The political game is different now: there are more players and more interests to be accommodated. Politicians and interest groups can anticipate all this, however. And because they can, their task ex ante is not simply to create an agency with a desirable mandate, but also to design structures for ensuring that the agency subsequently does what its creators want it to do. They must, in other words, design a governance structure that links them to the public agency—through legislative oversight, presidential management, control over appointments, and other means.

The result is a two-tiered hierarchy: one tier is the internal hierarchy of the agency, the other is the political control structure linking it to politicians and groups.[6] If we think of business firms as governance structures that include their creators, then, the closest analogy in the public sector is not the public agency itself, but rather this extended hierarchy of public authority that begins at the top with politicians and interest groups and moves down through bureaucratic leaders to the lowest reaches of the organization. This is the "organization" we need to understand.

To turn the comparison around: this two-tiered hierarchy actually does have a reasonable analogy in the world of economic organization, namely, a more complicated and realistic version of the firm in which ownership is separated from managerial control. Here, owners—stockholders—have the authority to create and control a firm for purposes of their own economic gain, but they will not actually be part of the internal hierarchy of the firm itself; the firm is run by managers and staffed by employees. Thus, just as politicians and interest groups create new participants to work for them, so do owners. And just as politicians and interest groups have to be concerned about designing a second hierarchy for controlling their new creation, so owners also have to design a structure for linking themselves to the lower tier.

The point, then, is not that there are no relevant analogies. In fact, it seems clear that work by economists on the separation of ownership from control should have useful applications to politics. The real point to be made here is that the political firm, the organization we want to understand in building a theory of public bureaucracy, consists of the entire two-tiered hierarchy linking politicians, interest groups, and bureaucrats. It is not limited to the public agency itself. A theory of public bureaucracy is unavoidably a theory about politics and political organization more generally.

Political Uncertainty

As Williamson (1985) develops the theory, individuals are boundedly rational, opportunistic, and operate in an uncertain economic and strategic environment. Under these conditions, he argues, the most important factor explaining the emergence and ultimate form of economic organization is asset specificity, which refers to transaction-specific investments that parties to a contract may have to make to carry out its terms over time. Consider, for example, a worker who becomes highly skilled over time at an idiosyncratic but important job. The worker's asset specificity makes him more valuable to his employer, but also more dependent on him, for there is little market on the outside for his company-specific skills. Similarly, the employer becomes more dependent on the worker because he cannot turn to the market for an equally valuable replacement at the same wage. As their mutual dependence grows, their contractual options narrow. They are driven to find some way to harmonize and safeguard their relationship.

Asset specificity tends to bring about what Williamson calls the fundamental transformation, in which market-based transactions are transformed over time into bilateral arrangements in which the parties have incentives to design and adopt a mutually acceptable governance structure. In our example, the specialized worker may demand seniority rules and other protections against layoffs and firing, while the employer may build in various mechanisms to ensure that the worker will not quit, for example, pension programs that vest only after a fairly long period of employee service. These sorts of contractual safeguards—aspects of the "internal labor market" (Doeringer & Piore 1971), in this case—give each party incentives to cooperate in a mutually beneficial, long-term relationship.

This cannot do justice to Williamson's theory of organization, but it does help to illustrate the kind of explanation that economists provide. Generally speaking, the new economics explains organization by exploring what I call the technical side of the choice problem. Property rights are taken as given and contracts are legally enforceable. The focus is on how individuals can put their property to efficient use by entering into contractual agreements with others. There are commodities to be produced, services to be performed, investments to be made. Individuals have to make choices about these things, and their choices are fundamentally shaped by transaction costs, uncertainty, and asset specificity.

But suppose their property rights were not guaranteed. Suppose, in particular, that the struggle for economic advantage were to take place within a framework in which some actors occasionally succeeded in usurping the property rights of others. In this sort of economic world, an analysis of economic choice and organization would surely look quite different. Economic actors would be concerned with more than simply making efficient choices about the use and disposition of their property. They would also be concerned with taking action to protect their rights from usurpation— and with making current choices about their property that recognize and adjust for the possibility that other actors might seize their rights to the property in the future. In this kind of world, in fact, it is not clear that transaction costs and asset specificity are consistently the keys to choice.

Something even more fundamental is now at work, shaping everyone's calculations and decisions—uncertainty about the very basis of all transactions.

Welcome to politics. This kind of uncertainty is right at its heart. The point is quite obvious if we stick to economic property rights, since these rights are clearly determined by political choice and can be changed by it. From a political standpoint, economic property rights are always up for grabs, and all economic actors have to take this into account in devising their strategies—resulting in, among other things, the allocation of resources to political pressure. But although this line of analysis is clearly important, the point I want to make about politics is a different one. It concerns what we might call political property rights rather than economic property rights.

As I argued earlier, the right to exercise public authority can be thought of as a property right of sorts. These rights are used, formally by politicians and informally by the interest groups that influence them, to make choices about policy and the structure of government. No set of individuals, however, has a perpetual claim on these rights. In a democracy, political property rights are uncertain. Some actors may be very powerful today, but they cannot count on maintaining their positions of power in the future. New politicians may arrive on the scene. New committees may claim jurisdiction over an issue or agency. Interest groups may rise and fall in political influence.

This "political uncertainty," as I call it, has a profound effect on the choices of political actors when they are fortunate enough to be in power. In particular, they know that whatever policies and structures they put in place today may be subject to the authoritative direction of other actors tomorrow, actors with very different interests who could undermine or destroy their hard-won achievements. If today's authoritative decisions are to have staying power and continue generating benefits for their creators into the future, they must somehow be insulated from tomorrow's exercise of authority.

An interest group, for example, may currently be powerful enough to bring about the creation of a new public agency with a mandate to carry out programs beneficial to the group. Yet it knows its current political power may not last and its opponents may someday be able to apply public authority toward their own ends to control, redirect, and perhaps undermine the agency and its policies. The group can anticipate all this and will have strong incentives to take preventive action ex ante. Its strategic task is not simply to get the policies and structures it wants in the current period, but also to design them in such a way that they have the capacity to survive and prosper in an uncertain political future. It needs to shield them from the public authority that its opponents might gain.

As I argue later, it can try to do this in various ways. In general, an interest group in a position to create a public agency tends to demand structures that entail the "separation of politics from administration." They do this not because they are uninterested in controlling the bureaucracy. On the contrary, they would desperately like to. They do it because they do not want "their" agencies to fall under the control of opponents. And given the way public authority is allocated and exercised in a democracy, they often can only shut out their opponents by shutting themselves out too. In many cases, then, they purposely create structures that even they cannot control.

Political uncertainty is surely of fundamental importance in distinguishing politics from economics. An explanation of economic organization has the luxury of focusing on transaction costs and asset specificity because economists can reasonably assume the existence of a legal framework guaranteeing property rights. With this as a foundation, all actors can simply concern themselves with the technical task of putting their property to its most efficient uses. But politics lacks such a foundation. Indeed, most of the political struggle is about who will have the rights, formal and informal, to make authoritative decisions for society, and the struggle never ends. Because of this uncertainty, the task of designing political organization is not simply a technical problem of finding an efficient governance structure linking current power-holders to their creations. The more fundamental task for political actors is to find and institute a governance structure that can protect their public organizations from control by opponents.

Political Compromise

Economic actors need not have identical interests to agree on a system of rules by which their relationships are to be governed. Some of their interests may even be in direct conflict—as is obviously true, for instance, for management and labor. They need only have sufficient common ground to enable gains from trade. Whatever their underlying interests might be, and whatever their ultimate roles in the firm to be created, economic actors will mutually agree to arrangements that leave them all at least as well off as they were without them, and they are not forced to accept any arrangements they do not like. In addition, they have incentives to move toward systems of rules that appear to be optimal, in the sense that no one could be made better off and someone would be worse off if some other system were chosen.

This might be understood as a process of compromise. In the bargaining and haggling that leads to the final contract, actors normally have to make all sorts of comprises to arrive at a mutually acceptable agreement. No one can have everything he or she might want. However costly some of the compromises might seem, though, the system of rules to come out of all this is advantageous to everyone, and people are always free to leave if they have better opportunities elsewhere. Compromise is therefore a means by which individuals with conflicting interests create efficient organizations for themselves.

In politics, compromise means something very different for the structure of public organizations. Structural choice is a process in which those who are able to exercise public authority can impose their preferred outcomes on everyone else. The losers need not have agreed to the structures so chosen. Nor, when faced with organizational arrangements that promise to make them worse off, can they walk away and choose to create other arrangements more to their liking. Public bureaucracies are not structures of mutual advantage. However benign or beneficent their public purposes might appear to be, they are essentially structures of coercion.

This is always true, even when structural politics involves substantial compromise. The nature of the compromises that occur, moreover, are crucially different from those we expect from the voluntary exchanges among economic actors. The designers of economic organizations have something to exchange, some mutual benefit to work toward. But in the politics of structural choice, the losers often have a stake in the proposed bureaucratic arrangement precisely because the whole point of setting up a new bureaucracy is to impose costs on them. In its fundamentals, the situation is frequently zero-sum.

When an Occupational Safety and Health Administration (OSHA) is proposed to regulate business, for instance, its very purpose is to force business firms to engage in costly behaviors they would not have undertaken on their own. What would happen, then, if business groups were somehow allowed to participate in the structural design of a public agency like OSHA? They would hardly favor arrangements that promote the efficient pursuit of its proposed mandate. These are goals they flatly oppose, and that are being imposed on them by the other side through the coercive powers of public authority. If business firms were allowed to help design OSHA, they would try to structure it in such a way that it could not do its job. They would try to cripple it.

This is not a hypothetical case. Interest groups representing business actually did participate in the design of OSHA, they did use their portion of public authority to impose structures intended to cripple OSHA's performance—and these structures had the intended effect. OSHA is an administrative nightmare, in large measure because some of its influential designers fully intended to endow it with structures that would not work (Moe 1989).

Why were business groups allowed to do this? The reason, when all is said and done, is that the American separation of powers system throws up so many obstacles to legislative victory that compromise among opposing forces is usually necessary if the more powerful side is to achieve anything at all. In the politics of structure, however, compromise means that the losing side is granted concessions—sometimes of great consequence—in the design of public bureaucracies whose policy mandates they oppose.

This allows them to weigh these organizations down with wholly unsuitable structures that promote ineffectiveness and failure.

This is unavoidable. Structure cannot somehow be taken out of politics, divorced from the necessities of compromise, and designed according to technical requirements of effectiveness and efficiency. Interest groups and politicians know that there is no meaningful disjunction between policy and structure. Structural choices have all sorts of important consequences for the content and direction of policy, and, because this is so, choices about structure are implicitly choices about policy. They are part and parcel of the same thing, and political compromise necessarily involves both. Just as policy can get watered down through compromise, so can structure—and it almost always does. Thus, however grand and lofty the policies that emerge from the political process, it is virtually guaranteed that the bureaucratic arrangements that go along with them are the products of compromise and thus, in part, are designed by opponents to ensure that the policies are not achieved.

In the economic system, organizations are generally designed by participants who want them to succeed. In the political system, public bureaucracies are designed in no small measure by participants who explicitly want them to fail.

MODELING POLITICAL ORGANIZATION

One might have expected that, when the new economics of organization burst onto the scene with much fanfare and promise, political scientists would have begun debating how best to use it to understand politics. The sorts of issues raised earlier should have been hashed over years ago. In fact, something analogous did happen in sociology. Sociologists reacted almost immediately to the new economics by attempting to reconcile it with what was distinctive about the theoretical and substantive concerns of sociology. But little of this has yet happened in political science (Moe 1984; Shepsle 1986).

One reason, in my view, is that there is an influential rational choice community within political science and a fast-growing positive theory of institutions. The value of the new economics was not a matter of controversy within this community, nor, for the most part, were questions of how it might best be applied to politics. Efforts were quickly launched to fit its components into a preexisting tradition of positive theory and to employ it in ways generally consistent with the accepted analytics of the tradition. Let me offer a little perspective on what those are.

The positive theory of institutions (PTI) arose out of the larger social choice literature, which has its roots in the pioneering work of Arrow (1963). The emphasis in social choice has traditionally been on voting, and particularly on the instabilities of majority rule. What it could not explain was the evident stability that characterizes so much of the actual political world. The positive theory of institutions has proceeded on social choice foundations to offer an answer: voting processes are constrained by institutions to bring stability out of chaos. More generally, PTI has been concerned with explaining how institutions emerge from self-interested behavior and what their consequences are for political choice.[7]

The substantive focus has mostly been on Congress, which is clearly a useful vehicle for studying social choice under a variety of institutional conditions. Within Congress, attention has centered on the agenda powers of committees and their chairs, their capacity to use these powers to shape legislative outcomes, and the strategies available to other legislators—on the floor and in the party leadership—to prevent committee or chair domination. When PTI has looked beyond Congress to address other institutions, virtually all its work has concerned congressional–bureaucratic relations. Much of this has to do with the question of political control: to what extent can congressional committees control bureaucratic agencies (e.g., Weingast & Moran 1983)? Steps have also been taken to address issues of delegation: when will Congress choose to create a bureaucracy, and what kind of bureaucracy will it create (Fiorina 1982a,b, 1986; McCubbins 1985)?

The new economics has already played a prominent role in this work, contributing fresh insights to the study of legislative institutions (Weingast 1984; McCubbins 1985; Weingast & Marshall 1988; Calvert 1987; Fiorina & Shepsle 1988). It has contributed far less, however, to the study of other political institutions, and it has not yielded new perspectives on politics as a whole. The new economics could be used to better advantage, it seems to me, if PTI's "normal science" were less constraining. Above all, theory-building should be freed from the deeply entrenched notion that voting is the primordial political act and the proper foundation of our political theories. This constraint is the legacy of social choice. Because of it, positive political theory is almost entirely about politicians, constituents, and their voting behavior. Constituents vote in elections to choose politicians to represent them, and politicians then vote in the legislature on public policy—always with an eye to how their votes will affect their prospects for reelection.

PTI focuses primarily on politicians and secondarily on voters. Voters influence politicians, but they do it indirectly, passively, and at a considerable distance. They are, after all, back home in the district. Politicians take policy positions based on "benefits to the district" or some such calculation about what voters want. This calculation, usually left implicit in institutional analyses, is the basis for politicians' "ideal points" on policy issues and the key to understanding what they are trying to achieve as they control agendas, control the bureaucracy, and otherwise participate in institutional politics.

The new economics, by contrast, is fundamentally about actors who enter into exchanges with one another: they bargain, they haggle, they design structural solutions to their mutual problems. The actors on both sides of the exchange have interests at stake, goals to achieve, information and resources to use on their own behalf, and strategies to formulate and follow. The theory tries to understand the kinds of arrangements at which these actors will arrive. In the positive theory of institutions, the automatic application of the exchange framework has been to politicians. They are the ones who enter into exchanges—with one another. They are the ones who make the crucial decisions about structure and control.

It would be analytically awkward, to say the least, to include voters explicitly in a model of political exchange or contracting. Fortunately, voters are the wrong social actors to include anyway. The fact is that most citizens do not care about the arcane details of public administration. In elections, they choose among candidates on the basis of party, policy positions, and the like. Where the candidates stand on issues of structure— for example, on whether the Consumer Product Safety Commission should be moved into the Commerce Department, or whether it should be required to carry out cost-benefit analysis prior to proposing a formal rule— is hardly the stuff that political campaigns are made of. People just do not know or care much about such things.

Organized interest groups, on the other hand, do care. They are active and informed in their own policy domains, and they understand that the advantages they seek from government depend crucially on precisely those fine details of structure that cause voters' eyes to glaze over. Structure is valuable to them, and they have every incentive to mobilize their political resources to get what they want. They are very likely, as a result, to be the only source of political demands and pressures when structural issues are at stake. Structural politics is interest group politics.

The best way to put the new economics to use in gaining insight about the politics of structure, it seems to me, is to stop thinking of constituency purely in terms of voters and to start thinking of it in terms of interest groups. Chicago School economists have been doing this for years in moving toward their own theory of politics, beginning with Stigler's (1971) capture theory and culminating most recently in Becker's (1983) generalized model of interest group competition, which is essentially a formalized version of political pluralism. Yet they ignore the new economics of organization—indeed, they proudly ignore institutions altogether. Moreover, their theory is premised on a state of nature in which groups suddenly emerge, organize, and lobby in response to political issues. Theirs is really a theory of group mobilization, not of government behavior (see Moe 1987b).

What I am proposing is different and a good deal simpler. For the time being, we should forget about group mobilization and states of nature. When a political issue rises to the top of the agenda, it is counterproductive to pretend that Olson's (1971) logic of collective action cranks up to generate brand new interest groups. The reality is that these new groups would arrive on the scene too late to play the game. For most issues most of the time, a set of organized interest groups already occupies and structures the upper reaches of political decision making, and these are the players. If we want to understand how public policy is decided, we need to understand how existing groups participate in political choice.

This interest-group perspective offers a very different view of the origins of public bureaucracy than we get from the positive theory of institutions. Positive theorists have tended to view structural decisions as the domain of politicians, who make their decisions free of specific constituent demands on structure. Yet this is hardly plausible when the environment contains interest groups instead of simple-minded, detached voters. Interest groups take an active part in the politics of structural choice, and politicians have strong incentives to be sensitive to their interests and demands. If we want to explain where public bureaucracy comes from and what it looks like, it does not make much sense to start with politicians as the prime movers. We should start with the groups and then try to understand their relationships with politicians. The groups are the prime movers in the politics of structural choice.

A group perspective also encourages us to think a bit differently about politicians than positive theorists usually do. The standard notion is that politicians are motivated by reelection. This is a very useful simplification that, for legislators anyway, is not far from the truth. The irony is that positive theorists have not seriously explored what the reelection motive actually implies for the behavior of politicians. Under what conditions, for instance, do they actually have incentives to control the bureaucracy? To what extent can politicians act autonomous of constituency interests? And when they can, what in the world do they do with their autonomy? After all, they do not want anything but to be reelected.

In an environment of atomized, faceless voters, it is easy to model politicians by assigning them benefit functions or ideal points presumed to reflect constituency interests. In an interest group model, on the other hand, constituency is no longer a passive player. Politicians must deal directly with strategic actors who make demands and back them up with rewards and sanctions. As in the new economics, they are involved in exchange relationships with others, and our job is to understand the kinds of arrangements that arise from these relationships. So how do politicians make choices within these relationships, and what does this imply for the kind of bureaucracy they will create? These issues cannot be addressed through benefit functions or ideal points. With constituency an active player, we are forced to think more carefully about the reelection motive and its implications for political choice.

Finally, bureaucrats are obviously important players in politics, just as interest groups and politicians are. The positive theory of institutions has so far barely recognized that bureaucrats have goals, resources, and strategies of their own. In most analyses, they are objects that legislators seek to control—successfully. As I have argued elsewhere, this line of theory falters on both logical and empirical grounds (Moe 1987a). The logical problems are partly due to the absence of any model of bureaucracy. No theory of control is complete until both parties to the relationship have been modeled. They are also due to the absence of any strong link between the reelection motive and bureaucratic control. As I argue later, legislators often have incentives to design bureaucracies that they cannot control.

An empirical point is also worth making. By and large, PTI's empirical studies of congressional–bureaucratic relations are really studies of Congress; they have little to say about the bureaucracy (see, e.g., Weingast & Moran 1983). There is, however, an enormous literature outside this tradition that does center on public bureaucracy, and it is of more than passing relevance that this literature comes to quite a different conclusion about political control. The thrust of this research is that bureaucracy has a substantial degree of autonomy, that direct political control is typically rather weak (Wilson 1980). Could it be that, if a theory of bureaucracy were well specified, its logic would take us in precisely this direction?

An adequate theory requires, among other things, that we take the bureaucracy seriously and recognize its distinctive role in the political order. This has two important aspects. The first is that we need to treat bureaucrats as actors with goals, strategies, and resources. They are players in politics, just as interest groups and politicians are, and they can throw their weight around to get what they want. The second is that public agencies are structured, staffed, and overseen by their creators, interest groups and politicians. They are players, all right—but players who also happen to be creatures of the other participants' designs. Both sides of bureaucracy need to be recognized if its role in politics is to make sense.

TOWARD A THEORY OF PUBLIC BUREAUCRACY

The framework I am suggesting, then, is built around three types of actors—interest groups, politicians, and bureaucrats—who enter into exchanges within the hierarchical ordering of democratic politics. As promised, I will now try to put this framework to use in sketching the outlines of a theory of public bureaucracy.[8]

Again, my purpose here is not to apply the new economics to politics. It is to understand the politics of structural choice and to suggest how the new economics might figure into a larger theoretical perspective that can help us do that. A theory of politics that really does its job, it seems to me, will naturally lead to many of the issues, and many of the conclusions about them, that are already familiar to the political science community.

It will not look like an economic theory that happens to have been applied to politics. It will look like a political theory. The following exercise serves to illustrate more concretely why this is so.

Interest Groups: The Technical Problem of Structural Choice

Let's start with an extreme case that helps clarify the role of interest groups in structural politics. Suppose that, in a given issue-area, there is a single dominant group (or coalition) with a reasonably complex problem—pollution, poverty, job safety, health, transportation—it seeks to address through governmental action, and that the group is so powerful politicians are willing to enact virtually any proposal the group comes up with, subject to reasonable budget constraints. In effect, the group is in a position to exercise public authority on its own by writing legislation that is binding on everyone and enforceable in the courts. What kinds of structures would the group want to put in place?[9]

The dominant group is an instructive case because, as it makes choices about structure, it faces no political problems. It need not worry about losing its grip on public authority, nor does it have to compromise with opponents dedicated to crippling its bureaucratic creations. It has the luxury of concerning itself entirely with the technical requirements of effective organization. Its job is to identify and impose those structural arrangements that best realize its policy goals.

We might think that the group would use its power to tell everyone what to do. It would figure out what types of behaviors were called for by what types of people under what sets of conditions, and it would write legislation spelling all this out in the minutest detail. If an administrative agency were necessary to perform services, process applications, inspect business operations, or whatever, the job requirements of bureaucrats could be specified in such detail that they would have little choice but to do the group's bidding.

If the group's policy goals were simple, requiring, say, little more than transfer payments from the government, these strategies would be attractive. But they are quite unsuited to policy problems of any complexity. The reason is that, while the group has the political power to impose its will on everyone, it almost surely lacks the knowledge to do it well. It does not know what to tell people to do.

In part, this is an expertise problem. Society as a whole simply has not developed sufficient knowledge through the natural and social sciences to determine what causes most social problems or how they can be solved; and the group typically knows much less than society does, even when it hires experts of its own. These knowledge problems are compounded by uncertainty about the future. The world is subject to unpredictable changes over time, and some call for specific policy adjustments if the group's interests are to be pursued effectively. The group could attempt to specify all future contingencies in the current legislation and, through continuous monitoring and intervention, update it over time. But the knowledge requirements of a halfway decent job would prove enormously costly, cumbersome, and time-consuming.

A group with the political power to tell everyone what to do, then, will typically not find it worthwhile to try. A more attractive option is to write legislation in general terms, put experts on the public payroll, and grant them the authority to "fill in the details" and make whatever adjustments are necessary over time. This compensates nicely for the group's formidable knowledge problems, allowing it to pursue its own interests without knowing exactly how to implement its policies and without having to grapple with future contingencies. The experts do what the group is unable to do for itself. And because they are public officials on the public payroll, the arrangement economizes greatly on the group's resources and time.

But it has a downside: reliance on expert agents raises problems of control. This is typical of principal–agent relationships generally, the kind that all of us have to deal with in everyday life as we choose doctors, lawyers, and auto mechanics to act on our behalf. Our control over these agents is inherently imperfect, for two basic reasons. First, our agents know more than we do, both about the substantive issues and about their own traits, such as honesty and diligence. As a result, we cannot know why they make the decisions they do and thus whether they are making the right choices on our behalf. This is the "adverse selection" problem. Second, agents have their own interests to pursue, and they will do what is best for us only if it is also best for them. This would not be such a problem if we could perfectly observe their behavior and detect shirking. But this is usually not possible. What appears on the surface to be a good job may be nothing of the kind. This is the "moral hazard" problem.

When an interest group's political power is assured, as we assume it is here, these control problems are at the heart of structural choice. The most direct approach is for the group to impose a set of rules to constrain bureaucratic behavior. Among other things, these rules might specify the criteria and procedures bureaucrats are to use in making decisions; shape incentives by specifying how bureaucrats are to be evaluated, rewarded, and sanctioned; require them to collect and report certain kinds of information on their internal operations; and set up oversight procedures by which their activities can be monitored. These are basic components of bureaucratic structure.

Yet, even if the group knows enough to design its rules well, the unobservables that give rise to adverse selection and moral hazard problems cannot be rendered entirely observable in this way. At least some slippage remains in the control relationship. Fortunately for the group, however, it can do more than impose a set of rules on its agents. It also has the power to choose its agents, and wise use of this power could make the extensive use of rules unnecessary.

But how to make wise use of it? The major sticking point here is adverse selection: the relevant traits of potential agents—their expertise, their policy preferences, their diligence, their honesty—are unobservable. The group needs to know these things if it is to assess how well various agents will pursue the group's interests, and also if it is to design an appropriate set of rules. But all rational agents in search of a job will claim to be experts, to be honest and diligent, and to have whatever policy preferences the group is looking for. How can the group learn each agent's true "type" when it cannot be observed?

Consider an everyday analogy. How do we find an expert, honest mechanic to repair our car if we know nothing about cars? The fact is we do not have to know much. Since mechanics know that customers value honesty and expertise, some (not all) will invest in building reputations for being mechanics of that type, for example, by guaranteeing their work and refusing to do repairs that customers request but do not need. This might make them more expensive, but it also reveals information about their type. When we look for a mechanic, then, we need not simply guess about honesty and expertise; we can search for one with a solid reputation for these qualities. Having chosen on this basis, moreover, we can be reasonably confident that he will behave as expected. By cheating us, he bears the risk of undermining a reputation in which he has invested heavily. It is in his own self-interest not to cheat. And this, of course, is the best protection we could ask for.

An interest group relies on reputation for precisely the same reason. At bottom, reputation is valuable because it allows predictability in an uncertain world. The group has compelling reason to believe that agents will behave in ways consistent with their reputations, and this makes their behavior predictable. Predictability, in turn, facilitates control. If it is known that, in certain areas, agents will automatically make decisions consistent with group interests, then no elaborate set of rules is needed. If desirable choices are not automatic, the predictability of their behavior allows for the design of rules specifically adapted to their types.

To see more concretely how this works, consider one of the most important reputational syndromes in politics, indeed in society generally: professionalism. If individuals are known to be accountants or securities lawyers or highway engineers, the group immediately knows a great deal about their types. They will be experts in certain issues. They will have specialized educational, training, and occupational experiences. They will apply theories, analyze issues, collect data, and propose solutions in characteristic ways. They will hew to the norms and standards of their professional communities. Particularly when professionalism is combined with reputational information of a more personal nature, the behavior of these experts is highly predictable.

The link between predictability and control seems especially problematic in this case, since professionals are widely known to demand autonomy in their work. As far as restrictive rules and hierarchical directives are concerned, their demand for autonomy does indeed pose problems. But we have to remember that the group is forced to grant experts discretion anyway because of its knowledge problems. What professionalism does, by means of reputation, is allow the group to anticipate how expert discretion will be exercised under various conditions; it can then plan accordingly as it designs a structure that takes best advantage of their expertise. In the extreme, we might think of professionals as automatons, programmed to behave in specific ways. Knowing how they are programmed, the group can select those with the desired programs, place them in a structure designed to accommodate them, and turn them loose to exercise free choice. The professionals would see themselves as independent decision makers. The group would see them as under control. And both would be right (see Moe 1987b).

The purpose of this illustration is not to emphasize professionalism per se, but rather to clarify a general point about the technical requirements of organizational design: a politically powerful group, acting under uncertainty and concerned with solving a complex policy problem, is normally best off if it resists using its power to tell bureaucrats exactly what to do. It can use its power more productively by selecting the right types of bureaucrats and designing a structure that, although strategically constraining their behavior, still affords them substantial discretion and autonomy. Reputation and predictability make this an especially attractive strategy of group control compared to a strategy of detailed formal command. Through the judicious allocation of bureaucratic roles and responsibilities, incentive systems, and structural checks on bureaucratic choice, a select set of bureaucrats can be unleashed to follow their expert judgments, free from detailed formal instructions.

Interest Groups: The Political Problem of Structural Choice

Political dominance is an extreme case for purposes of illustration. In the real world of democratic politics, interest groups cannot lay claim to unchallenged legal authority. Because this is so, they face two fundamental problems that a dominant group does not: political uncertainty and political compromise. Both have enormous consequences for the strategic design of bureaucracy, consequences that entail substantial departures from effective organization.

A dominant group's approach to structural choice is like that of a capitalist who wants to create a business enterprise and hire a team of managers and workers to run it. Both the interest group and the capitalist are faced with technical problems of organizational design and control. But in the real world of structural choice, the interest group is plagued by a fundamental source of uncertainty that the capitalist is not. The capitalist has property rights, backed by the legal system, that guarantee his ownership of and authority over the business organization he creates. It is "his," and so are the benefits it generates over time. This is not true for the interest group.[10]

Political uncertainty is inherent in democratic government. No one has a perpetual hold on public authority nor, therefore, a perpetual right to control public agencies. An interest group may be powerful enough to exercise public authority today, but tomorrow its power may ebb and its right to exercise public authority may then be usurped by its political opponents. Should this occur, they would become the new "owners" of whatever the group had created, and they could use their authority to destroy, quite legitimately, everything the group had worked so hard to achieve.

A group that is currently advantaged must anticipate all this. Precisely because its own authority is not guaranteed, the group cannot afford to focus entirely on technical issues of effective organization. It must also design its creations so that they have the capacity to pursue its policy goals in a world in which its enemies may achieve the right to govern. The group's task in the current period, then, is to build agencies that are difficult for its opponents to gain control over later. Given the way authority is allocated and exercised in a democracy, this often means building agencies that are insulated from public authority in general—and thus from formal control by the group itself.

The group can try to protect and nurture its bureaucratic agents by various structural means:[11]

1. It can write detailed legislation that imposes rigid constraints on the agency's mandate and decision procedures. While these constraints tend to be flawed, cumbersome, and costly on technical grounds, they serve to remove important types of decisions from future political influence. The reason they are so attractive is rooted in the American separation-of-powers system, which sets up obstacles that make formal legislation of any kind extremely difficult to achieve and, if achieved, extremely difficult to overturn. Should the group's opponents gain in political power, there is a good chance they would still not be able to pass corrective legislation of their own.

2. It can impose specific deadlines for specific agency actions as a means of front-loading the benefits of agency policy. These requirements, again, may be entirely unjustified on scientific grounds, and they may promote ineffective and chaotic administration. But the price may seem well worth it, given a future in which opponents could take control.

3. It can place even greater emphasis on professionalism than is technically justified, since professionals generally act to protect their own autonomy and resist political interference. For similar reasons, the group can be a strong supporter of the career civil service and other personnel systems that insulate bureaucratic jobs, promotion, pay, and the like from direct

political intervention. And it can try to minimize the power and numbers of political appointees, since these, too, are routes by which its opponents can exercise influence.

4. It can oppose formal provisions that enhance political oversight and involvement. The legislative veto, for example, is bad because it gives opponents a direct mechanism for reversing agency decisions. Sunset provisions, which require reauthorization of the agency after some period of time, are also dangerous because they give opponents opportunities to overturn the group's legislative achievements.

5. It can see that the agency is given a safe location in the scheme of government. Most obviously, it might try to place the agency in a friendly executive department, where it can be sheltered by the group's allies. Or it may favor formal independence, which provides special protection from presidential removal and managerial powers.

6. It can favor judicialization of agency decision making as a way of insulating policy choices from outside interference. It can also favor making various types of agency decisions, or failure to make decisions, appealable to the courts. It must take care to design these procedures and checks, however, so that they disproportionately favor the group over its opponents in administrative practice.

The driving force of political uncertainty, then, causes the winning group to favor structural designs it would never favor on technical grounds alone: designs that place detailed formal restrictions on bureaucratic discretion, impose complex procedures for agency decision making, minimize opportunities for oversight, and otherwise insulate the agency from politics. The group has to protect itself and its agency from the dangers of democracy, and it does so by imposing structures that appear strange and incongruous indeed when judged by almost any reasonable standards of what an effective organization ought to look like.

But this is only part of the story. The departure from technical rationality is still greater because of a second basic feature of American democratic politics: legislative victory of any consequence almost always requires compromise. This means that opposing groups have a direct say in how the agency and its mandate are constructed. One form this can take, of course, is the classic compromise over policy that is written about endlessly in textbooks and newspapers. But there is no real disjunction between policy and structure, and many of the opponents' interests can and will be pursued through demands for structural concessions. What sorts of arrangements should they favor?

1. Opponents want structures that work against effective performance. They fear strong, coherent, centralized organization. They like fragmented authority, decentralization, federalism, checks and balances, and other structural means of promoting weakness, confusion, and delay.

2. They resist formal deadlines for agency action that might front-load

policy benefits. They favor specific structural means (see following) of delaying and stretching out the flow of policy benefits, giving them more time to assert control.

3. They want structures that allow politicians to get at the agency. They do not want to see it placed within a friendly department, nor, all else being equal, do they favor formal independence. They are enthusiastic supporters of legislative veto and reauthorization provisions. They favor imposing onerous requirements for collecting and reporting information, monitoring agency operations, and reviewing agency decisions—thus laying the basis for active, interventionist oversight by politicians.

4. They want appointment and personnel arrangements that allow for political direction of the agency. They also want more active and influential roles for political appointees and less extensive reliance on professionalism and the civil service.

5. They favor agency decision-making procedures that allow them to participate, to present evidence and arguments, to appeal adverse agency decisions, to delay, and, in general, to protect their own interests through formal, legally sanctioned rules. This means that they tend to push for cumbersome, heavily judicialized decision processes and that they favor an active, easily triggered role for the courts in reviewing agency decisions.

6. They want agency decisions to be accompanied by, and partially justified in terms of, "objective" assessments of their consequences: environmental impact statements, inflation impact statements, and cost-benefit analysis. These are costly, time-consuming, and disruptive. Even better, agency methods and conclusions can be challenged in the courts, providing new opportunities for delaying or quashing agency decisions.

Political compromise ushers the fox into the chicken coop. Opposing groups are dedicated to crippling the bureaucracy and gaining control over its decisions, and they will pressure for fragmented authority, labyrinthine procedures, mechanisms of political intervention, and other structures that subvert the bureaucracy's performance and open it up to attack. In the politics of structural choice, the inevitability of compromise means that agencies will be burdened with structures fully intended to cause their failure.

In short, democratic government gives rise to two major forces that cause the structure of public bureaucracy to depart from technical rationality. First, those currently in a position to exercise public authority often face uncertainty about their own grip on political power in the years ahead, and this prompts them to favor structures that insulate their achievements from politics. Second, opponents also have a say in structural design and, to the degree they do, impose structures that subvert effective performance and enhance their own control.

Legislators and Structural Choice

If politicians were nothing more than conduits for political pressures, structural choice could be understood without paying much attention to them. But politicians, especially presidents, do sometimes have preferences about the structure of government that are not simple reflections of what the groups want. When this is so, they can use their control of public authority to make their preferences felt in structural outcomes.

The conduit notion is not so wide of the mark for legislators, owing to their almost paranoid concern for reelection. In structural politics, well-informed interest groups make demands, observe legislators' responses, and accurately assign credit and blame as decisions are made and consequences realized. Legislators therefore have strong incentives to do what groups want and, even in the absence of explicit demands, to take entrepreneurial action in representing group interests. They cannot satisfy groups with empty position taking. Nor can they "shift the responsibility" without cost by delegating tough decisions to the bureaucracy (Fiorina 1982a, b). Interest groups, unlike voters, are not easily fooled.

Yet this does not mean that legislators always do what groups demand of them. Autonomous behavior can arise even among legislators who are motivated by nothing but reelection. This happens because politicians, like groups, make their choices with an eye to the future: they recognize that their current choices are not just means of responding to current pressures, but are also means of imposing structure on their political lives. This sometimes leads them to make unpopular choices today—choices contrary to group demands—in order to reap political rewards later on. Unpopular choices are investments in the future.

These investments are especially attractive in conflict situations. Legislators hate conflict because it virtually guarantees that one side will be alienated. Their ideal is a world in which they can make everyone happy and alienate no one. This, moreover, is an ideal they can pursue by making the right structural choices. They can favor structures, regardless of whether the groups demand them, that reduce the occasions for conflict, promote the routine resolution of disputes, and put distance between themselves and whatever conflicts arise. The groups recognize these as "shift the responsibility" maneuvers, and they may penalize legislators for misbehaving. For legislators, these are the costs of autonomy. But their investments also promise payoffs down the line, chiefly by freeing them from a great many more of these painful conflicts in the future.

The question is whether the expected benefits outweigh the costs. Most often, I suspect, they do not. The costs are concentrated in the current period and can be heavy indeed if the groups are deadly serious about the ongoing structural battle. The benefits are largely realized in future periods, and they are uncertain as well; thus they are subject to double discounting. Although conflict is painful and legislators would like to avoid it, an autonomous response is probably the exception rather than the rule.

Much the same applies to questions of legislative control. Interest groups have their own views on political control issues, and these views are reflected in their structural demands. In effect, they tell legislators what kinds of controls, if any, the latter should exercise and by what structural means. Do legislators have their own reasons for valuing control, and will they take autonomous action to obtain it regardless of what the groups demand of them?

Given the division of labor within Congress, control over the bureaucracy inevitably means that certain critically situated legislators—subcommittee chairs, for instance—are endowed with special powers and expertise that others do not possess. This is a kind of asset specificity. The more of it they have, the more groups depend on them to get what they want, and the more politically valuable and powerful they become. This in itself makes control electorally attractive. But the attractiveness of control is diluted by other factors. First, current-period pressures may run strongly against such structures; most obviously, the winning group—the more powerful side— normally pressures to have its victories removed from political influence. Second, the capacity for control can be a curse for legislators in later conflict, since both sides will descend on them repeatedly. Third, oversight for purposes of serious policy control is time-consuming, costly, and difficult to do well; legislators typically have much more productive ways to spend their scarce resources (Dodd & Schott 1979).

The result is that legislators do not typically invest in general policy control. Instead, they value "particularized" control: they want to be able to intervene quickly, inexpensively, and in ad hoc ways to protect or advance the interests of particular clients in particular matters (Mayhew 1974; McCubbins & Schwartz 1984). This sort of control can be managed by an individual legislator without collective action; it has direct payoffs; it is generally carried out behind the scenes; and it does not involve or provoke conflict. The bottom line is that it generates political benefits with few political costs. Moreover, it fits nicely with the kind of bureaucratic structure that is likely to result anyway from interest group politics: an agency that is highly constrained by complex procedural requirements offers all sorts of opportunities for particularistic interventions.

The more general point is that legislators, by and large, can be expected either to respond to group demands in structural politics or to take entrepreneurial action in trying to please them. They will not be given to flights of autonomous action or statesmanship.

Presidents and Structural Choice

Presidents are motivated differently. Governance is the driving force behind the modern presidency. All presidents, regardless of party, are expected to govern effectively and are held responsible for taking action on virtually the full range of problems facing society. To be judged successful in the eyes of history—arguably the single most important motivator for presidents—they must appear to be strong leaders, active and in charge. They need to achieve their policy initiatives, their initiatives must be regarded as socially valuable, and the structures for attaining them must appear to work (Moe 1985).

This raises two basic problems for interest groups. The first is that presidents are not very susceptible to the appeals of special interests. They want to make groups happy, to be sure, and sometimes responding to group demands contributes nicely to governance. But this is often not so. In general, presidents have incentives to think in grander terms about what is best for society as a whole, or at least broad chunks of it, and they have their own agendas that may depart substantially from what even their more prominent group supporters might want. Even when they are simply responding to group pressures—which, of course, is more likely during their first term—the size and heterogeneity of their support coalitions tend to promote moderation, compromise, opposition to capture, and concern for social efficiency.

The second problem is that presidents want to control the bureaucracy. While legislators eagerly delegate their powers to administrative agencies, presidents are driven to take charge. They do not care about all agencies equally, of course. Some agencies are especially important because their programs are priority items on the presidential agenda. Others are important because they deal with sensitive issues that can become political bombshells if something goes wrong. But most agencies impinge in one way or another on larger presidential responsibilities—for the budget, for the economy, for national defense—and presidents must have the capacity to direct and constrain agency behavior in basic ways if these larger responsibilities are to be handled successfully. They may often choose not to use their capacity for administrative control; they may even let favored groups use it when it suits their purposes. But the capacity must be there when they need it.

Presidents therefore play a unique role in the politics of structural choice. They are the only participants who are directly concerned with how the bureaucracy as a whole should be organized. And they are the only ones who actually want to run it through hands-on management and control. Their ideal is a rational, coherent, centrally directed bureaucracy that strongly resembles popular textbook notions of what an effective bureaucracy, public or private, ought to look like (Seidman & Gilmour 1986).

In general, presidents favor placing agencies within executive departments and subordinating them to hierarchical authority. They want to give important oversight, budget, and policy coordination functions to department superiors—and, above them, to the Office of Management and Budget and other presidential management agencies—so that the various components of the bureaucracy can be brought under unified direction. While they value professionalism and the career civil service for their contributions to expertise, continuity, impartiality, and other foundations of bureaucratic effectiveness, they want authority and responsibility to rest in the hands of their own political appointees, and they want to choose appointees whose types appear most conducive to presidential objectives and leadership.

This is just what the winning group and its legislative allies do not want. They want to protect their agencies and policy achievements by insulating them from politics, and presidents threaten to ruin everything by trying to direct and control these agencies from above. The opposing groups are delighted with this, but they cannot always take comfort in the presidential approach to bureaucracy either. For presidents tend to resist complex procedural protections, excessive judicial review, legislative veto provisions, and many other means by which the losers try to protect themselves and cripple the agency. Presidents want agencies to have discretion, flexibility, and the capacity to take direction. They do not want them to be hamstrung by rules and regulations—except, of course, for presidential rules and regulations designed to enhance presidential control.

Legislators, Presidents, and Interest Groups

Obviously, presidents and legislators have very different orientations to the politics of structural choice. Interest groups can be expected to anticipate these differences from the outset and devise their own strategies accordingly.

Generally speaking, groups on both sides find Congress a comfortable place in which to do business. Legislators are not bound by any overarching notion of what the bureaucracy as a whole ought to look like. They are not intrinsically motivated by effectiveness, efficiency, coordination, management, or any other design criteria that might limit the kind of bureaucracy they are willing to create. They do not even want to retain political control for themselves. They are, by and large, willing to go along with whatever organizational monstrosity happens to emerge from the group struggle.

The key thing about Congress is that it is open and responsive to what the groups want. It willingly builds, piece by piece—however grotesque the pieces, however inconsistent with one another—the kind of bureaucracy interest groups incrementally demand in their structural battles. This "congressional bureaucracy" is not supposed to function as a coherent whole. Only the pieces are important. That is the way groups want it.

Presidents, of course, do not want it that way. Interest groups may find them attractive allies on occasion, especially when their interests and the presidential agenda coincide. But, in general, presidents are a fearsome presence on the political scene. Their broad support coalitions, their grand perspective on public policy, and their fundamental concern for a coherent, centrally controlled bureaucracy combine to make them maverick players in the game of structural politics. What they want is a "presidential bureaucracy" that is fundamentally at odds with the congressional bureaucracy everyone else is busily trying to create.

To the winning group, presidents are a major source of political uncertainty over and above the risks associated with the future power of the group's opponents. This gives it even greater incentives to pressure for structures that are insulated from politics and, when possible, disproportionately insulated from presidential politics. Because of the seriousness of the presidency's threat, the winning group places special emphasis on limiting the powers and numbers of political appointees, locating effective authority in the agency and its career personnel, and opposing new hierarchical powers—of review, coordination, veto—for units in the Executive Office or even the departments.

The losing side is much more pragmatic. Presidents offer important opportunities for expanding the scope of conflict, imposing new procedural constraints on agency action, and appealing unfavorable decisions. Especially if presidents are not entirely sympathetic with the agency and its mission, the losing side may actively support all the trappings of presidential bureaucracy, but only, of course, for the particular case at hand. Thus, although presidents may oppose group efforts to cripple the agency through congressional bureaucracy—burdensome procedures, legislative vetoes, and the like—groups may be able to achieve much the same end through presidential bureaucracy. The risk, however, is that the next president could turn out to be an avid supporter of the agency, in which case presidential bureaucracy might indeed be targeted to quite different ends. If there is a choice, sinking formal restrictions into legislative concrete offers a much more secure and permanent fix.

Bureaucracy

Bureaucratic structure emerges as a jerry-built fusion of congressional and presidential forms, their relative roles and particular features determined by the powers, priorities, and strategies of the various designers. The result is that each agency, whatever the technical requirements of effective organization might seem to be, cannot help but begin life as a unique structural reflection of its own politics.

Once an agency is created, the political world becomes a different place. Agency bureaucrats are now political actors in their own right: they have career and institutional interests that may not be entirely congruent with their formal missions, and they have powerful resources—expertise and delegated authority—that might be employed toward these "selfish" ends. They are new players whose interests and resources alter the political game.

It is useful to think in terms of two basic types of bureaucratic players, political appointees and careerists. Careerists are the pure bureaucrats. As they carry out their jobs, they are concerned with the technical requirements of effective organization but also face the same problem that all other political actors face: political uncertainty. Changes in group power, committee composition, presidential administration, and all the rest represent serious threats to things that bureaucrats hold dear. Their mandates could be restricted, their budgets cut, their discretion curtailed, their reputations blemished, their aspirations dashed. Like groups and politicians, bureaucrats cannot afford to concern themselves solely with technical matters. They must take action to reduce their political uncertainty.

One attractive strategy is to nurture mutually beneficial exchange relationships with groups and politicians whose political support the agency needs. If these are to provide real security, they must be more than isolated quid pro quos; they must be part of an ongoing stream of exchanges that give all participants expectations of future gain, and thus incentives to resist short-term opportunities to profit at one another's expense. This is most easily done with the agency's initial supporters. Over time, however, the agency is driven to try to broaden its support base, and it may move away from some of its creators, as regulatory agencies sometimes have, for example, in currying favor with the business interests they are supposed to be regulating (Bernstein 1955). All agencies have incentives to move away from presidents, who, as temporary players, are inherently unsuited to participation in stable, long-term relationships. Presidents are unreliable allies.

Political appointees are also unreliable allies. They are not long-term participants, and no one treats them as though they are. They have no concrete basis for participating in the exchange relationships of benefit to careerists. Indeed, they may not want to, for they have incentives to pay special attention to White House policy, and they try to forge alliances that further those ends. Their focus is on short-term presidential victories, and relationships that stabilize politics for the agency may get in the way and have to be challenged.

As this begins to suggest, the negotiated-environment strategy is inherently limited. In the end, important aspects of the environment remain out of control. This prompts bureaucrats to rely on a second, complementary strategy of uncertainty avoidance: insulation. If the environment cannot be controlled, they can seek to shut themselves off as much as possible from sources of political disruption. The president is particularly dangerous and to be guarded against. Legislators are less threatening, but their institutions can cause unexpected trouble as well. With one election or the demise of a committee chair, an agency's political world can suddenly shift from friendly to hostile.

Bureaucrats have various means of insulating themselves from these and other sources of political uncertainty. They can promote further professionalization and more extensive reliance on civil service. They can formalize and judicialize their decision procedures. They can base decisions on technical expertise, operational experience, and precedent, thus making it "objective" and agency-centered. They can try to monopolize the information necessary for effective political oversight. These insulating strategies are designed, moreover, not simply to shield the agency from its political environment, but also to shield it from the very appointees who are formally its in-house leaders.

In their pursuit of autonomy, whether through negotiation or insulation, bureaucrats are better armed as time goes on. The major reason has to do with the "small numbers" problem (see Williamson 1985) that characterizes their relationships with groups and politicians. In the delegation phase, groups and politicians have the freedom to select their agents and impose a structure on their behavior. Over time, however, bureaucrats accumulate job-specific expertise through the normal performance of their duties, and this asset specificity alters the original relationships. Experienced bureaucrats become valuable in ways that alternative agents cannot readily duplicate, and their wholesale replacement is less and less a live option. Groups and politicians must "deal" with the agents they once selected. And in these dealings the bureaucrats have an advantage in technical and operational expertise (Niskanen 1971). As a result, they are increasingly empowered to pursue their own ends, notably greater autonomy.

All of this raises an obvious question: why cannot groups and politicians anticipate the autonomy problem from the outset and design a structure ex ante that adjusts for it? The answer is that they can and do. To be sure, their best efforts are destined to mitigate the problem without completely solving it. At the margins, groups and politicians cannot stop bureaucrats from shirking and thus making structural changes that promote their own autonomy. But the fundamental point is that groups and politicians do base their designs on anticipations about the future. The autonomy problem may cause presidents to push for stronger hierarchical control and greater formal power for appointees than they otherwise would. Group opponents may place even greater emphasis on opening the agency up to political oversight. The winning group may rely more heavily on placing detailed formal restrictions on agency decision-making criteria and procedures, and so on. The agency's design, therefore, should from the beginning incorporate everyone's anticipations about its incentives to form alliances and promote its own autonomy.

Thus, however active the agency is in forming alliances, insulating itself from politics, and otherwise shaping political outcomes, it would be a mistake to regard it as a truly independent force. It is literally manufactured by the other players as a vehicle for advancing and protecting their own interests, and their structural designs are based on anticipations about the roles the agency and its bureaucrats will play in future politics. The whole point of structural choice is to anticipate, program, and engineer bureaucratic behavior. Although groups of politicians cannot do this perfectly, the agency is fundamentally a product of their designs, and so is the way it plays the political game. That is why, in this attempt to understand the structure and politics of bureaucracy, we turn to bureaucrats last rather than first.

Structural Choice as a Perpetual Process

The game of structural politics never ends. An agency is created and given a mandate, but, in principle at least, all of the choices that have been made in the formative round of decision making can be reversed or modified later. Battles lost today can be won tomorrow, and vice versa.

As the politics of structural choice unfolds over time, three basic forces supply its dynamics. First, group opponents are constantly on the lookout for opportunities to impose structures of their own that will inhibit the agency's performance and open it up to external control. Second, the winning group must constantly be ready to defend its agency from attack—but it may also have attacks of its own to launch. The prime reason is poor performance: because the agency is burdened from the beginning with a structure unsuited to its lofty goals, the supporting group is likely to be dissatisfied and to push for more productive structural arrangements. Third, the president will try to ensure that agency behavior is consistent with broader presidential priorities, and he will take action to impose his own structures on top of those already put in place by Congress. He may also act to impose structures on purely political grounds in response to the interests of either the winning or opposing group.

All of this goes on all the time, generating pressures for structural change that find expression in both the legislative and executive processes. These are potentially of great importance for bureaucracy and policy, and all the relevant participants are intensely aware of it. In the final analysis, however, the choices about structure that are made in the first period, when the agency is designed and empowered with a mandate, are normally far more enduring and consequential than those made later. They constitute an institutional base that is protected by all the impediments to new legislation inherent in our separation of powers system, as well as by the political clout of the agency's supporters. Most of the pushing and hauling in subsequent years is likely to produce only incremental change. This, obviously, is very much on everyone's minds in the first period.

PUBLIC BUREAUCRACY, POLITICS, AND THE NEW ECONOMICS

I have tried to sketch the broad outlines of a political theory of public bureaucracy, and thus to provide at least a general indication of how such a theory might be constructed and where it is likely to lead. Throughout, I have not put the new economics of organization to as much use as I might have. It seems clear to me that, were the logic of this framework developed more extensively, various aspects of the new economics might take on more important roles than I have indicated here. Among other things, agency theory stands to tell us more about efforts by interest groups to control politicians and the efforts of both to control bureaucracies; economic theories of the separation of ownership and management may shed light on the governance problems faced by groups and politicians as they design bureaucratic arrangements; and a focus on asset specificity may help explain how groups, politicians, and bureaucrats gain power in the ongoing politics of structure.

The reason I have not pursued these sorts of things here is that they do not strike me as fundamental. I have tried to map out a theoretical path oriented by distinctive features of politics: public authority, political firms, political uncertainty, and political compromise. These features require that we understand public bureaucracy in a different way than economists have sought to understand economic organization. We cannot copy or mimic economic explanation. We have to put its tools to selective use, and we can make productive decisions only when we understand what is fundamental about our own subject matter.

In the new economics, organizations arise out of voluntary contractual agreements among individuals whose property rights to engage in such transactions are guaranteed. No one is forced to participate. No one fears that his or her property rights will suddenly be taken away. Their organizational problem is a technical one: to arrive at a structure of rules for governing relationships among them, a structure that constrains and coordinates their behaviors to the advantage of all.

A political theory cannot explain public organization this way. Bureaucracy emerges from the exercise of public authority. It is imposed on losers by winners, and the losers have no choice but to live with it. While the winners are the principal designers of bureaucratic arrangements, even they do not demand efficiency or effectiveness in its design. These technical concerns are rivaled and can be overwhelmed by political uncertainty, which causes them to favor complex, restrictive, often bizarre administrative arrangements that insulate their creations from control by opponents. They consciously impose structures that hobble and undermine bureaucratic performance because they do not have the luxury of knowing that their property rights to public authority and political control are guaranteed. They have to protect themselves from the uncertainties of democratic politics.

The departure from technical rationality is still greater—and more devastating—because the winners are not the only ones participating in the design of public bureaucracy. The American separation of powers system virtually guarantees that the losers, opposing interest groups, will have enough power to participate in some fashion as well. The losers, however, are dedicated to crippling the bureaucracy and gaining control over its decisions, and they pressure for fragmented authority, cumbersome procedures, intrusive mechanisms of political oversight, and other structures that subvert the bureaucracy's performance and open it up to attack. Their integral role in the politics of structural choice ensures that, in some measure, public bureaucracy is literally designed to fail.

Presidents, too, are a major source of trouble for public agencies and their principal designers. They are responsive to a broad national constituency, they are held responsible for almost every aspect of the nation's well-being, and they have strong incentives to build an institutional capacity for exercising centralized, hierarchical control over the federal bureaucracy. Agencies are single-minded in pursuit of their congressional mandates, but presidents do not want them to be; presidents want them to make balanced decisions consistent with economic growth and other presidential priorities. Interest groups and legislators create whatever labyrinthine bureaucratic arrangements suit their political purposes, but presidents resist their organizational monstrosities and try to rationalize them. Presidents may also be responsive to opposing groups, using their institutional leverage to impose structures that directly undermine bureaucratic performance. In general, presidents are a continuing and formidable threat to congressional bureaucracy. They are constitutionally empowered and politically induced to control executive agencies, and they cannot be stopped from imposing structures of their own—presidential bureaucracy—that may be quite incompatible with those prescribed by the participants who most want public agencies to achieve their mandated goals.

Public bureaucracy therefore cannot bear much resemblance to the rational organization of the new economics. Winning groups, losing groups, legislators, and presidents combine to produce bureaucratic arrangements that, by economic standards, appear to make no sense at all. Agencies are not built to do their jobs well. Strange and incongruous structures proliferate. Presidential bureaucracy is layered on top of congressional bureaucracy. No one is really in charge.

There is, in fact, a rational explanation for all this, but it arises from foundations wholly different from those presumed by economists. Public bureaucracy is a product of American democracy and, in particular, of the characteristic ways in which its political institutions shape the incentives and opportunities of those who exercise public authority. A theory of public bureaucracy is, at bottom, a theory about democratic politics and its consequences for bureaucratic organization. As such, it is unavoidably a theory about separation of powers, legislators and presidents, professionals, civil service, capture, subgovernments, and a range of topics immediately familiar to political scientists but absent from economic theories of organization. A theory of public bureaucracy, however much it may benefit from aspects of the new economics, cannot help but be a thoroughly political theory in this sense—a theory that, in the end, is about roughly the same cast of characters and issues political scientists have been studying for ages.

My purpose here is not to indict the new economics. The fact is I think it is superior to other schools of organization theory in what it stands to contribute to our understanding of political organization. I use it here because I believe it is the best place to begin in moving toward a theory of public bureaucracy and because, as the best of what organization theory has to offer, its inadequacies for political analysis are particularly instructive.

The analytical foundations of new economics were not built to explain government organization or to address salient issues in the study of politics. The same is true for the other schools of thought within the organization literature. In general, all theories of organization that political scientists have relied on over the years to understand public bureaucracy have been motivated and shaped by the theoretical perspectives and substantive interests of other disciplines—sociology, social psychology, economics. These theories were simply designed to do other things. That is why organization theory as a whole has never had much that was original or insightful to say about public bureaucracy. It is also why political scientists have never been very successful in their attempts to put it to use.

I make no profound claims about the political theory of organization I have tried to construct here. For the most part, I view it as a rather primitive step in what seems to me the right direction, and I regard its function to be largely suggestive. As I have said, I do think it captures certain fundamentals of politics with pervasive consequences for the nature of bureaucratic organization. And in building on these fundamentals, it provides a very different perspective on public bureaucracy from those currently and traditionally popular in the literature. It suggests, in concrete terms and at some length, why the organization of public bureaucracy is inextricably bound up with politics. It also suggests that a theory integrating politics and organization is not an intractable problem, and thus that there is no practical reason why public administration should continue to tolerate an intellectual structure that implicitly separates them.

Whatever the merits of my own efforts at theory-building, the more general point is this. A political theory of organization that really does the job is unlikely to emerge from further efforts by political scientists to borrow, apply, or modify theories that were really designed to do something else. A role shift is in order. Political scientists need to take the initiative in creating organization theories of their own—theories that are about politics at least as much as they are about organization, theories that are designed for the explicit purpose of mapping out and exploring the political foundations of public bureaucracy. They need to become organization theorists again.

NOTES

The first draft of this paper was presented at the Conference on Society and Economy, Santa Barbara, California, in May 1988. The second draft was presented at the annual meeting of the American Political Science Association in

Washington, D.C. on September 1–4, 1988. I would like to extend my special
thanks to Gary J. Miller, who collaborated with me during the early stages of
this project.

1. I put it this way for effect. It would be more accurate to say that although a
   small number of political scientists have been and still are important contributors to organization theory, their theories are about the generics of organization and are not specifically designed to reflect or explain the distinctive
   organizational features of government. For the most part, I am referring here
   to those scholars responsible for developing what has been called the behavioral or decision-making tradition: Herbert A. Simon, James G. March, Johan
   P. Olsen, and Michael Cohen.
2. For an exception, see Warwick 1975.
3. The more successful and interesting attempts to anchor bureaucratic politics
   in organization theory have almost always relied on the decision-making tradition. See, for example, Allison 1971; Lindblom 1965; and Steinbruner 1974.
4. Economists, following Williamson (1985), tend to refer to this body of work
   as the "new institutional economics," whereas within political science positive
   theorists sometimes call it the "new institutionalism." I find both of these
   labels unsatisfying. The new institutionalism does not refer to anything in particular and is liberally employed to stand for a grabbag of institutionally oriented approaches (March & Olsen 1984). The new institutional economics
   does refer specifically to the right body of literature but urges us to think of it
   as a branch of economics, which seems to me unnecessarily parochial. In my
   view, we are best off characterizing it as a contribution to the general, interdisciplinary study of organizations. My purpose in labeling it the "new economics of organization" is to cast it, first and foremost, as a body of organization theory.
5. My brief summary statements about the new economics largely follow the
   transactions costs approach of Williamson (1985). Readers who want more
   detail on this or any of the other approaches within the new economics are
   referred to Williamson's book, which provides a nice overview.
6. I do not mean to imply by this that the two tiers are somehow separate. In
   fact, they are jointly conceived and designed by the agency's creators and constitute a single control structure for ensuring that the agency acts in the best
   interests of the creators.
7. The PTI literature is huge, and I will not try to cite even its more prominent
   works here except as they directly bear on my argument. For overviews and
   extensive citations, see Moe (1987b), Shepsle (1986), and Weingast and Marshall (1988).
8. This theoretical argument is a slightly more discursive version of the one presented in Moe (1989).
9. The reasoning about the technical foundations of choice follows that of recent
   work on contingent-claims contracting, agency theory, and other components
   of the new economics of organization. For overviews, see Williamson (1985),
   Moe (1984), and Kreps (1984).
10. A capitalist might worry about hostile takeovers, power plays within the firm,
    and the like, but these sources of uncertainty do not entail the usurpation of
    property rights. The capitalist "victims" of hostile takeovers, for example, are

financially compensated for the property that is "taken" from them; these are transactions that follow legally prescribed rules. By contrast, an interest group that loses its grip on public authority also loses its right to control public agencies. But it has no right to compensation; its property rights are simply seized.

11. Obviously the structural positions advanced by each side depend on exactly what the other side is pushing, what is politically feasible at the time, and how the various elements of feasible structural "packages" fit together with one another. My discussion here is abstracted from all this and is meant to be more suggestive than definitive.

REFERENCES

Allison, Graham T. 1971. *The Essence of Decision.* Boston: Little, Brown.

Arrow, Kenneth J. 1963. *Social Choice and Individual Values.* Rev. ed. New York: Wiley.

Barnard, Chester A. 1938. *The Functions of the Executive.* Cambridge, Mass.: Harvard University Press.

Becker, Gary. 1983. A theory of competition among pressure groups for political influence. *Quarterly Journal of Economics* 98:329–47.

Bernstein, Marver H. 1955. *Regulating Business by Independent Commission.* Princeton, N.J.: Princeton University Press.

Calvert, Randall. 1987. Reputation and legislative leadership. *Public Choice.* 55:81–120.

Coase, Ronald. 1937. The nature of the firm. *Economica* 4 (November): 386–405.

Cohen, Michael D., James G. March, and Johan P. Olsen. 1972. A garbage can model of organizational choice. *Administrative Science Quarterly* 17:1–25.

Cyert, Richard M., and James G. March. 1963. *A Behavioral Theory of the Firm.* Englewood Cliffs, N.J.: Prentice-Hall.

Dodd, Lawrence C., and Richard L. Schott. 1979. *Congress and the Administrative State.* New York: Wiley.

Doeringer, Peter B., and Michael J. Piore. 1971. *Internal Labor Markets and Manpower Analysis.* Boston: D.C. Heath.

Downs, Anthony. 1957. *An Economic Theory of Democracy.* New York: Harper & Row.

Fiorina, Morris P. 1982a. Legislative choice of regulatory forms: Legal process or administrative process? *Public Choice* 39:33–66.

Fiorina, Morris P. 1982b. Group concentration and the delegation of legislative authority. In *Regulatory Policy and the Social Sciences,* ed. Roger G. Noll. Berkeley: University of California Press.

Fiorina, Morris P. 1986. Legislator uncertainty, legislative control, and the delegation of legislative power. *Journal of Law, Economics, and Organization* 2:33–51.

Fiorina, Morris P., and Kenneth A. Shepsle. 1988. Formal theories of leadership: agents, agenda-setters, and entrepreneurs. Paper presented at the Hoover Institution Conference on Legislative Institutions, Practices, and Behavior, February 26–27. Stanford University, Palo Alto, Calif.

Granovetter, Mark. 1985. Economic action and social structure: the problem of embeddedness. *American Journal of Sociology* 91:481–510.

Jensen, Michael C. 1983. Organization theory and methodology. *Accounting Review* 8:319–37.

Kreps, David M. 1984. Corporate culture and economic theory. Unpublished manuscript. Graduate School of Business, Stanford University.

Lindblom, Charles. 1965. *The Intelligence of Democracy.* New York: The Free Press.

March, James G., and Johan P. Olsen. 1984. The new institutionalism: organizational factors in political life. *American Political Science Review* 78:734–49.

March, James G., and Herbert A. Simon. 1958. *Organizations.* New York: The Free Press.

Mayhew, David. 1974. *Congress: The Electoral Connection.* New Haven, Conn.: Yale University Press.

McCubbins, Mathew D. 1985. The legislative design of regulatory structure. *American Journal of Political Science* 29:721–48.

McCubbins, Mathew D., and Thomas Schwartz. 1984. Congressional oversight overlooked: police patrols versus fire alarms. *American Journal of Political Science* 28:165–79.

Moe, Terry M. 1984. The new economics of organization. *American Journal of Political Science* 28:739–77.

Moe, Terry M. 1985. The politicized presidency. In *The New Direction in American Politics,* ed. John E. Chubb and Paul E. Peterson. Washington, D.C.: The Brookings Institution.

Moe, Terry M. 1987a. An assessment of the positive theory of congressional dominance. *Legislative Studies Quarterly* 12:475–520.

Moe, Terry M. 1987b. Interests, institutions, and positive theory: the politics of the NLRB. *Studies in American Political Development* 2:236–99.

Moe, Terry M. 1989. The politics of bureaucratic structure. In *Can the Government Govern?* ed. John E. Chubb and Paul E. Peterson. Washington, D.C.: The Brookings Institution.

Niskanen, William A. 1971. *Bureaucracy and Representative Government.* Chicago: Rand McNally.

Olson, Mancur. 1971. *The Logic of Collective Action,* 2d ed. Cambridge: Harvard University Press.

Ouchi, William G. 1980. Markets, bureaucracies, and clans. *Administrative Science Quarterly* 25:129–41.

Peltzman, Sam. 1976. Toward a more general theory of regulation. *Journal of Law and Economics* 19:211–40.

Perrow, Charles. 1981. Markets, hierarchies, and hegemony: a critique of Chandler and Williamson. In *Perspectives on Organization Design and Behavior,* eds. Andrew Van de Ven and William Joyce. New York: Wiley Interscience.

Perrow, Charles. 1986. *Complex Organizations: A Critical Essay,* 3d ed. New York: Random House.

Romer, Thomas, and Howard Rosenthal. 1978. Political resource allocation, Controlled agendas, and the status quo. *Public Choice* 33:27–43.

Seidman, Harold, and Robert Gilmour. 1986. *Politics, Position, and Power.* New York: Oxford University Press.

Shafritz, Jay M., and Albert C. Hyde. 1987. *Classics of Public Administration*. Chicago: Dorsey Press.

Shepsle, Kenneth A. 1986. Institutional equilibrium and equilibrium institutions. In *Political Science: The Science of Politics*, ed. Herbert F. Weisberg. New York: Agathon Press.

Simon, Herbert A. 1947. *Administrative Behavior*. New York: Macmillan.

Simon, Herbert A. 1951. A formal theory of the employment relation. *Econometrica* 19:293–305.

Steinbruner, John. 1974. *The Cybernetic Theory of Decision*. Princeton, N.J.: Princeton University Press.

Stigler, George J. 1971. The theory of economic regulation. *Bell Journal of Economics and Management Science* 2:3–21.

Tiebout, Charles M. 1956. A pure theory of local expenditures. *Journal of Political Economy* 64:416–24.

Warwick, Donald P. 1975. *A Theory of Public Bureaucracy*. Cambridge, Mass.: Harvard University Press.

Weingast, Barry R. 1984. The congressional–bureaucratic system: a principal-agent perspective. *Public Choice* 44:147–92.

Weingast, Barry R., and William Marshall. 1988. The industrial organization of Congress. *Journal of Political Economy* 96:132–63.

Weingast, Barry R., and Mark Moran. 1983. Bureaucratic discretion or congressional control: regulatory policymaking by the Federal Trade Commission. *Journal of Political Economy* 91:765–800.

Williamson, Oliver E. 1975. *Markets and Hierarchies*. New York: The Free Press.

Williamson, Oliver E. 1985. *The Economic Institutions of Capitalism*. New York: The Free Press.

Wilson, James Q. 1980. *The Politics of Regulation*. New York: Basic Books.

7

An Economist's Perspective
on the Theory of the Firm

OLIVER HART

This chapter examines the ways in which economists have recently come to think about firms. Interestingly, the evolving economic conception of the firm is broadly consonant with that advanced by Chester Barnard in 1938. This chapter does not pretend to be a systematic survey of this area; rather, it serves to highlight those ideas I think are particularly important. For other perspectives on the same material, I refer the reader to three recent surveys: Holmstrom and Tirole (1989), Milgrom and Roberts (1988), and Williamson (1988).

An outsider to the field would probably take it for granted that economists have a highly developed theory of the firm. After all, firms are the engines of growth of modern capitalistic economies, and so economists must surely have fairly sophisticated views of how they behave. In fact, this is far from the truth. On the one hand, most formal models of the firm are extremely rudimentary, with the firm in question bearing little relation to the complex organizations we see in the world. On the other hand, those theories that attempt to incorporate real-world features of corporations, partnerships, and the like often lack precision and rigor, and have therefore by and large not been accepted in the theoretical mainstream.

THE NEOCLASSICAL THEORY

An example of the first category—an approach that is rigorous but rudimentary—is the standard neoclassical theory of the firm. This theory, which has been developed over the last hundred years or so, is the staple of modern economists and is what one will find in any modern-day textbook (see,

This article originally appeared in Vol. 89, Number 7, of the *Columbia Law Review* (1989), pp. 1757–74.

e.g., Varian 1978). In fact, in most textbooks, it is the *only* theory of the firm presented.

According to this theory, the firm is a collection or set of feasible production plans, presided over by a manager who, buying and selling inputs and outputs in a spot market, chooses the plan that maximizes owners' welfare.[1] Welfare is usually taken to be represented by profit or, if the firm's environment is uncertain and profit maximization is not well defined, by expected net present value of profit (possibly discounted for risk) or market value.

To most noneconomists—and many economists, too—this is a caricature of the modern firm. Why has it survived for so long? Let me offer three reasons (in no particular order of importance): (1) the theory lends itself to an elegant and general mathematical formalization; (2) it is very useful for analyzing how a firm's production choice responds to exogenous changes in the environment, for example, an increase in wages or a sales tax (see Varian 1978 or Bishop 1968); and (3) it is also very useful for analyzing the consequences of strategic interaction between firms under conditions of imperfect competition (see, e.g., Tirole 1988); for example, it can help us to understand the relationship between the degree of concentration in an industry and that industry's output and price level.

Granted these strengths, neoclassical theory has some very clear weaknesses. It does not explain how production is organized within a firm, how conflicts of interest between the firm's various constituencies—its owners, managers, workers, and consumers—are resolved, or, more generally, how the goal of profit maximization is achieved. More subtly, neoclassical theory begs the question of what a firm is. In particular, since each firm's size (or extent) is taken as given, the theory does not tell us what would happen if two firms chose to merge to become a single firm (Would the assumption of profit maximization become less reasonable?), or if one firm split into two smaller firms. To put it in another way, the theory tells us nothing about the *structure* of firms.

PRINCIPAL-AGENT THEORY

Some of the weaknesses of the neoclassical approach are addressed in an important development of the theory that has occurred in the last fifteen years: principal-agent theory.[2]

Principal-agent theory introduces conflicts of interest between different economic actors through the inclusion of asymmetries of information or observability problems. In this theory, the firm is still viewed as a production set, but now the production decisions are made by a professional manager who chooses actions, which are unobservable to the firm's owners, or has information about the firm's profitability that the owners do not have. In addition, the manager is assumed to have goals other than the owners' welfare, for example, on-the-job perks, an easy life, or empire building. Under these conditions, it is impossible for the owners to implement the profit-maximizing plan directly—say, through a contract with the manager; in general, they cannot even tell, ex post, whether the manager has chosen the right plan. Instead, the owners try to align the manager's objectives with their own by putting the manager on an incentive scheme. Even under an optimal scheme, however, the manager will put some emphasis on his or her own objectives at the expense of the owners', and a conflict of interest remains. Hence we have the beginnings of a managerial theory of the firm.[3]

Principal-agent theory enriches neoclassical theory significantly, but still fails to answer the vital question of what a firm is (or what determines its boundaries). To see why, consider the example of Fisher Body, which for many years has supplied car bodies to General Motors. Principal-agent theory can explain why it might make sense for GM and Fisher to write a profit-sharing agreement, whereby part of Fisher Body's reward is based on GM's profit from car sales (since this encourages Fisher to supply high-quality input). The theory does not tell us, however, whether it matters if this profit-sharing agreement is accomplished through the merger of Fisher and GM into a single firm, with GM having authority over Fisher management, whether GM and Fisher should remain as separate firms, or whether they should merge with Fisher management having authority over GM's management.[4] The point is that principal-agent theory tells us about optimal incentive schemes but not directly about organizational form. Hence, in the absence of a parallel between the two (which turns out to be difficult to draw), principal-agent theory, by itself, can make no predictions about the nature and extent of the firm.[5]

TRANSACTION COST ECONOMICS

While the neoclassical paradigm was progressing along these lines, a very different approach to the theory of the firm was being developed under the heading of transaction cost economics. Starting with Coase's famous 1937 article, transaction cost economics traces the existence of firms to the thinking, planning, and contracting costs that accompany any transaction but are usually ignored in the neoclassical paradigm. The idea is that in some situations these costs will be lower if a transaction is carried out within a firm rather than through the market. According to Coase, the main cost of transacting in the market is that of learning and haggling over the terms of the trade; this cost can be particularly large if the transaction is a long-term one in which learning and haggling must be performed repeatedly. This cost can be reduced by giving one party (or group) authority over the terms of trade, at least within limits. But, according to Coase, this is precisely what defines a firm: within a firm, the price mechanism is suppressed and transactions occur as a result of instructions or orders issued by a boss.[6]

Such an arrangement brings costs of its own, however: concentrating authority in one person's hands is likely to increase the cost of errors and also to lead to greater administrative rigidity. In Coase's view, the boundaries of the firm occur at the point where the cost savings from transacting within the firm are, at the margin, just offset by these additional error and rigidity costs.

Coase's ideas, although recognized as highly original from early on, took a long time to catch on.[7] There are probably two reasons for this. First, they remain to this day very hard to formalize. Second, they contain a conceptual weakness, which was pointed out by Alchian and Demsetz in their 1972 paper. Alchian and Demsetz questioned Coase's dichotomy between the role of authority within the firm and the role of consensual trade within the market. Consider, for example, Coase's notion that an employer has authority over an employee, that is, an employer can tell an employee what to do. For Alchian and Demsetz the crucial question is: what ensures that the employee obeys the employer's instructions? To put it another way, what happens to the employee if he disobeys these instructions? Will he be sued for breach of contract? Unlikely. Probably, the worst that can happen is that the employee will be fired. But firing is typically the sanction that one independent contractor imposes on another whose performance he does not like. To paraphrase Alchian and Demsetz, it is not clear that an employer can tell an employee what to do any more than I can tell my grocer what to do (what vegetables to sell me at what prices); in either case, a refusal is likely to lead to a termination of the relationship, that is, firing. (In the case of the grocer, this means that I shop at another grocer.)[8]

Thus, Coase's view that firms are characterized by authority relations does not really stand up. It should further be noted that the second part of Coase's thesis, namely, that the price mechanism is suppressed within firms, is also not convincing. Transfer pricing within a multidivisional firm— probably a more common phenomenon now than it was in Coase's day— is a fairly obvious counterexample.

Finding Coase's characterization of the firm wanting, Alchian and Demsetz developed their own theory, based on joint production and monitoring. Alchian and Demsetz argued that transactions involving joint or team production require careful monitoring, so that each agent's contribution can be assessed. According to Alchian and Demsetz, the best way to provide the monitor with appropriate incentives is to give him the following bundle of rights, which effectively define ownership of the capitalist firm: (1) to be a residual claimant, (2) to observe input behavior, (3) to be the central party common to all contracts to inputs, (4) to alter memberships of the team, and (5) to sell rights 1 through 4 (see Alchian & Demsetz [1972], p. 783). We will return to some of Alchian and Demsetz's ideas later, but at this stage it is enough to note that their theory suffers from the same problem that they pointed out in Coase's theory: it is unclear why the problems of joint production and monitoring cannot also be solved through the market (i.e., through a contract), and in fact one does not need to look far to see examples of joint ventures or auditing between independent contractors.

At the same time that doubts were being expressed about the specifics of Coase's theory, Coase's major idea—that firms arise to economize on transaction costs—was becoming increasingly accepted. But what exactly was the nature of these transaction costs? What lay behind the learning and haggling costs which, according to Coase, are a major component of market transactions? The deepest and most far-reaching analysis of these costs is to be found in the work of Williamson (1975, 1985) (see also Goldberg 1976; Klein, Crawford, & Alchian 1978). Williamson recognized that transaction costs are likely to be particularly important when economic agents make relationship-specific investments, that is, investments to some extent specific to a particular set of individuals or assets. Examples of such investments are the location of an electricity generating plant next door to a coal mine that is going to supply it, a firm's expansion of capacity to satisfy the demands of a particular customer, the training a worker undertakes to operate a particular set of machines or to work with a particular group of individuals, or a worker's relocation to a town where he has a new job.

In situations like these, although there may be plenty of competition before the investments are made—for example, many coal mines an electricity generating plant can locate near or many towns to which a worker can move—once the investments are made, the parties are locked into each other (at least to some extent). As a result, external markets do not provide a guide to the parties' opportunity costs once the relationship is underway. Moreover, this lack of information can be significant because, given the size and degree of the specific investment, one would expect these relationships to be long-lasting.

In an ideal world, the lack of ex-post market signals would not be a problem, since the parties could always write a long-term contract in advance of the investment that spelled out each agent's obligations and the terms of the trade in every conceivable state of the world. In practice, however, thinking, negotiation, and enforcement costs usually make such a contract prohibitively expensive. As a result, many of the terms of the relationship have to be negotiated by the parties as they go along. Williamson argues that this leads to two sorts of costs. First are ex-post costs associated with the negotiation itself; for example, the parties may engage in collectively wasteful activities to increase their own share of the ex-post surplus. Also, some gains from trade may not be realized because of asymmetries of information. Second, and perhaps more fundamentally, since bargaining power and resulting share of the ex-post surplus bear little relation to the ex-ante investment, parties have the wrong investment incentives at the ex-ante stage. A far-sighted agent thus chooses his investment inefficiently, from the point of view of the group as a whole, because he realizes that part of his investment will be expropriated by the others at the ex-post stage.

In Williamson's view, bringing a transaction from the market into the firm (i.e., integration) mitigates this opportunistic behavior and improves investment incentives. The idea is that agent A is less likely to hold up agent B if A is an employee of B than if A is an independent contractor. However, Williamson does not spell out in precise terms the mechanism by which this opportunism is reduced. Moreover, integration presumably must be accompanied by some costs, since otherwise all transactions would tend to be carried out in firms, that is, the market would cease to be used at all. The precise nature of these costs is also left unclear, however.[9]

THE FIRM AS A NEXUS OF CONTRACTS

All the theories discussed so far suffer from the same weakness: although they can throw light on the nature of contractual failure, none explains in a convincing or rigorous manner how this failure is mitigated by bringing a transaction into the firm.

One reaction to this weakness is to argue that it is not really a weakness at all. According to this point of view, often associated with Jensen and Meckling (1976), the firm is simply a nexus of contracts, and there is therefore little point in trying to distinguish between transactions within a firm and those between firms; rather, both categories of transactions are part of a continuum of types of contractual relations, with different firms or organizations simply representing different points on this continuum—that is, particular *standard form* contracts. An example of such a standard form contract is a public corporation, which is characterized by limited liability, indefinite life, and free transferability of shares (and votes). In principle, one could create a set of contracts with these characteristics each time it is needed, but, given that the characteristics are likely to be found useful in many different contexts, it is much more convenient to be able to appeal to a standard form. Closely held corporations or partnerships are other examples of useful standard forms.

Jensen and Meckling's view of the firm as a nexus of contracts is helpful in drawing attention to the fact that contractual relations with employees, suppliers, customers, creditors, and others are an essential aspect of the firm. Also, it "serves to make it clear that the personalization of the firm implied by asking questions such as 'what should be the objective function of the firm' . . . is seriously misleading. *The firm is not an individual.* . . . The 'behavior' of the firm is like the behavior of a market, i.e., the outcome of a complex equilibrium process" (Jensen & Meckling 1976, p. 311).

At the same time, the Jensen and Meckling approach does less to resolve the questions of what a firm is than to shift the terms of the debate. In particular, it leaves open the question of why particular standard forms are chosen. And, perhaps more fundamental, it begs the question of what limits the set of activities covered by a standard form. For example, let us accept that corporations are characterized by limited liability, free transferability of shares, and indefinite life. One still wants to know what limits their size—in other words, what are the economic consequences of two corporations merging or one corporation splitting into two? Given that mergers and breakups occur all the time, and at considerable transaction cost, it seems unlikely such changes are cosmetic. Presumably there are some real effects on incentives and opportunistic behavior, but what are they?

THE FIRM AS A SET OF PROPERTY RIGHTS

One way to resolve the question of how integration changes incentives is spelled out in recent literature that views the firm as a set of property rights (see Grossman & Hart 1986; Hart 1988; Hart & Moore 1988; and Holmstrom & Tirole 1989).[10] The approach is very much in the spirit of the transaction cost literature of Coase and Williamson, but focuses attention on the role of physical, or at least nonhuman, assets in a contractual relationship.

To understand this approach, consider an economic relationship of the type analyzed by Williamson, in which relationship-specific investments are important, and where for transaction cost reasons, it is impossible to write a comprehensive, long-term contract to govern the terms of the relationship (i.e., the initial contract is incomplete). Consider the nonhuman assets that, in the postinvestment stage, make up this relationship. Given that the initial contract has gaps or missing provisions (or is ambiguous), states of the world will typically occur in which some aspects of the use of these assets are not specified: for example, a contract between GM and Fisher might leave open certain aspects of maintenance policy for Fisher machines, or might neglect to specify the speed of the production line or the number of shifts per day.

Take the position that the right to choose these missing aspects of usage resides with the *owner* of the asset. Ownership of an asset goes together with the possession of residual rights of control over that asset, that is, the owner has the right to use the asset any way that is not inconsistent with a prior contract, a custom, or any law. So in the preceding examples, the owner of Fisher assets would have the right to choose maintenance policy and production line speed to the extent that the initial contract was silent about these.[11]

Finally, identify a firm with all the nonhuman assets that belong to it (i.e., that the firm's owners possess by virtue of being owners of the firm).

Included in this category are machines, inventories, buildings or locations, and cash, as well as client lists, patents, copyrights, and the rights and obligations embodied in outstanding contracts, to the extent these are transferred with ownership. Human assets are not included, however. The reason is that, although one can argue that when GM buys up Fisher it gets control over all Fisher's physical or nonhuman assets, one cannot make the same argument for human assets: given antislavery laws, Fisher management and workers own their human capital both before and after a merger.

We now have the basic ingredients of a theory of the firm. In a world of transaction costs and incomplete contracts, ex-post residual rights of control are important because, through their influence on asset usage, they affect ex-post bargaining power and the division of ex-post surplus in a relationship. This division, in turn, affects the incentives of agents to invest in that relationship. Hence, when contracts are incomplete, the boundaries of firms matter. In particular, a merger of two firms does not yield unambiguous benefits: to the extent that the (owner-)manager of the acquired firm loses control rights, his incentive to invest in the relationship falls. In addition, the shift in control may lower the investment incentives of workers in the acquired firm, as we shall see. In some cases these investment reductions are sufficient that nonintegration is preferable to integration.[12]

It is also worth noting that integration in which firm A buys firm B is not the same as integration in which firm B buys firm A. The reason is that, in the former case, all the residual control rights shift to (owner-)manager A, and he can use these to hold up manager B and firm B's workers; in the latter case, however, all the residual control rights shift to (owner-)manager B, and he can use these to hold up (owner-) manager A and firm A's workers. In other words, in assessing the effects of integration, one needs to know not only the characteristics of the firms merging, but also who owns the merged company.

It will be helpful to illustrate these ideas in the context of the Fisher Body–General Motors relationship. Suppose these companies have an initial contract specifying that Fisher must supply a certain number of car bodies a week. Imagine that demand for GM cars now rises and GM wants to increase the quantity Fisher supplies. Suppose also that the initial contract is silent about this possibility (say, because it was hard to predict Fisher's costs of increasing supply in advance). Then, with Fisher a separate company, GM presumably needs to get Fisher's permission to increase supply. That is, the status quo point in any contract renegotiation is where Fisher does *not* provide the extra bodies. (In particular, GM does not have the right to go into Fisher's factory and set the production line so that the extra bodies are supplied; Fisher, as owner, has the residual right of control.) The situation is very different if Fisher is a subdivision or subsidiary of GM, in which case GM owns Fisher's factory. In this case, if Fisher management refuses to supply the extra bodies, GM has the option to fire management and hire someone else to supervise the factory and supply extra bodies (they could even run Fisher themselves on a temporary basis). The status quo point in the contract renegotiation is therefore quite different.

To put it very simply, when Fisher is a separate firm, Fisher management can threaten to make both Fisher assets and their own labor unavailable for the uncontracted-for supply increase. In contrast, when Fisher belongs to GM, Fisher management can only threaten to make their own labor unavailable. The latter threat is generally much weaker than the former.[13]

Although the status quo point in the contract renegotiation may depend on whether GM and Fisher are one firm rather than two, it does not follow that the outcomes after renegotiation will differ. In fact, if the benefits to GM of the extra bodies exceed the costs to Fisher of supplying them, we might expect the parties to agree that the bodies should be supplied, regardless of the status quo point. However, the divisions of surplus in the two cases are very different. If GM and Fisher are separate, GM may have to pay Fisher a large sum to persuade it to supply the extra bodies. In contrast, if GM owns Fisher's plant, it may be able to enforce the extra supply at much lower cost since, as we have seen in this case, Fisher management has greatly reduced bargaining and threat power.

Anticipating the way surplus is divided, GM will typically be much more prepared to invest in machinery specifically geared to Fisher bodies if it owns Fisher than if Fisher is independent, because the threat of expropriation is reduced.[14] The incentives for Fisher may be quite the opposite, however. Fisher management will generally be much more willing to come up with cost-saving or quality-enhancing innovations if they are an independent firm than if they are part of GM. The reason is that Fisher management is more likely to see a return on its activities if it is independent, since it can then extract some of GM's surplus by threatening to deny GM access to the assets embodying these innovations. In contrast, if GM owns the assets, Fisher management faces total expropriation, to the extent that the innovation is asset-specific rather than management-specific, and GM can threaten to hire a management team to incorporate the innovation.[15]

So far, we have discussed the effects of control changes on the incentives of top management. But workers' incentives are also affected. Consider, for example, the incentive of someone who works with Fisher assets to improve the quality of Fisher's output, for example, by learning better some aspect of the production process. Suppose, further, that this improvement in car body quality is of specific interest to GM, that is, none of Fisher's other customers cares about it. The worker might be rewarded for this in a number of ways, but one important possibility is that the worker's value to the Fisher–GM venture will rise in the future and, because of his additional skills, he will be able to extract some of these benefits through a higher wage or promotion. Note, however, that, in the example given, the worker's ability to do this is likely to be greater if GM controls the assets than if Fisher does. In the former case, the worker bargains directly with the party who benefits from the worker's increased skill—GM[16]; in the latter case, the worker bargains with a party (Fisher) that receives only a fraction of these benefits and must, in turn, bargain with GM to parlay these benefits into dollars (by assumption, the benefits are specific to GM). Consequently, the worker's share of the surplus will typically be lower in the second case, and so his incentive to make the improvement decreases.

In other words, since the worker is liable to be held up no matter who owns the Fisher assets (assuming that he, himself, does not), his incentives are greater if the number of possible hold-ups is smaller. With Fisher management in control of the assets, there are two potential hold-ups: Fisher can deny the worker access to the assets, and GM can decline to pay more for the improved product.[17] As a result, we might expect the worker to get, say, a third of his increased marginal product (equal division with Fisher and GM). With GM management in control of the Fisher assets, only one potential hold-up exists, since the power to deny the worker his increased marginal product is concentrated in one agent's hands. As a result, we might expect the worker in this case to get, say, half of his increased marginal product (equal division with GM).[18]

This reasoning applies to the case in which the improvement is specific to GM. Exactly the opposite conclusion would be reached, however, if the improvement were specific to Fisher, for example, the worker learns how to reduce Fisher management's costs of making car bodies, regardless of Fisher's final customer (but the cost reduction cannot be enjoyed by any substitute for Fisher management). In that event, the number of hold-ups is reduced by giving control of Fisher assets to Fisher management rather than GM. With Fisher management in control, the worker bargains with the party who benefits directly from his increased productivity, whereas with GM management in control, he must bargain with an indirect recipient; GM must then bargain with Fisher management to benefit from the reduction in costs.

So far we have taken it as a given that GM management will control GM assets. However, this need not be the case; in some situations (maybe unrealistic ones) it might make more sense for Fisher management to control these assets, that is, for Fisher to buy up GM. One thing we can be sure of is that if GM and Fisher assets are sufficiently complementary, and initial contracts sufficiently incomplete, the two sets of assets should be under common control. This is because, with extreme complementarity, no agent—whether manager or worker—can benefit from any increase in his marginal productivity unless he has access to both sets of assets. Giving control of these assets to two different management teams is therefore bound to be bad, since it increases the number of parties with hold-up power (for details, see Hart & Moore 1988). This result confirms Klein, Crawford, and Alchian's insight that when lock-in effects are extreme, integration dominates nonintegration; Klein, Crawford, and Alchian do not provide a formal justification for their conclusions, however.

These ideas can be used to build up a theory of the firm's boundaries. First, as we have seen, highly complementary assets should be owned in common, which may provide a minimum size for the firm. Second, as the firm grows beyond a certain point, the manager at the center becomes less and less important, as far as operations at the periphery are concerned, in that increases in marginal product at the periphery are unlikely to be specific either to this manager or to the assets at the center. At this stage, a new firm should be created, since giving the central manager control of the periphery increases hold-up problems there without any compensating gains. It should also be clear from this line of argument that, in the absence of significant lock-in effect, nonintegration is always better than integration; that is, it is optimal to do things through the market. Again, the reason is that integration only increases the number of potential hold-ups without any compensating gains.[19]

Finally, it is worth noting that the property rights approach has the following important implication: the purchase of physical assets leads to control over human assets. To see this, consider again the GM–Fisher example. We showed that someone working with Fisher assets is more likely to improve Fisher's output in a way that is of value specifically to GM if GM owns these assets than if Fisher does (the reverse conclusion holds with respect to improvements of value specific to Fisher). This result is expressed more informally as follows: a worker will put more weight on an agent's objectives if that agent is the worker's boss, that is, controls the assets the worker works with, than otherwise. The conclusion is quite Coasian in spirit, but the logic underlying it is very different. Coase obtains the conclusion by assuming that a boss can tell a worker what to do; in contrast, the property rights approach obtains it by showing that it is in a worker's self-interest to behave in this way, since it puts him in a stronger bargaining position with his boss later.

To put it slightly differently, the reason an employee is likely to be more responsive to what his employer wants than a grocer is to what his customer wants is that the employer has much more leverage over his employee than the customer has over his grocer. In particular, the employer can deprive the employee of the assets he works with (and hire another employee to work with these assets), while the customer can only deprive the grocer of his business (and if the customer is small, it is presumably not difficult for the grocer to find another customer).

FURTHER REMARKS

The property rights approach shares features with each of the approaches described previously. It is based on maximizing behavior (like the neoclassical approach), emphasizes incentive issues (like the principal-agent approach), emphasizes contracting costs (like the transaction cost approach), treats the firm as a standard form contract (as in Jensen & Meckling 1976),[20] and relies on the idea that a firm's owner has the right to alter membership of the firm, that is, to decide who uses the firm's assets and who does not (as in Alchian & Demsetz 1972). It has the advantage over these other approaches, however, of being able to explain both the costs and the benefits of integration; in particular, it shows how incentives change when one firm buys another one.

One reaction to the property rights approach is skepticism that a firm can be characterized completely by the nonhuman assets under its control. That is, there is a feeling that one should be able to make sense of a firm as a mode of organization, even with no definable assets on the scene. For example, Klein (1988), in his analysis of GM's decision to acquire Fisher Body in 1926, argues that getting control over Fisher's organizational assets rather than their physical capital was the crucial factor. Klein writes that "by integrating with Fisher, General Motors acquired the Fisher Body organizational capital. This organization is embedded in the human capital of the employees at Fisher but is in some sense greater than the sum of its parts. The employees come and go but the organization maintains the memory of past trials and the knowledge of how best to do something (that is, to make automobile bodies)" (p. 208).

Klein's conclusion is in no way inconsistent with the property rights approach, since, as we have seen, that approach shows that control of physical capital can lead to control of human assets, that is, organizational capital (the observation that the whole of organizational capital is typically greater than the sum of its parts is equivalent to the observation that total output of a group of workers typically exceeds the sum of the workers' individual outputs, to the extent that there are complementarities). However, Klein appears to argue that his conclusion would hold true even if physical assets were irrelevant. The problem with this point of view is that, in the absence of physical assets, it is unclear how GM can get control over an intangible asset like organizational capital by purchasing Fisher. For example, what is to stop Fisher management from trying to reassert control of the organizational capital after the merger? Klein writes, "a threat that all the individuals will simultaneously shirk or leave if their wages were not increased to reflect the quasi-rents on the organizational capital generally will not be credible. After vertical integration the Fisher brothers will not be able to hold up General Motors by telling all the employees to leave General Motors and show up on Monday morning at a new address" (p. 208).

This conclusion is reasonable when physical capital is important, since it would be hard (impossible?) for Fisher employees to find a substitute for this capital, particularly by Monday morning. However, it is not reasonable in the absence of physical assets. In this case, to paraphrase Alchian and Demsetz yet again, the Fisher brothers have no more ability to hold up GM by telling all the employees to leave GM, or more generally by countermanding GM's instructions, when Fisher is separate than when Fisher belongs to GM. Their ability to do so is determined by factors such as the motivation, talent, knowledge, and charisma of the Fisher brothers, the quality of worker information,[21] and the degree of worker inertia—factors that do not seem to have anything to do with ownership structure. To put it another way, GM's response to a hold-up attempt by the Fisher brothers will be the same whether GM owns Fisher or Fisher is independent: to try to persuade Fisher workers to desert the Fisher brothers and join GM.[22]

Before we conclude, an important lacuna in the property rights approach should be mentioned. As it stands, the approach makes no distinction between ownership and control. We have talked throughout this chapter as if those who own assets also manage them. In most of the formal models that have been developed, such an arrangement turns out to be optimal, since agents are assumed to be risk neutral and to have sufficient wealth to buy any asset. If managers were risk-averse and had limited wealth, however, this conclusion would no longer be valid. Moreover, from a descriptive point of view the assumption that owners manage is seriously inadequate; although it may apply to small firms such as partnerships or closed corporations, it certainly does not apply to open corporations.

In principle, it ought to be possible to extend the existing models to public corporations, too. A public corporation is still usefully thought of as a collection of assets, with ownership providing control rights over these assets. Now, however, the picture is more complicated since, although owners (i.e., shareholders) typically retain some control rights, such as the right to replace the board of directors, in practice they delegate many others to management, at least on a day-to-day basis.[23] In addition, some of the shareholders' rights shift to creditors during periods of financial distress. Developing a formal model of the firm that contains all these features, and that also includes an explanation of the firm's financial structure, is an important and challenging task for future research. Fortunately, recent work suggests that the task is not an impossible one.[24]

I began this chapter by observing that the portrayal of the firm in neoclassical economics is a caricature of the modern firm. I then discussed some other approaches that try to develop a more realistic picture. The end product to date is still, in many ways, a caricature, but perhaps not quite such an unreasonable one. One promising sign is that the different approaches economists have used to address this issue—neoclassical, principal-agent, and transaction cost—appear to be converging. The hope is that in the next few years the best aspects of each of these approaches can be drawn on to develop a more comprehensive and realistic theory of the firm, one that captures the salient features of modern corporations as well as owner-managed firms, and is illuminating to economists and noneconomists alike.

NOTES

Helpful comments from Jeffrey Gordon, Bengt Holmstrom, and Jean Tirole are gratefully acknowledged. This chapter is based in part on the author's Fisher-Schultze lecture, delivered to the Econometric Society in Bologna, Italy, in August 1988. Some of the work was done while the author was visiting the Harvard Business School as a Marvin Bower Fellow. He would like to thank that institution for its hospitality and financial support. The author would also like to acknowledge financial assistance from the Guggenheim and Olin Foundations, the Center for Energy and Policy Research at MIT, and the National Science Foundation.

1. For example, one feasible plan might be to use ten person-hours and one acre of land to produce one hundred pounds of wheat, while another feasible plan might be to use twelve person-hours and one and a half acres to produce fifty pounds of corn.
2. See, e.g., Holmstrom (1979) and Shavell (1979); or, for a recent survey, Hart and Holmstrom (1987).
3. It is also possible to analyze extensions of the principal-agent view of the firm in which conflicts of interest between managers and workers and managers and consumers are explored (see e.g., Calvo and Wellisz 1978).
4. As a matter of history, GM and Fisher started off as separate firms linked by a long-term contract, but after a dispute GM bought Fisher in 1926. For interesting discussions of the relationship, see Klein, Crawford, and Alchian (1978) and Klein (1988).
5. Drawing a parallel might be possible if, say, profit- or cost-sharing arrangements were only found within a single firm. Then one might conclude that GM and Fisher would have to merge. This is not the case, however. For example, consider cost-plus contracts between the U.S. government and private defense contractors.
6. A related idea can be found in Simon (1951). It is also worth noting that the superior adaptive properties of the employment relation were being emphasized by Barnard (1938) at around the same time that Coase was writing.
7. In Coase's words, they were "much quoted but little used" (until the 1970s).
8. Masten (1988) has recently pointed out that an employee owes an employer a duty of loyalty that one independent contractor does not owe another (see also Coase [1937]). This may give the employer additional leverage over the employee in some circumstances. The empirical significance of this difference is unclear, however.
9. Williamson (1985) argues that a major benefit of integration comes from the fact that the party with authority can resolve disputes by fiat (as opposed to going through litigation); a major cost occurs because the party with authority cannot commit himself to intervene selectively in the affairs of others. Williamson is not very clear about what mechanisms are at work here, however. For example, a boss may try to resolve a dispute, but what guarantee is there that the parties will follow his edicts? To paraphrase Alchian and Demsetz, what disciplinary power does a boss have that an independent contractor does not? A similar issue arises regarding selective intervention. In what activities will the boss intervene, and how will this intervention be enforced? What power

to intervene does a boss have that an independent contractor does not have?

As will become clear later, I believe these questions can be answered, but only by expanding the picture of a firm to include nonhuman assets under its control, as well as human assets.

10. This literature owes a lot to the earlier property rights literature on the efficiency of private property in an externality-free world (see, e.g., Demsetz 1967).

11. This view of ownership seems consistent with the standard one adopted by lawyers. For example, Oliver Wendell Holmes (1881, p. 246) writes: "But what are the rights of ownership? They are substantially the same as those incident to possession. Within the limits prescribed by policy, the owner is allowed to exercise his natural powers over the subject-matter uninterfered with, and is more or less protected in excluding other people from such interference. The owner is allowed to exclude all, and is accountable to no one but him."

12. It is important to emphasize that the property rights approach distinguishes between ownership in the sense of possession of residual control rights over assets and ownership in the sense of entitlement to a firm's (verifiable) profit stream. In practice, these rights often go together, but they do not have to. The property rights approach takes the point of view that it is the possession of control rights that is crucial for the integration decision. That is, if firm A wants to acquire part of firm B's (verifiable) profit stream, it can always do this through a contract. It is only if firm A wants to acquire control over firm B's assets that it needs to integrate.

13. If current Fisher management is indispensable for the operation of Fisher assets, there is, of course, no difference between the two threats. It is rare, however, that current management is completely irreplaceable.

14. It should be emphasized that there is no inconsistency in assuming that an initial contract is incomplete and at the same time that the parties anticipate how the ex-post surplus will be divided as a result of this incompleteness. For example, suppose many individually unlikely states exist with similar characteristics to an uncontracted-for increase in demand. For the parties to contract for each of these states may be prohibitively expensive, and yet they may be well aware of the average degree to which their investments will be expropriated as a result of not contracting for these states.

15. Under some conditions expropriation or hold-up problems can be avoided regardless of organizational form. One possibility is for the parties to write an ex-ante profit-sharing agreement. However, a profit-sharing agreement is an insufficient tool to encourage ex-ante investments to the extent that some returns from an asset's use are unverifiable. Examples of unverifiable returns are effort costs, nonmonetary rewards such as perks, and monetary returns that can be diverted so that they do not show up in the firm's accounts (i.e., are not verifiable).

Another way the parties might overcome expropriation problems is to share investment expenditures. For example, if Fisher and GM are independent, Fisher could compensate GM for its later hold-up power by contributing toward GM's initial Fisher-specific investment. Note, however, that this strategy only works to the extent that either GM's investment can be contracted on, or Fisher can make part of the investment on GM's behalf. Otherwise, GM can use an upfront payment from Fisher to make a *non*-relationship-specific investment.

16. This is not quite correct, since the worker actually bargains with GM management rather than with GM shareholders, who are arguably the ultimate beneficiaries. However, it is approximately correct to the extent that, perhaps because GM management is on an incentive scheme, GM management benefits from an increase in GM's profit or market value. For the remainder of the discussion, we will, at a cost in both precision and realism, ignore the distinction between management and shareholders, and also treat management as a monolithic group. (See, however, note 19 and the comments in the "Further Remarks" section.)

17. We are assuming that the initial contract was incomplete in the sense that no payment was specified for the improved product.

18. For a formal analysis of this, see Hart and Moore (1988).

19. In the preceding we have concentrated on ownership by an individual or by a homogeneous and monolithic group ("management"). However, the analysis can be generalized to include more complicated forms of group ownership, such as partnerships, or worker, manager, or consumer cooperatives. It turns out that these will be efficient when increases in agents' marginal products are specific to a group of individuals of variable composition, rather than to a fixed group. For example, if the increase in an agent's marginal product can be realized only if the agent has access to a majority of the members of a management team, as well as to a particular asset, then it will be optimal to give each of the managers an equal ownership share (i.e., vote) in the asset and adopt majority rule. For details, see Hart and Moore (1988).

20. *The firm* is shorthand for a collection of assets, and *ownership* is shorthand for the possession of residual rights of control over these assets.

21. See Mailath and Postlewaite (1988).

22. This is not without qualification. It can be argued that if GM acquires Fisher, Fisher workers become liable for damages if they try to organize a new firm since, as employees, they owe GM a duty of loyalty (see Masten 1988). Since employees do in practice leave to form new firms, and the courts often do not enforce covenants not to compete even when they are explicit, it is unclear how important this factor could have been in the GM–Fisher acquisition.

23. See for example, Clark (1985), Easterbrook and Fischel (1983), and Fama and Jensen (1983).

24. See, for example, Aghion and Bolton (1988), Harris and Raviv (1988), Huberman and Kahn (1988), and Grossman and Hart (1988).

REFERENCES

Aghion, P., and P. Bolton. 1988. An "incomplete contracts" approach to bankruptcy and the optimal financial structure of the firm. Harvard University Economics Dept., mimeographed.

Alchian, A., and H. Demsetz. 1972. Production, information costs and economic organization. *American Economic Review* 62:777–95.

Barnard, C. 1938. *The Functions of the Executive.* Cambridge, Mass.: Harvard University Press.

Bishop, R. L. (1968). The effects of specific and ad valorem taxes. *Quarterly Journal of Economics* 82:198–218.

Calvo, G., and S. Wellisz. 1978. Supervision, loss of control and the optimal size of the firm. *Journal of Political Economy* 86:943–52.

Clark, R. 1985. Agency costs vs. fiduciary duties. In *Principles and Agents: The Structure of Business,* eds. J. Pratt and R. Zeckhauser. Cambridge, Mass.: Harvard Business School Press.

Coase, R. 1937. The nature of the firm. *Economica* 4, 386–405; reprinted in G. Stigler and K. Boulding eds. 1952. *Readings in Price Theory.* Homewood, Ill: Richard D. Irwin.

Demsetz, H. 1967. Toward a theory of property rights. *American Economic Review* 57:347–48.

Easterbrook, F., and D. Fischel. 1983. Voting in corporate law. *Journal of Law and Economics* 26:395–428.

Fama, E., and M. Jensen 1983. Separation of ownership and control. *Journal of Law and Economics,* 26:301–25.

Goldberg, V. 1976. Regulation and administered contracts. *Bell Journal of Economics* 7:426–48.

Grossman, S., and O. Hart. 1986. The costs and benefits of ownership: a theory of vertical and lateral integration. *Journal of Political Economy* 94:691–719.

Grossman, S., and O. Hart. 1988. One share—one vote and the market for corporate control. *Journal of Financial Economics* 20:175–202.

Harris, M., and A. Raviv. 1988. Corporate governance: voting rights and majority rules. *Journal of Financial Economics* 20:203–35.

Hart, O. 1988. Incomplete contracts and the theory of the firm. *Journal of Law, Economics, and Organization* 4(1):119–39.

Hart, O., and B. Holmstrom. 1987. The theory of contracts. In *Advances in Economic Theory,* ed. T. Bewley. Fifth World Congress, Cambridge: Cambridge University Press.

Hart, O., and J. Moore. 1988. Property rights and the nature of the firm. MIT Discussion Paper, M.I.T.

Holmes, O. W. 1881. *The Common Law.* 1946 reprint. Boston: Little Brown.

Holmstrom, B. 1979. Moral hazard and observability. *Bell Journal of Economics* 10:74–91.

Holmstrom, B., and J. Tirole. 1989. The theory of the firm. In *The Handbook of Industrial Organization,* eds. R. Schmalensee and R. Willig. Amsterdam: North-Holland.

Huberman, G., and C. Kahn. 1988. Default, foreclosure, and strategic renegotiation. Mimeographed, University of Chicago, Chicago, Ill.

Jensen, M., and W. Meckling. 1976. Theory of the firm: managerial behavior, agency costs and ownership structure. *Journal of Financial Economics* 3:305–60.

Klein, B. 1988. Vertical integration as organizational ownership: the Fisher Body–General Motors relationship revisited. *Journal of Law, Economics, and Organization* 4(1):199–213.

Klein, B., R. Crawford, and A. Alchian. 1978. Vertical integration, appropriable rents and the competitive contracting process. *Journal of Law and Economics* 21:297–326.

Mailath, G., and A. Postlewaite. 1988. Workers versus firms: bargaining over a firm's value. University of Pennsylvania Working Paper #88-11, University of Pennsylvania, Philadelphia, Pa.

Masten, S. 1988. A legal basis for the firm. *Journal of Law, Economics, and Organization* 4:181–98.

Milgrom, P., and J. Roberts. 1988. Economic theories of the firm: past, present, and future. *Canadian Journal of Economics* XXI(3):444–58.

Shavell, S. 1979. Risk sharing and incentives in the principal and agent relationship. *Bell Journal of Economics* 10:55–73.

Simon, H. 1951. A formal theory of the employment relation. *Econometrica* 19:293–305.

Tirole, J. 1988. *The Theory of the Industrial Organization*. Cambridge, Mass.: MIT Press.

Varian, H. 1978. *Microeconomic Analysis*. New York: W. W. Norton and Company.

Williamson, O. 1975. *Markets and Hierarchies: Analysis and Antitrust Implications*. New York: Free Press.

Williamson, O. 1985. *The Economic Institutions of Capitalism*. New York: Free Press.

Williamson, O. 1988. The logic of economic organization. *Journal of Law, Economics, and Organization* 4(1):65–94.

8

Chester Barnard and the
Incipient Science of Organization

OLIVER E. WILLIAMSON

This chapter argues that an incipient science of organization has been taking shape over the past ten and fifteen years and that it is inspired, directly and indirectly, by Chester Barnard's classic book, *The Functions of the Executive*. Interestingly, Barnard observed in the last chapter of that book that there was a need for, but that we did not have, a "science of organization" (p. 290).[1] Although that unrealized need remains today, we have nonetheless made recent progress.

The incipient science of organization to which I refer involves an interdisciplinary joinder of law, economics, and organization theory. Barnard is everywhere recognized for his path-breaking contributions to the field of organization theory,[2] and this is the main use I make of Barnard here. Barnard's intuitions, however, were very much those of an economist. Thus, although he expressed dismay that economic theory and thought had not helped him in the least—indeed, had gotten in the way of his understanding of the problems of organization (pp. x–xi)—Barnard approached the study of organization very much in a rational spirit, which is to say, "in the spirit of an economist" (Arrow 1974, p. 16).

As discussed later, economics and organization theory form the main axis of the incipient science of organization. I argue that each needs to inform and be informed by the other. Law, however, also plays a role—albeit of a background or supporting kind.[3]

The first two sections of this chapter examine leading developments in organization theory, with special emphasis on Barnard. The third section indicates how transaction cost economics draws on parts of these, rejects others, and combines economics with organization theory to effect a joinder. The simple contractual schema and the generic trade-off out of which transaction cost economics works are then sketched in the fourth section. Concluding remarks follow.

BARNARD

Barnard came to the study of organization as a deeply perceptive practitioner. It was his experience that executives in large organizations could communicate easily about "essential problems of organization, provided that the questions are stated without dependence upon the technologies of their respective fields" (p. viii). Presumably there were underlying regularities and a common conceptual core to which individuals experienced in and skilled at organization could and did relate. What were these?

Barnard's first and insistent point was that formal organization was important. What was obvious to him, however, was evidently not so obvious to others, since the study of formal organization had been neglected by social scientists.[4] Believing this to be a remediable condition, he set about to correct it. This required that a new conceptual framework be fashioned, out of which a theory of formal organization could be developed.

Spontaneous Versus Induced Cooperation

The invisible hand of Adam Smith and the marvel of the market to which Friedrich Hayek referred have spontaneous origins: "The price system is . . . one of those formations which man has learned to use . . . after he stumbled on it without understanding it" (Hayek 1945, p. 528). Karl Menger's approach to economics was similar. He averred that the most noteworthy problem in the social sciences was to ascertain how "institutions which serve the common welfare and are extremely significant for its development came into being without a *common will* directed toward establishing them" (Menger 1963, p. 147).

What interested Barnard, however, was not spontaneous cooperation but induced cooperation. He simply asserted that in his experience formal organization was important and undervalued, where formal organization was defined as "that kind of cooperation among men that is conscious, deliberate, purposeful" (p. 4).

The self-conscious, intentional cooperation with which Barnard was concerned was widely believed to be of lesser importance than cooperation that results from organic evolution. Thus Hayek observed that "If social phenomena showed no order except insofar as they were consciously designed, there would be . . . only problems of psychology. It is only insofar as some sort of order arises as a result of individual action but without being designed by any individual that a problem is raised which demands theoretical exploration" (1955, p. 39). The plain meaning of this is that if "the task of social science is to explain planned behavior or consciously planned social institutions, then all that remains to be studied are the preferences of the planner" (Schotter 1981, p. 21).

The long tradition within economics of treating firms "of the category of the individual agent" (Kreps 1984, p. 8) contributed to this condition. Inasmuch as individual agents were described by utility functions and consumption sets, profit functions and production possibility sets were arguably the appropriate terms with which to describe firms. The neoclassical scheme of things simply made no place for "conscious, deliberate, purposeful" efforts to craft formal structures in support of internal organization.

Barnard's experience told him otherwise. Since there was little theory to which he could appeal, he set out to supply it.

Adaptation as Central Problem

Barnard observed that the main concern of organization was that of adaptation to changing circumstances, the reason being that problems of organization in a steady state are comparatively trivial.

The remarkable adaptive properties of markets were ignored by Barnard. What concerned him was internal organization. Confronted with a continuously fluctuating environment, the "survival of an organization depends upon the maintenance of an equilibrium of complex character. . . . [This] calls for readjustment of processes internal to the organization . . . , [whence] the *center of our interest* is the processes by which [adaptation] is accomplished" (p. 6; emphasis added).

Moreover, adjustments of cooperative systems are not piecemeal but require "balance of the various types of organizational activities. The capacity for making these adjustments is a limiting factor . . . ; for if cooperation cannot adjust to attack new limitations in the environment, it must fail. The adjustment processes become management processes, and the specialized organs are executives and executive organization. . . . Barring extraordinary cataclysms, . . . [such processes and organs] are in fact the most important limitations in most, and especially in complex, cooperative systems" (p. 35).

Efficacious adaptations to changing circumstances were thus the central concern of Barnard. Interestingly, despite his emphasis on intentionality, he fully appreciated that most cooperative efforts fail: "successful cooperation in or by formal organizations is the abnormal, not the normal, condition" (p. 5). One possibility, albeit unmentioned by Barnard, is that those who craft cooperative systems often err for lack of a (more or less correct) conceptual framework. Whether for that reason or otherwise, Barnard decided to supply one.

The Framework

Instead of technology, Barnard examined the human attributes of organization. Instead of focusing on markets, Barnard focused entirely on internal organization. Of special importance were the following: (1) a theory of authority, (2) the employment relation, (3) informal organization, and (4) an economizing orientation. We consider these each in turn.

Authority The natural and usual approach to the origin and nature of authority—in both the theory of the state and the theory of internal organization—is to regard authority as originating at the top. Sometimes this top-down imposition of authority is believed to have societal benefits—as in Thomas Hobbes's theory of state, in which the law is a means by which to "compel men equally to perform their covenants" (1928, p. 94). More often, authority is believed to be a means by which one group (e.g., bosses) exploits another (e.g., workers) (Marglin 1974).

Barnard argued that authority is a solution to a complex problem of coordination/adaptation and that it arises out of mutual consent. He was influenced in this by his study of Eugen Ehrlich's book on the *Fundamental Principles of the Sociology of Law* (1936). In Ehrlich's view, "the center of gravity of legal development lies not in legislation, nor in juristic science, nor in judicial decision, but in society itself" (1936, p. xv). Barnard held the thesis of this study to be "that all law arises from the formal and especially informal understandings of the people as socially organized." Such was "broadly consistent with the facts" of organization as he had experienced them (p. x).

Barnard thus viewed authority as an instrumental solution to the problems of cooperation/coordination that were posed by the adaptive needs of complex organization. Moreover, Barnard insisted that rather than being top down, authority rested on the acceptance or consent of subordinates (p. 164). It was his experience that orders are commonly disobeyed (p. 162), which is unsurprising if the "decision as to whether an order has authority . . . lies with the person to whom it is addressed" (p. 163). If authority implies compliance, then lower-level consent is needed.

To be sure, long-run versus short-run distinctions may be pertinent. Thus orders that are refused in the long run (possibly by reallocating resources) may be binding in the short run. Given the added degrees of freedom that the long run affords, attempts to impose law on unwilling participants— be they individuals or organizations—are apt to be fatuous (pp. 181–82).

Although one could complain that this concept of authority can be pushed too far and is contradicted by authoritarian states and the like,[5] the consensual view of authority—more generally, the consensual view of contract—has been enormously influential for reconceptualizing the study of economic organization. Barnard's novel theory of the employment relation works out of this consensual orientation.

The employment relation Barnard maintained that both the decision of an individual to join an organization and the decision to continue reflected a comparative net benefit assessment. Presented with different employment scenarios, persons consciously "choose whether or not they will enter into a specific cooperative system" (p. 17). Continuation thereafter depends on whether or not net gains can be projected (p. 85).

The need was to craft a contractual relation that would facilitate adaptability. The distinguishing feature of the employment relation, according to Barnard, is that employees (implicitly and explicitly) agree to accede to authority within a "zone of acceptance."[6] The size and nature of this zone of acceptance, moreover, is priced out: the zone "will be wider or narrower depending upon the degree to which the inducements exceed the burdens and sacrifices which determine the individual's adhesion to the organization" (p. 169). At the outset, therefore, expanding a zone to include greater (potential) burdens or sacrifices must be attended by greater inducements.

To be sure, things can get complicated once an employment relation has been agreed to. Although workers will not thereafter have the same degree of choice, they are not without resources. If an order is "believed to involve a burden that destroys the net advantage of connection with the organization, . . . [the] net inducement, [which] is the only reason for accepting *any* order as having authority," vanishes (p. 166). In the extreme, the individual will quit. But there are many other ways to deflect, defeat, or otherwise frustrate orders: "Malingering and intentional lack of dependability are the more usual methods" (p. 166). Also, as described later, informal organization is pertinent.

In effect, Barnard examined the employment relation from something akin to a rational expectations point of view—with all the burdens and benefits that accrue thereto. This contrasts with myopic contracting, according to which participants approach contract noncomparatively and incur commitments (make investments in human assets) the future ramifications of which are not worked out. Instead, Barnard treats the ex-ante bargain and the ex-post contractual relation in a unified way—a much more sophisticated conception of contracting.

Informal organization   Barnard argued that formal and informal organization always and everywhere coexist (p. 20) and that informal organization contributes to the viability of formal organization in three significant respects: "One of the indispensable functions of informal organizations in formal organizations . . . [is] that of communication. . . . Another function is that of maintaining the cohesiveness in formal organizations through regulating the willingness to serve and the stability of objective authority. A third function is the maintenance of the feeling of personal integrity, of self-respect, and independent choice" (p. 122).

These effects occur spontaneously, as a consequence of or in conjunction with formal organization. Presumably firm and market organization differ in informal organization respects—which differences should be taken into account in the decision to use one or the other. The comparison of markets and hierarchies was not, however, a concern of Barnard's. Also, arguably, informal organization could be supported or suppressed. Although this latter is closer to Barnard's concerns, he was silent on that aspect as well.

The communication benefits of informal organization include coding, rumors, and the like. These effects are familiar and widely conceded. More subtle is the claim that informal organization serves to stabilize authority (p. 169):

> Since the efficiency of organization is affected by the degree to which individuals assent to orders, denying the authority of an organization communication is a threat to the interests of all individuals who derive a net advantage from their connection with the organization, unless the orders are unacceptable to them also. Accordingly, at any given time there is among most of the contributors an active personal interest in the maintenance of the authority of all orders which to them are within the zone of [acceptance]. The maintenance of this interest is largely a function of informal organization.

Inasmuch as the third function of informal organization—that of protecting personal integrity and self-respect—affords "opportunities for reinforcement of personal attitudes," this function is often "deemed destructive of formal organization" (p. 122). That, however, construes things too narrowly if such protections are "a means of maintaining the personality of the individual against certain effects of formal organizations which tend to disintegrate the personality" (p. 122).

Not only can informal organization give succor to individuals that are devalued or demeaned by formal organization, but informal organization may be a means by which collective dissent from authority is supported. Thus, just as contributors have the aforementioned "active personal interest in the maintenance of the authority of all orders which to them are within the zone of indifference" (p. 169), so likewise do they have an interest in resisting or securing clarification on problematic claims of authority. Albeit unmentioned by Barnard, this too can play a useful role.

A fourth effect of informal organization that may, in fact, undercut the efficacy of internal organization also goes unmentioned by Barnard. This is that informal organization can lead to resource misallocation distortions—including on-the-job leisure, waste, investment distortions, and other forms of subgoal pursuit. Barnard's frequent references to moral codes, moral factors, moral elements, and so forth—in the context of executive responsibility—are, perhaps, his way of dealing with (finessing) concerns over subgoal pursuit (Chapter 17).

The economy of incentives Barnard disputed the efficacy of material incentives, which he associated with the prevailing economic approach to organization (pp. x, 143), and asserted that "Inducements of a personal, non-materialistic character are of great importance to secure cooperative effort above the minimum material rewards essential to subsistence. The opportunities for distinction, prestige, personal power, and the attainment of dominating position are much more important than material rewards in the development of . . . commercial organizations" (p. 145).

Although Barnard advanced these and related arguments in a chapter titled "The Economy of Incentives," and might have developed the argument that nonmaterial incentives are substitutes for material incentives and that this has comparative institutional significance, he pulled up short in both respects. There is at least a hint of such broader significance, however, in his expansive treatment of incentive issues.

SIMON AND OTHERS

The Science of Administration

One could conclude that a splendid start had been made toward the development of a new science of organization. That Herbert Simon's book, *Administrative Behavior,* which relies on Barnard and is expressly designed to advance the science of administration, was published in 1947 must be counted as an auspicious development. In Simon's judgment, the study of organization suffered for lack of "adequate linguistic and conceptual tools for realistically and significantly describing even a simple administrative organization—describing it, that is, in a way that will provide the basis for scientific analysis of the effectiveness of its structure and operation" (1957, p. xlv). Using Barnard's earlier work as framework, Simon set out to develop more relevant concepts and a more precise vocabulary (1957a, p. xlv): "Before we can establish any immutable 'principles' of administration, we must be able to describe, in words, exactly how an administrative organization looks and exactly how it works. . . . I have attempted to construct a vocabulary which will permit such description."

Of Simon's numerous and important contributions to the science of administration, I focus on five features: bounded rationality, microanalytics, the employment relation, hierarchy, and subgoal pursuit.

Bounded rationality Although the term *bounded rationality* was not coined until 1957, Simon's approach to the study of organization has consistently been of a bounded rationality kind. Albeit sometimes confused with irrationality, nonrationality, and the like, bounded rationality refers to behavior that is *"intendedly* rational, but only *limitedly* so" (Simon 1957a. p. xxiv).

Bounded rationality is important to the study of economic organization in several respects. For one thing, it is "only because individual human beings are limited in knowledge, foresight, skill, and time that organizations are useful instruments for the achievement of human purpose" (Simon 1957b, p. 199). But for bounded rationality, all issues of organization collapse in favor of comprehensive contracting of either Arrow-Debreu or mechanism design kinds.

A second (related) way in which bounded rationality is relevant is that mind now becomes a scarce resource (Simon 1978). The study of organization as a means by which to economize on mind as the scarce resource is thus suggested. Simon, however, chose to emphasize a different lesson. He insistently argued that social scientists (especially economists) should give up maximizing in favor of "satisficing."

Simon defined the principle of bounded rationality as follows: "The capacity of the human mind for formulating and solving complex problems is very small compared with the size of the problems whose solution is required for objectively rational behavior in the real world" (Simon 1957b, p. 198; emphasis omitted). He averred that the "key to the simplification of the choice process . . . is the replacement of the goal of *maximizing* with the goal of *satisficing*, of finding a course of action that is good enough . . . [T]his substitution is an essential step in the application of the principle of bounded rationality" (Simon 1957b, pp. 204–5; emphasis in original).

This turned out to be a fateful choice. Rather than encourage economizing reasoning, to which economists could easily relate and usefully contribute, bounded rationality became identified with aspiration level mechanics instead—which has wide appeal but is more closely associated with psychology. Simon's repeated insistence that satisficing was the way to go (1959, 1962, 1972) and some specific economic applications (especially Cyert & March 1963) notwithstanding, a cumulative research tradition within economics did not develop. It is now generally agreed that the satisficing approach has not been broadly applicable (Aumann 1985, p. 35).

As discussed later, economics could have (and, more recently, has) gleaned another and, as it turns out, less controversial lesson from bounded rationality: *all complex contracts are unavoidably incomplete.* That is, however, another story.

Microanalytics Simon's contrast between the physical sciences and economics in microanalytic respects is instructive. As he observes (1984, p. 40), "In the physical sciences, when errors of measurement and other noise are found to be of the same order of magnitude as the phenomena under study, the response is not to try to squeeze more information out of the data by statistical means; it is instead to find techniques for observing the phenomena at a higher level of resolution. The corresponding strategy for economics is obvious: to secure new kinds of data at the micro level."

But this immediately poses the questions: What particulars of organization are pertinent? What is the basic unit of analysis? As Simon had earlier remarked, "It is not possible to build an adequate theory of human behavior unless we have an appropriate unit of analysis," to which he responded that the "decision *premise* is . . . the appropriate unit for the study of human behavior" (1957a, p. xxxii). Although Simon and others have used very microanalytic methods to study human problem solving to good advantage (Newell & Simon 1972), the use of the decision premise as the unit of analysis for studying organization has never been shown to have general application.

The employment relation   Simon specifically adopted and refined Barnard's concept of authority and of the employment relation. Of special importance was his 1951 article, "A Formal Theory of the Employment Relation." In it he described the zone of acceptance to which an employee could be induced to agree and compared sales contracts, in which actions are stipulated in advance, with employment contracts, in which actions can be decided later, depending on state realizations. Unsurprisingly, the employment relation is favored as uncertainty increases. Simon also makes the sophisticated point that worker and firm are faced with a complex incentive problem: "If the worker had confidence that the employer would take account of his preferences [once the wage had been agreed to], the former would . . . be willing to work for a smaller wage than if he thought these satisfactions were going to be ignored in the employer's exercise of authority and only profitability to the employer taken into account" (1957b, p. 192). This has been a recurrent theme in much of the subsequent labor economics literature.

Hierarchy   Simon regards hierarchy as an instrument and observes that complex biological, physical, and social systems are all characterized by hierarchy (1962a, p. 468): "The central theme that runs through my remarks is that complexity frequently takes the form of hierarchy, and that hierarchic systems have some common properties that are independent of their specific content. Hierarchy . . . is one of the central structural schemes that the architect of complexity uses."

Simon notes that a condition of "near-decomposability" is commonly associated with hierarchy and serves to distinguish interactions between subsystems from interactions within subsystems (Simon 1962a, p. 473). In hierarchical systems with near-decomposability, not only are "intracomponent linkages . . . generally stronger than intercomponent linkages" but the short-run or "higher frequency dynamics are associated with the subsystems" and the longer-run or "lower frequency dynamics with the larger systems" (Simon 1962a, p. 477). W. Ross Ashby's (1960) analysis of adaptive systems that employ double feedback—one of a frequent and short-run kind; the other of a less frequent but longer-run kind—can be interpreted in precisely these terms. In organizational terms, operating and strategic levels of decision making correspond to the higher and lower frequency dynamics, respectively. These are natural outcomes of an unconvoluted, evolutionary kind (Simon 1962a)—although, to be sure, design distortions can be and sometimes are introduced into hierarchies as well. It is nonetheless vital to understand that hierarchy is a basic organizing principle for all complex social systems—which is a message that some students of economic organization resist or deny (Marglin 1974).

Subgoal pursuit Subgoal pursuit makes its appearance in March and Simon (1958) but is not a subject with which Simon (before or since) has been greatly concerned. As indicated, factoring complex problems into manageable parts is something that has been of continuous interest to Simon. Such factoring can lead to subgoal pursuit of both instrumental and strategic kinds.

The general argument is that "members of an organizational unit [tend] to evaluate action only in terms of subgoals, even when these are in conflict with the goals of the larger organization" (March & Simon 1958, p. 152). Selective perceptions are partly responsible. Within-group reinforcement is another factor. Selective exposure to problems is a third (March & Simon 1958, pp. 152–53). Goal distortions, bargaining, and coalition formation result (March & Simon 1958, p. 156). Strategic subgoal pursuit gets little attention and possible remedies go unremarked.

Subsequent Developments

As previous chapters in this book make clear, organization theory is an enormously rich field. Only a few subsequent developments are treated here. These are: (1) posterior rationality, (2) resource dependency, and (3) disciplinary borrowing.

Posterior rationality The behavior of individuals who engage in satisficing will be stabilized if these same individuals are given to ex-post rationalization. A substantial literature on "posterior rationality" (Weick 1969; March 1973) developed along these lines. As James March puts it, "Posterior rationality models maintain the idea that action should be consistent with preferences, but they conceive action as being antecedent to goals" (1988, pp. 273–74). Though this is instructive, one of the consequences of work along these lines is that it discouraged the analysis of what I refer to later as "incomplete contracting in its entirety." A disjunction between organization theory and economics developed as a consequence.

Resource dependency Jay Barney and William Ouchi remark that throughout "the 1960s and 1970s, the dominant theoretical frameworks in organization theory were drawn from sociology and social psychology and relied heavily on the concept of power" (1986, p. 12). Specifically, the resource dependency approach to organization works out of a power perspective. The argument is that (Scott 1987, p. 111) "The need to acquire resources creates dependencies between organizations and outside units. How important and how scarce these resources are determine the nature and extent of organizational dependency. Dependency is the obverse of power (Emerson 1962). Economic dependencies give rise to political problems and may succumb to political solutions."

As discussed later, many dependency issues can be addressed in efficiency terms, whereupon power considerations largely vanish. It suffices for my purpose here merely to remark that power, for a long time, has been the congenial organization theory perspective—March's early conclusion that "power is a disappointing concept" (1966, p. 70) notwithstanding.

Borrowing   Research in organization theory has a history of borrowing from other disciplines (Barney & Ouchi 1986, p. xi):

> This borrowing began . . . early . . . [with borrowing] from psychology and social psychology to establish what became known as the human relations school. Later, concepts and a way of thinking were borrowed from sociology and political science to develop the contingency and resource dependence theories. More recently, concepts from biology have been borrowed in the development of the population ecology model, and anthropology has been a source of concepts and a way of thinking for those studying organizational cultures.

The latest discipline from which organization theory has begun to borrow is economics (Barney & Ouchi 1986, pp. xi–xii). Although this is often described as a one-way street, whereby economics informs organization theory (Jensen 1983), I submit that economics and organization theory ought to inform each other. Indeed, as this book testifies, that has been happening.

One of the distinctive things that economics brings to organization theory—and to the study of the "contiguous disciplines" more generally—is a systems orientation. Ronald Coase maintains that this is what explains the success of economics in moving into the other social sciences: economists "study the economic system as a unified interdependent system and, therefore, are more likely to uncover the basic interrelationships within a social system than is someone less accustomed to looking at the working of a system as a whole," one consequence of which is that "economics makes it more difficult to ignore factors which are clearly important and which play a part in all social systems" (1978, pp. 290–91). These views are pertinent to my discussion of transaction cost economics, which follows.

TRANSACTION COST ECONOMICS: CONCEPTS

Kenneth Arrow queries "Why . . . has the work of Herbert Simon, which meant so much to all of us, . . . had so little direct consequence? Why did the older institutional school fail so miserably, though it contained such able analysts as Thorstein Veblen, J. R. Commons, and W. C. Mitchell?" (1987, p. 734). He ventures two answers, one of which is that the issues are intrinsically difficult. But he further remarks that the New Institutional Economics movement, of which transaction cost economics is a part, has made more headway. He attributes this headway to the fact that the New Institutional Economics "does not consist primarily of giving new answers to the traditional questions of economics—resource allocation and degree of utilization. Rather it consists of answering new questions, why economic institutions have emerged the way they did and not otherwise; it merges into economic history, but brings sharper nanoeconomic . . . ('nano' is an extreme version of 'micro') reasoning to bear than has been customary" (1987, p. 734). R. C. O. Mathews similarly concludes that whereas institutional economics had until recently been relegated to the pages of the history of thought, the economics of institutions has, over the past decade, "become one of the liveliest areas in our discipline" (Mathews 1986, p. 903).

My purpose in this section is to examine the transaction cost economics branch of the New Institutional Economics movement, mainly in relation to the organization theory literature referred to earlier. The uses that are made of earlier organization theory work are discussed first, after which some of the significant differences are treated.

Uses

Barnard   Transaction cost economics concurs with Barnard's assessment that formal organization is important and that the study of induced cooperation deserves a prominent place on the research agenda. The firm is therefore not described as a technological unit to which a profit maximization purpose is ascribed but is described instead as an organizational unit, the efficacy of which is to be examined in comparative institutional (mainly, transaction cost economizing) terms.

Barnard's view that the central problem of organization is that of adaptation is likewise embraced. Of special interest in this connection is how parties engaged in a long-term contract can adapt effectively to disturbances. The need to craft contractual structures in which they have mutual confidence is plainly posed.

The zone of acceptance within the employment relation was Barnard's way of introducing an adaptive capacity. His view of contract and, more generally, of the law as being farsighted and consensual are both noteworthy. Transaction cost economics relates constructively to both "incomplete contracting in its entirety" and the importance of private ordering (as opposed to legal centralism).

As discussed in the section entitled A Simple Contractual Schema, the implementation of an incomplete contract viewed in its entirety requires that price, technology, and contractual safeguards all be addressed simultaneously. Not only will wider zones of acceptance be priced out, as Barnard indicated, but they will also be embedded in protective governance structures. Much more concerted attention to the design of governance in this latter respect is needed.

Also, real differences between the employment relation and all other forms of contracting notwithstanding, our understanding of contract and of economic organization more generally will benefit from a realization that very strong similarities recur across markets of all kinds—labor, intermediate product, and capital included. Transaction cost economics emphasizes and works out the ramifications of these commonalities, as a consequence of which it supports a broader approach to economic organization than exclusive focus on the employment relation yields. Indeed, the canonical transaction, for the purposes of transaction cost economics, is not the employment relation but vertical integration.

Focusing on the make-or-buy decision has advantages of two kinds. For one thing, intermediate product market contracting is easier to address in instrumental terms than is labor market contracting.[7] For another, the study of vertical integration invites the query, what is responsible for limitations to firm size? This is a central query to which the economics of organization should be expected to speak[8] but which does not arise—as easily or at all—in conjunction with the study of the employment relation.

Like Barnard, transaction cost economics works out of a private ordering rather than legal centralism approach to contract law. The legal centralism approach to contract law assumed that efficacious rules of law regarding contract disputes were in place and were applied by the courts in an informed, sophisticated, and low-cost way. Purportedly, "disputes require 'access' to a forum external to the original social setting of the dispute [from which] remedies will be provided as prescribed in some body of authoritative learning and dispensed by experts who operate under the auspices of the state" (Galanter 1981, p. 1). But the facts disclose otherwise: most disputes, including many that under current rules could be brought to a court, are resolved by avoidance, self-help, and the like (Galanter 1981, p. 2).

To be sure, a private ordering approach to contract requires support. For one thing, good intentions or mere agreements are prone to breakdown. This invites precisely the type of analysis of credible commitments with which transaction cost economics is concerned. Also, as discussed later in the subsection on Incomplete Contracting in Its Entirety, private ordering benefits from having the law available for purposes of ultimate appeal.

Barnard's notion of "informal organization" is useful to transaction cost economics in two respects. First, informal organization arguably helps to safeguard the security and integrity needs of employees. This is a governance structure feature, the ramifications of which need to be taken into account. For another, informal organization may be a manifestation of a more general condition of "atmosphere," the effects of which serve to distinguish market and hierarchical modes of organization. Such distinctions support comparative analysis of a discrete structural rather than (as is more customary) of a marginal analysis kind.

Finally, although the economy of incentives to which Barnard refers is a narrow use of economizing reasoning, an economizing approach, broadly conceived, is what transaction cost economics holds to be the main case (to which alternative main case scenarios should be compared). The issues here are discussed further in the next section on Differences.

Simon Simon's concept of bounded rationality is specifically embraced by transaction cost economics. Moreover, both parts of the definition—*intended* but *limited* rationality—are accorded respect. Intentionally rational agents are attempting to cope effectively. This is plainly in the "rational spirit" tradition. But their limitations also need to be admitted. The principal lessons of bounded rationality for transaction cost purposes are these: (1) all complex contracts are unavoidably incomplete, on which account the hitherto neglected study of ex-post governance is placed at the very center of the research agenda[9]; and (2) economizing on bounded rationality is a leading purpose of economic organization.

Microanalytics is likewise a matter of special concern to transaction cost economics.[10] This is partly tied up with the choice of a unit of analysis (see Differences, next). But the study of process considerations is also implicated. Transaction cost economics maintains that there are no shortcuts and that economic organization needs to be examined in a "modest, slow, molecular, definitive" way.[11]

This view contrasts with the much more widely held opinion that "if one wishes to model the behavior of organizations such as firms, then study of the firm as an organization ought to be high on one's agenda. This study is not, strictly speaking, necessary: one can hope to divine the correct 'reduced form' for the behavior of the organization without considering the micro-forces within the organization" (Kreps and Spence 1985, pp. 374–75).

The Kreps–Spence remarks appear to relegate the study of microanalytics to others or, alternatively, turn on the hope that economists will be lucky. The main risks with the first of these conditions are that those to whom the study of the details are relegated will either make the wrong observations or report the right observations in ways that mask their economic significance. Hoping to get lucky is even more problematic. Accordingly, Kreps and Spence conclude that the "study of organization is likely to help in the design of reduced forms that stress the important variables" (1985, p. 375).

Transaction cost economics maintains that the details matter in assessing the efficacy of alternative forms of organization. That franchise bidding is an effective way of dealing with natural monopoly cannot, therefore, rest entirely on an imaginative formulation of the issues (Demsetz 1968; Stigler 1968; Posner 1972). Instead, both the attributes of transactions (with special attention to the assets) and the details of the contracting process need to be carefully examined. There is no other way adequately to deal with the franchise bidding hypothesis except by moving beyond the general description to assess the underlying attribute and contractual microanalytics (Williamson 1985a, chap. 13).

The same is true in assessing the assertion that transactions can be moved out of markets and into firms without loss of incentive intensity (Grossman & Hart 1986). Convenient though this assumption is, a microanalytic examination of the effort to preserve high-powered incentives within firms discloses that such an effort elicits adverse cost consequences (Williamson 1985; 1988a). *Incentive differences,* rather than unchanged incentive intensity, *thus characterize firm and market organization.*

More generally, the argument is this: although several different tradeoff scenarios may yield similar crude, qualitative predictions, that is not the only test. A second test is whether the trade-offs postulated are plausible. Assessing this normally requires that the underlying microanalytics be examined—tiresome and troublesome as such an effort may be. Nonetheless, "study the microanalytics" is the unchanging message of transaction cost economics. Or, as Stephen Jay Gould puts it, "God dwells in the details" (1987, p. 32).

Understanding the employment relation and the differences between sales and employment contracts are of central interest to transaction cost economics.[12] Also, hierarchy, especially the differences between markets and hierarchies, is prominently featured in the transaction cost economics scheme of things. Like Simon, hierarchy is treated instrumentally—principally with reference to its transaction cost economizing properties. This is pertinent both in assessing the decision to take a transaction out of the market (or not) and, for those transactions that are organized internally, for purposes of choosing between alternative hierarchical designs. (In fact, of course, these two decisions are related.)

Finally, transaction cost economics subscribes to subgoal pursuit. Indeed, it goes beyond the March and Simon formulation and argues that "opportunism" is a behavioral assumption of such pervasive reach and importance that it deserves coequal status with bounded rationality in any concerted effort to assess the comparative efficacy of alternative modes of contracting. Thus, just as the absence of bounded rationality would vitiate the need for internal organization, since all of the relevant contracting action could be concentrated in a comprehensive ex-ante agreement, so likewise would the absence of opportunism vitiate the need for added safeguards, since "contract as promise" could be used to annihilate ex-post defections from even incomplete contracts.[13]

Differences

That transaction cost economics relies very substantially on the "science of administration" of Barnard and Simon is apparent from the foregoing.

But transaction cost economics aspires to move beyond administration to deal symmetrically with all forms of organization. The eventual object is to realize a science of organization. Work toward that purpose is in progress.

The numerous and important dependencies of transaction cost economics on organization theory notwithstanding, there are also real differences, which are the matters of concern here. With reference to Simon, these are (1) the rejection of the decision premise as the unit of analysis in favor of the transaction and (2) the rejection of satisficing in favor of economizing. Also (3) a myopic treatment of contracting (the power perspective) is rejected in favor of incomplete contracting in its entirety. Moreover, an economic theory of organization poses further needs. Of special importance are the needs to (4) explicate opportunism, (5) make selective appeal to contract law, with special reference to "excuse doctrine," (6) work through crucial process-related particulars of a firm and market kind, and (7) develop the applications. The core features and recurrent variations are captured in (8) the simple contractual schema and (9) the generic trade-off. These last two are treated in the section entitled Transaction Cost Economics: Apparatus.

Unit of analysis   Simon proposed that the decision premise be made the basic unit of analysis. This is a highly microanalytic unit of analysis—arguably more microanalytic than is needed to examine issues of economic organization that are of interest even to institutional economists. In any event, that question is moot: the decision premise as a unit of analysis has never been operationalized in such a way as to give it broad and general application.

An alternative unit, proposed earlier by John R. Commons, has proved more promising. Thus, Commons saw the problem of economic organization as that of dealing simultaneously with conflict, mutual dependence, and order, whereupon the criterion for the "ultimate unit of economic activity . . . [should] contain in itself the three principles of conflict, mutuality and order" (Commons 1925, p. 4). The transaction, in his view, was responsive to these principles and he proposed that it be made the basic unit of analysis (Commons 1925, p. 4; 1934, pp. 4–8). But neither Commons nor his followers took the obvious next step: if the transaction is the basic unit of analysis, then what are the principal dimensions with respect to which transactions differ?

The transaction is a semimicroanalytic unit of analysis—more microanalytic than economics has characteristically been concerned with but a larger unit than the decision premise. It is also a unit that lends itself to dimensionalization. This permits the study of economic organization to be developed in a more operational way than had been hitherto feasible.

Transaction cost economics maintains that the key dimensions for describing transactions are (1) asset specificity, (2) uncertainty, and (3) frequency. Of the three, asset specificity is the most important and most distinctive. Investments in durable, specialized assets that cannot be redeployed from existing uses and users except at a significant loss of productive value are transaction specific. Contracting for goods and services that are produced with the support of transaction specific assets poses serious problems. Classical market contracting gives way to bilateral trading (or, more generally, hybrid modes of organization), which in turn gives way to unified ownership (hierarchies) as the condition of asset specificity builds up.[14]

The usual way in which the organization theory literature deals with asset specificity is in conjunction with "resource dependency." The general argument here is that exchanges of important and scarce resources "create dependencies." A power orientation is adopted, such dependencies being the obverse of power (Scott 1987, p. 111).

Albeit very much concerned with bilateral dependency conditions, transaction cost economics assumes that parties *anticipate such conditions and organize with respect to them.* Resource dependency therefore does not come as a "surprise" to unwitting victims. To the contrary, parties explore alternative supply scenarios. Each alternative node in the general contracting schema described later is characterized by (1) the supply technology, (2) the price at which product is traded, and (3) the governance structure (including safeguards) in which the contract is embedded. These three features—asset specificity, price, and governance—are determined simultaneously in an internally consistent way. Therefore, rather than interpret dependency in ex-post power terms, transaction cost economics examines ex-ante and ex-post contractual features simultaneously within an efficiency framework.

Put differently, whereas much of the resource dependency literature works out of a *myopic* incomplete contracting set-up, whereupon dependency is an unwanted surprise, transaction costs economics examines incomplete contracts in their *entirety*—hence the absence of surprise, victims, and the like. This is not to say that all outcomes are equally good. Often, however, contrived breach, expropriation, holdups, and so forth can be and are mitigated.

Economizing and discriminating alignment Upon supplanting hyperrationality with bounded rationality, Simon argued that the key analytical consequence was that maximizing be supplanted by satisficing. That placed Simon on a collision course with economics. Although it is perhaps still in doubt, most economists have concluded that satisficing never developed a cumulative and compelling research product and lost out to the economics mainstream in the contest that ensued.

Transaction cost economics embraces bounded rationality but urges that the principal ramification of bounded rationality for studying economic organization is that all complex contracts are unavoidably incomplete. If, moreover, mind is a scarce resource, then an economizing orientation, broadly construed to include organization, brings economics and organization theory together (rather than placing them in opposition or locating them on different domains). Frank Knight's views of economics are pertinent: "Men in general, and within limits, wish to behave economically, to make their activities *and their organization* 'efficient' rather than wasteful. This fact does deserve the utmost emphasis; and an adequate definition of the science of economics . . . might well make it explicit that the main relevance of the discussion is found in its relation to social policy, assumed to be directed toward the end indicated, of increasing economic efficiency, of reducing waste" (1941, p. 252; emphasis added).

Transaction cost economics maintains that the economic institutions of capitalism have the main purpose and effect of economizing on transaction costs. To be sure, economic organization is very complex and a variety of economic and noneconomic purposes are normally at work. If, however, all are not equally important, our understanding of the weight to be ascribed to each will be promoted by examining economic organization from several well-focused perspectives. Qualifications, extensions, refinements, and so forth can then be introduced into each main case which, in such a contest, qualifies as a finalist. But the incipient science of organization needs to start somewhere. That is what the choice of a main case is all about.

The main case hypothesis out of which transaction cost economics works is this: align transactions (which differ in their attributes) with governance structures (which differ in their costs and competencies) in a discriminating (mainly transaction cost economizing) way. This discriminating alignment hypothesis predicts a large number of organizational regularities. The preliminary data are broadly corroborative (Joskow 1988; Williamson 1985a).

Incomplete contracting in its entirety Not every transaction poses defection hazards, and it may not be possible to safeguard all that do. However, where the potential hazards that beset contracts are evident to the parties from the beginning—possibly because they have previously had bad experience, possibly by noting the experience of others, possibly by consciously working the contracting ramifications through—studies of contract and of contracting institutions should start at the beginning.

That contracts are incomplete does not, therefore, imply myopia. Instead, alternative contracting scenarios are described and their ramifications compared. Manifestly bad games, of which the prisoners' dilemma is one, will be avoided or reorganized in a larger contracting context in which the incentives to defect are attenuated. The use of reciprocity to equilibrate hazards is an example (Williamson 1985a, chap. 8).

Opportunism and credible commitments Most organization theorists subscribe to bounded rationality and count it a distinct gain that bounded rationality has made inroads into economics. To be sure, many might emphasize different aspects from those to which I refer here. But the argument that both markets and hierarchies need to come to terms with bounded rationality is uncontroversial.

By contrast, most organization theorists avoid making express reference to, much less relying on, the assumption of opportunism. Instead, assumptions of opportunism, moral hazard, agency costs and the like are regarded as demeaning variations on the familiar assumption of self-interest seeking, on which economics has long relied.

I submit, however, that organization theorists were familiar with and had an extensive literature dealing with opportunism long before economists got around to it. And I further submit that the assumption is less jaundiced than it first appears.

To be sure, there were (and are) language differences between economics and organization theory. The terms *unofficial rewards, managerial discretion,* and *subgoal pursuit* are the organization theory counterparts for opportunism, moral hazard, shirking, agency costs, and the like.[15] Whereas economists were reluctant to grant these conditions, preferring instead to work out of a profit-maximization set-up, organization theorists came to terms easily with these conditions.

Economists are thus late comers to the opportunism scene. When they arrived, however, they pulled in new paraphernalia and wrung out different implications. Rather than regard opportunism in myopic terms, they instead viewed it from the aforementioned standpoint of incomplete contracting in its entirety.

The contrast between the Machiavellian treatment of promise and that of transaction cost economics is instructive. Machiavelli advised his prince that "a prudent ruler ought not to keep faith when by so doing it would be against his interest, and when the reasons which made him bind himself no longer exist. . . . [L]egitimate grounds [have never] failed a prince who wished to show colourable excuse for the promise" (Gauss 1952, pp. 92–93). But reciprocal or preemptive opportunism is not the only lesson to be gleaned from an awareness that human agents are not fully trustworthy. Indeed, that is a very primitive response.

The more important lesson, for the purposes of studying economic organization, is this: Transactions that are subject to ex-post opportunism will benefit if appropriate safeguards can be devised ex ante. Rather than reply to opportunism in kind, therefore, the wise prince is one who seeks both to give and to receive "credible commitments." Incentives may be realigned, or superior governance structures within which to organize transactions may be devised.

So regarded, the transaction cost economics assumption of opportunism is less offensive than it at first appears. To assume, moreover, that human agents are opportunistic does not mean that all are continually given to opportunism. Rather, the assumption is that *some* individuals are opportunistic *some* of the time and that it is costly to ascertain differential trustworthiness ex ante. H. L. A. Hart's remarks help to put the issues into perspective: "Neither understanding of long-term interest, nor the strength of goodness of will . . . are shared by all men alike. All are tempted at times to prefer their own immediate interests. . . . 'Sanctions' are . . . required not as the normal motive for obedience, but as a *guarantee* that those who would voluntarily obey shall not be sacrificed by those who would not" (1961, p. 193; emphasis in original). Lest the world be reorganized to the advantage of the more opportunistic agents, checks against opportunism are needed.

Taken together, the overall import of bounded rationality and opportunism for transaction cost economics is this: organize transactions so as to economize on bounded rationality while simultaneously safeguarding the transactions in question against the hazards of opportunism. That is a message to which both economists and organization theorists can relate.

Contract law   Although transaction cost economics emphasizes private ordering over legal centralism, and thus pushes contract law into the institutional background, contract law nonetheless has two important roles to play. One of these is to serve as ultimate appeal, thereby delimiting threat positions. Karl Llewellyn's concept of contract as framework is pertinent (Llewellyn 1931, pp. 736–37):

> The major importance of legal contract is to provide a framework for wellnigh every type of group organization and for well-nigh every type of passing or permanent relation between individuals and groups . . . a framework highly adjustable, a framework which almost never accurately indicates real working relations, but which affords a rough indication around which such relations vary, an occasional guide in cases of doubt, and a norm of ultimate appeal when the relations cease in fact to work.

The norm of ultimate appeal is a factor that delimits threat positions— should it happen, as it sometimes does, that push comes to shove.

Additionally relevant in this connection is the important role played by "excuse doctrine." Thus, parties that are able to enforce the terms of the contract in court might do this not only for good but also for poor cause. If, for example, a party asked that the letter of a contract be enforced for state realizations of a very low probability kind for which literal enforcement would impose egregious hardship on the other, then contract would be made to serve a purpose for which it was not originally intended. The use of contract, compared with internal organization, would suffer relatively if such punitive uses of contract were permitted.

Contract excuse doctrine is arguably intended to relieve such contractual "abuses." More generally, the "less than total commitment to the keeping of promises" by the legal system to which Ian Macneil refers is pertinent (1974, p. 730):

> Contract remedies are generally among the weakest of those the legal system can deliver. But a host of doctrines and techniques lies in the way of even

those remedies: impossibility, frustration, mistake, manipulative interpretation, jury discretion, consideration, illegality, duress, undue influence, unconscionability, capacity, forfeiture and penalty rules, doctrines of substantial performance, severability, bankruptcy laws, statutes of fraud, to name a few; almost any contract doctrine can and does serve to make the commitment of the legal system to promise keeping less than complete.

To be sure, there are trade-offs. One way of examining these is to assume that the object is to encourage the use of contracting (as opposed to internal organization). Both "too lax" and "too strict" contract enforcement are then to be avoided. Assessing the balance is a matter to which transaction cost reasoning can be and, to a degree, has been applied (Williamson 1985b).

Process particulars   Two processes of special relevance to an understanding of economic organization are the Fundamental Transformation and the impossibility of selective intervention. The first of these deals with the transformation of what had been a large numbers bidding competition at the outset into one of bilateral exchange during contract execution and at contract renewal intervals. The second explains why internal organization is not able to beat markets everywhere by combining replication (where markets work well) with selective intervention (where markets do poorly).

Both the Fundamental Transformation and the impossibility of selective intervention are tedious process arguments and are developed at length elsewhere (Williamson 1975, 1985a). Suffice it to observe here that process analysis (1) goes to the very core of economic organization, (2) is needed to evaluate the plausibility of alternative trade-off scenarios, and (3) invites further application—to life cycle and reputation effect features of organization (Weizsacker 1980; Fama 1980; Kreps 1984), among other things.

Examples of issues to which the new economics of organization can be or has been applied include the following:

The Theory of Economic Organization

1. If the firm is a governance structure, then the boundary of the firm ought to be set with reference to the capacity of the firm (compared with the market) to provide useful organizational functions. Accordingly, an organizational theory of the firm needs to take its place alongside a technological theory of the firm. That has been occurring.

2. If the benefits of supplying contractual safeguards against breakdown and premature breach vary systematically with the attributes of transactions, then an economic theory of contract will prescribe significant safeguards for some transactions and fewer safeguards for others. It does and the data line up.[16]

3. If the preceding theory of contract has general application, it should apply—with variation—to labor, intermediate product, and capital market transactions alike. It does.

     a. Labor. The collective organization of labor (unions) and the governance structures within internal labor markets should vary systematically with the attributes of labor. The preliminary evidence suggests that they do.

     b. Intermediate product. Make or buy decisions should vary systematically with the attributes of transactions. The evidence is abundant. They do.[17]

4. Leakage. The need to seal off some technologies or protect some investments against loss of appropriability will predictably elicit leakage attenuation of a discriminating kind. It does.[18]

5. The limits of internal organization. Lest internal organization be overused, with adverse increases in cost, internal organization needs to be used in a discriminating way. The powers and limits of both markets and hierarchies need to be worked out. The basic trade-offs need to be displayed. The data need to be worked up. Nuances need to be discovered. More generally, market failure and organizational failure need to be put on a parity. Work of this kind is in progress but will take a decade and more to work out.

6. Integrity. The relentless emphasis on efficiency should not obscure the needs of individuals—especially for personal integrity. The integrity-respecting (or demeaning) attributes of markets and hierarchies of different kinds need to be worked out. Albeit enormously difficult problems, they nevertheless need to be addressed.

Applications to Functional Areas

7. Finance. Debt and equity can be described as financial instruments. But it is misleading to think of debt and equity only in financial terms if the critical economic differences between these two instruments turn equally on their governance structure differences. A combined theory of corporate finance and corporate governance is needed. Alliance capitalism issues are implicated. Work on these matters has been progressing.[19]

8. Marketing. A contractual approach to marketing should lead to a discriminating theory of forward integration into distribution, the use of franchising, the use of agents, and so on. Work of this kind and evidence that pertains thereto are coming along.[20]

9. Comparative systems. A variety of approaches to the study of comparative economic systems have been employed, with varying degrees of success. An assessment of the incentive and bureaucratic features of capitalism and socialism—the powers, limits, contradictions—of each is sorely needed. The logic of economic organization to which I refer is germane and should be developed along these lines.

10. Business strategy. Strategic thinking is always appealing. But a lot of strategizing is mistaken and can be costly. A discriminating theory of strategy—when it pays, when it does not, what the instru-

ments are, how they work—is needed. The contractual approach supplies some of the needed framework.

11. Business history. Business history ought both to inform and to be informed by the combined study of economics and organization. Business history is a field that appears to be experiencing a new life.

Applications to Contiguous Disciplines

12. Politics. Contractual theories of how to organize regulatory agencies and how federalism should be structured would add greatly to our understanding of politics. Work of both kinds is in progress.[21]

13. Reconceptualizing the modern corporation in governance structure/ organizational terms has ramifications for the way in which the multinational corporation is interpreted. The selective use of the multinational corporation to facilitate technology transfer is one example. More generally, the multinational corporation is usefully thought of in transnational terms—which has ramifications for the theory of the nation state.[22]

14. Sociology. The new economics of organization has brought economics and sociology into active contact with one another whereas they used to operate at a distance. A rich dialogue is needed and is in prospect.[23]

15. The law. In addition to antitrust and regulation, the new economics of organization has an important bearing on corporate governance and on contract law. Among other things, new interpretations of "excuse doctrine," the rationale for which has been an ancient contract law puzzle, have been proposed.

Public Policy

16. Public policy toward business needs to be informed and reformed accordingly. That too has been going on. Antitrust has already been reshaped (especially with respect to vertical integration and vertical contracting practices) and more is in prospect—joint research ventures being an example.[24]

17. If contracts work well in some circumstances but predictably break down in others, then the merits of deregulation (moving out of regulation into autonomous contracting) ought to be susceptible to analysis. It is. Deregulation—including mistaken deregulation—has been examined along these lines.[25]

18. Policy implementation—in general but specifically with reference to developing countries—needs to be reexamined from an institutional point of view. The time has come and the apparatus is at hand to examine policy implementation in a disciplined, microanalytic way. Older theories—of neoclassical, rent seeking, and property rights kinds—simply fail to address pertinent institutional issues.

TRANSACTION COST ECONOMICS: APPARATUS

A Simple Contractual Schema[26]

Transaction cost maintains that the organization of economic activity involves variations on a theme. Once the basic structure of the contracting problem has been worked out in one context, the same general argument applies, with variation, to what had previously been thought to be disparate contractual issues. The pattern recognition to which Hayek referred is pertinent: "Whenever the capacity of recognizing an abstract rule which the arrangement of these attributes follows has been acquired in one field, the same master mould will apply when the signs for those abstract attributes are evoked by altogether different elements. It is the classification of the structure of relationships between these abstract attributes which constitutes the recognition of the patterns as the same or different" (1967, p. 50).

The variations on a theme to which I refer involve repeated application of the hypothesis of "discriminating alignment," which is the transaction cost economics translation of Knight's view that "activities and their organization" be made efficient.

The simple contractual schema set out here explicates this condition. It begins with a technological distinction, to which price and governance are then added. Thus, assume that a good or service can be supplied by either of two alternative technologies. One is a general-purpose technology, the other is a special-purpose technology. The latter requires greater investment in transaction-specific durable assets and is more efficient for servicing steady-state demands.

Using k as a measure of transaction-specific assets, transactions that use the general-purpose technology are ones for which $k = 0$. When transactions use the special-purpose technology, by contrast, a $k > 0$ condition exists. Assets here are specialized to the particular needs of the parties. Productive values would therefore be sacrificed if transactions of this kind were to be prematurely terminated. A bilateral monopoly condition thus applies to such transactions.

Whereas classical market contracting—"sharp in by clear agreement; sharp out by clear performance" (Macneil 1974, p. 738)—suffices for transactions of the $k = 0$ kind, unassisted market governance poses hazards whenever nontrivial transaction-specific assets are placed at risk. Parties have an incentive to devise safeguards to protect investments in transactions of the latter kind. Let s denote the magnitude of any such safeguards. An $s = 0$ condition is one in which no safeguards are provided; a decision to provide safeguards is reflected by an $s > 0$ result.

Figure 8.1 displays the three contracting outcomes corresponding to such a description. Associated with each node is a price. To facilitate comparisons between nodes, assume that suppliers (1) are risk-neutral, (2) are prepared to supply under either technology, and (3) will accept any safeguard

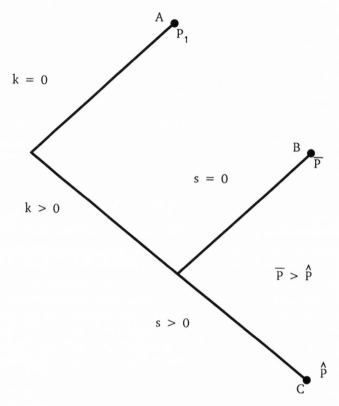

Figure 8.1 Simple contracting schema

condition whatsoever, as long as an expected break-even result can be projected. Thus, node A is the general-purpose technology $(k = 0)$ supply relation for which a break-even price of p_1 is projected. The node B contract
is supported by transaction-specific assets $(k > 0)$ for which no safeguard is
offered $(s = 0)$. The expected break-even price here is $\bar{p}$. The node C contract also employs the special-purpose technology. But since the buyer at
this node provides the supplier with a safeguard $(s > 0)$, the breakeven price,
$\hat{p}$, at node C is less than $\bar{p}$.

The protective safeguards to which I refer normally take on one or more
of three forms. The first is to realign incentives, which commonly involves
some type of severance payment or penalty for premature termination. A
second is to create and employ a specialized governance structure to which
to refer and resolve disputes. The use of arbitration, rather than litigation
in the courts, is thus characteristic of node C governance. A third form is
to introduce trading regularities that support and signal continuity intentions. Expanding a trading relation from unilateral to bilateral exchange—
through the concerted use, for example, of reciprocity—to effect an equi-

libration of trading hazards is an example of this third form of protective safeguard.

This simple contracting schema applies to a wide variety of contracting issues. It facilitates comparative institutional analysis by emphasizing that technology *(k)*, contractual governance/safeguards *(s)*, and price *(p)* are fully interactive and are determined simultaneously.

To summarize, the nodes, A, B, and C in the contractual schema set out in Figure 8.1 have the following properties:

1. Transactions that are efficiently supported by general-purpose assets $(k = 0)$ are located at node A and do not need protective governance structures. Discrete market contracting suffices. The world of competition obtains.
2. Transactions that involve significant investments of a transaction-specific kind $(k > 0)$ are ones for which the parties are effectively engaged in bilateral trade.
3. Transactions located at node B enjoy no safeguards $(s = 0)$, on which account the projected break-even supply price is great $(\bar{p} > \hat{p})$. Such transactions are apt to be unstable contractually. They may revert to node A (in which event the special-purpose technology would be replaced by the general-purpose $[k = 0]$ technology) or be relocated to node C (by introducing contractual safeguards that would encourage the continued use of the $k > 0$ technology).
4. Transactions located at node C incorporate safeguards $(s > 0)$, and thus are protected against expropriation hazards.
5. Inasmuch as price and governance are linked, parties to a contract should not expect to have their cake (low price) and eat it too (no safeguard). More generally, it is important to study *contracting in its entirety*. Both the ex-ante terms and the manner in which contracts are thereafter executed vary with the investment characteristics and the associated governance structures within which transactions are embedded.

The Generic Trade-off

The following deep puzzle of economic organization has been variously expressed: "Why is not all production carried on in one big firm?" (Coase 1952, p. 340). A second formulation is Why can a large firm not do everything that a collection of smaller firms can do and more? A third and more general formulation is Why aren't more degrees of freedom always better than fewer? But the most instructive way of putting the issue is in terms of selective intervention: if a firm can always do as well as the market, by replicating the market in those areas where the market performs well, and can intervene selectively, to improve on the market wherever expected net gains can be projected, then the firm will always be the superior form. The puzzle thus reduces to the following: What defeats selective intervention?

I mentioned this puzzle above and have addressed it elsewhere (Williamson 1985a, 6; 1988a). One of the things that emerges from a microanalytic examination of the factors responsible for the breakdown of selective intervention is that firms and markets are each characterized by a distinctive syndrome of attributes.

Without pretending to be exhaustive, governance structures can be described in terms of the following four attributes: (1) incentive intensity, (2) reliance on court ordering, (3) ease of making uncontested bilateral adaptation, and (4) reliance on monitoring and related administrative controls. Incentive intensity and adaptability are both valued performance features—where (within limits) greater incentive intensity elicits greater and more sustained effort and superior adaptability results in quicker restorations to positions on the shifting contract curve. By contrast, court ordering and administration refer to (interfirm and intrafirm) enforcement and control techniques.

Comparing markets and hierarchies in these respects, and using + and 0 to denote much and nil of each attribute, the vector that describes markets is (+, +, 0, 0) while hierarchies display an attribute reversal (0, 0, +, +). Accordingly, markets are well suited to govern transactions for which high-powered incentives are especially important, whereas a sacrifice of incentive intensity in favor of better adaptability is what firm governance entails.

Since incentive intensity is a valued performance attribute, markets will be the favored form of organization *if* bilateral adaptability is relatively unimportant. As a condition of bilateral dependency builds up, however, forms of organization that are better able to effect uncontested adaptability have more to recommend them—incentive disabilities notwithstanding. Transaction cost economics maintains that the condition of bilateral dependency varies systematically with (indeed, is defined by) the condition of asset specificity.

Using k to index asset specificity and letting $M(k)$ and $H(k)$ be market governance costs and hierarchical governance costs, respectively, the basic trade-off turns on the following two inequalities: $M(0) < H(0)$ and $M' > H'$. $M(0) < H(0)$ implies that hierarchical governance incurs added operating and bureaucratic costs compared with market governance. This reflects the aforementioned incentive disabilities of internal organization. $M' > H'$ is explained by the differential ease of effecting adaptations as the condition of asset specificity builds up. Figure 8.2 displays the relations.

Letting $\hat{k}$ be the value of k for which $M(k) = H(k)$, the predicted uses of markets and hierarchies are as follows: classical markets will be favored for those transactions for which $k << \hat{k}$; unified ownership and administration will be favored for those transactions for which $k >> \hat{k}$; and transactions for which k is in the neighborhood of $\hat{k}$ will be organized both ways, there being little governance cost difference between markets and hierarchies in this region.

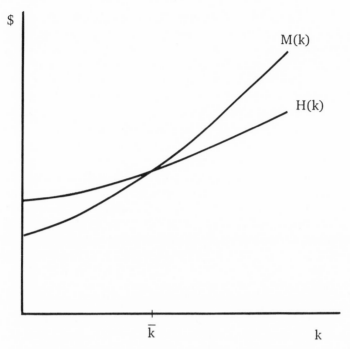

Figure 8.2 Governance costs: markets and hierarchies

Also, whereas the preceding discussion runs entirely in terms of inter-mediate product markets—the concern being whether the firm should pro-duce to its own requirements or procure the good or service in question from the market—it is noteworthy that the same generic trade-off charac-terizes "rules" governance versus "discretion" more generally. In the con-text of an employment relation, for example, piece rate employment with limited guarantees is the marketlike mode, whereas time rates supported by internal governance is the more hierarchical. The high-powered incen-tives of piece rates, according to this formulation, are more appropriate if the labor skills in question are easily redeployable (migrant farm labor being an example). Time rates with collective organization to serve as sup-porting governance become the superior mode as human asset specificity (nonredeployability) builds up. Debt and equity can be interpreted simi-larly, where debt is the more rules governed of the two and equity the more administrative form. Debt, according to this formulation, is the fi-nancial instrument/governance structure to use to finance redeployable as-sets (general-purpose buildings; assets on wheels), whereas equity is re-served for nonredeployable investments.

Significant interim accomplishments notwithstanding, all would agree that the "science of organization" to which Barnard referred fifty years ago has not been realized. The past ten and fifteen years have nonetheless witnessed a combined law, economics, and organizations assault on the issues—the effect of which has been to push the incipient science of organization across a threshold from which there is no returning. Economics and organization theory form the axis off of which this new work operates—to which contract law provides added support.

Although much of what is in progress differs from Barnard in many ways, Barnard's imprint throughout these fifty years remains highly visible. Plainly, this was a man with great knowledge and a deep understanding of organization.

The incipient new science of organization is not a separate discipline. As indicated, it works off of and integrates the underlying disciplines of law, economics, and organization. Note, moreover, that I refer to his new science not as the "science of administration," which is the organization theory way of describing things, but as the "science of organization." The latter subsumes the former as a special case.

The aspect of the new science of organization with which I have been especially concerned (in this chapter and elsewhere) is that of transaction cost economics. This approach is distinguished by the fact that it examines economic organization in a way that is simultaneously microanalytic, comparative institutional, and economizing in its orientation. The first of these has long been resisted by economics,[27] the last by organization theory.[28] I argue that the two go together and that the prospects for a science of organization are improved as a consequence.

NOTES

1. References to Barnard with page numbers only are to his 1938 book, *The Functions of the Executive.*
2. Even those who take vigorous exception with Barnard conceded his vast influence (Perrow 1986). Not only did Barnard's work influence the human relations approaches to organization, but the work of two giants in the study of organization—Philip Selznick's institutionalist views and Herbert Simon's theory of decision making—drew inspiration from Barnard. For a discussion, see W. Richard Scott (1987, pp. 61–68).
3. The New Institutional Economics distinction between institutional environment (political, social, and legal round rules) and institutional arrangements (governance) is pertinent in this connection (Davis & North 1971, pp. 6–7). The incipient science of organization encompasses both but puts principal emphasis on governance structures (which mainly implicates economics and organization) rather than on the institutional environment (where the law is more salient).
4. Barnard observed that while social scientists had studied "mores, folkways, political structures, institutions, attitudes, motives, propensities, [and] instincts . . . *in extenso,*" there was a general failure among social scientists "to sense the processes of coordination and decision that underlie a large part at least

of the phenomena they described. More important, there was lacking much recognition of formal organization as the most important characteristic of social life, and as being the principal structural aspect of society itself" (p. ix).

5. Even this might be questioned. Authoritarian states, such as Nazi Germany, and other controlled societies, such as prisons, are never totally controlled from the top in the manner that is often ascribed to them.

6. Mark Granovetter observes that Barnard originally described the zone as one of "indifference" and that Simon had substituted the term "acceptance" without explanation (1985, p. 495, *n* 5). Granovetter objects to this substitution because it undercuts "Barnard's emphasis on the problematic nature of obedience" (1985, p. 495, *n* 5). The reason for the substitution is this: several degrees of indifference are included within the zone of acceptance. Usually, only a very small subset of orders place an individual at the margin of indifference between staying and leaving.

One of Simon's main purposes was to develop a more scientific vocabulary for describing organizations (1957a, p. xlv). The substitution of acceptance for indifference in the context of the employment relation accomplishes that purpose.

7. Compared with the study of the employment relation, which implicates complicated emotive and dignitarian features, decisions to make or buy an intermediate good or service are much more instrumental.

I once attended a conference several years ago at which the participants were advised that the analysis of work organization should be informed by "unabashed rooting for the workers." Those are understandable sentiments. But it is not obvious that better analysis is promoted in this way.

8. Indeed, there is a long literature. For a summary and discussion, see Williamson (1985a, chap. 6).

9. Theories of comprehensive contracting, with and without private information, concentrate all of the contracting action on the ex-ante incentive alignment.

10. Recall that Arrow ascribed the differential success of the New Institutional Economics to its nanoeconomic orientation (1987, p. 734).

11. The quote is from Peguy (source unknown).

12. Note, however, that whereas the crucial feature for Simon is uncertainty, I focus mainly on the condition of asset specificity.

13. The argument is elaborated in Williamson (1985a, pp. 64–67).

14. Interestingly, the organization theory literature deals expressly, albeit in a somewhat different way, with both asset specificity and uncertainty. Cyert and March contend that the main way of dealing with uncertainty is by avoidance. One way of doing this is by focusing on the short run: rather than plan for an uncertain future, managers use short-run reactions to deal with current disturbances. It may also, however, be possible to mitigate uncertainty "by arranging a negotiated environment: [managers] impose plans, standard operating procedures, industry tradition, and uncertainty-absorbing contracts" (Cyert & March 1963, p. 119).

Mitigating uncertainty, especially "behavioral uncertainty," by supplanting interfirm by intrafirm organization is emphasized by transaction cost economics (Williamson 1985a; Helfat & Teece, 1987). The use of "excuse doctrine" in contract law also serves to limit uncertainty (Williamson 1985a). More generally, the comparative efficacy of alternative forms of organization for dealing with uncertainty through adaptive, sequential decision making is a recurrent concern in the transaction cost economics literature (Williamson, 19775, 1985a; Wiggins 1989). The degree to which transaction specific assets are implicated has an important bearing on such comparative assessments.

15. The following remarks of Simon are pertinent (1957b, p. 199): "Organization theory is centrally concerned with identifying and studying those limits to the achievement of goals that are, in fact, limits on the flexibility and adaptability of the goal-striving individuals and groups of individuals themselves. . . . The fact that these limits . . . are largely determined by social and even organizational forces creates problems of theory construction of great subtlety." Although the goal-striving "limits" to which Simon refers are not specifically identified, I submit that the absence of opportunism greatly relieves goal-striving strains.

16. See especially the papers by Joskow (1985, 1987, 1988) and references therein.

17. Much of this is summarized in Williamson (1985a, Chapter 5).

18. See the chapter in this volume by Terry Moe. See also Douglass North and Barry Weingast (1988) and Weingast and Marshall (1988).

19. See Erin Anderson and David Schmittlein (1984) and George John and Burton Weitz (1988).

20. See Teece (1986) and Jan Heide and George John (1988).

21. See Mark Granovetter (1985) and Oliver Williamson (1988b).

22. On this, see Robert Keohane (1988) and Beth and Robert Yarborough (1987).

23. See Williamson (1988b), Michael Gerlach (1987), and Eric Berglof (1989).

24. On the latter, see Thomas Jorde and David Teece (1988).

25. See Williamson (1985a, Chapter 13) and Joskow and Schmalensee (1983).

26. Parts of this subsection are taken from Williamson (1985a, pp. 32–35).

27. Compared with earlier economic approaches to the study of economic organization, transaction cost economics (1) is more microanalytic, (2) is more self-conscious about its behavioral assumptions, (3) introduces and develops the economic importance of asset specificity, (4) relies more on comparative institutional analysis, (5) regards the business firm as a governance structure, (6) places greater weight on the ex-post institutions of contract, with special emphasis on private ordering (compared with court ordering), (7) works out of a combined law, economics, and organization perspective, and (8) asserts that economizing on transaction costs is the main case.

28. Compared with a standard organization theory set-up, transaction cost economics (1) eschews satisficing in favor of economizing; (2) works out of a systems framework, whereupon myopia and/or posterior rationality are eschewed in favor of "incomplete contracting in its entirety"; (3) regards the transaction as the basic unit of analysis, the dimensionalization of which is thereafter pertinent; (4) repeatedly appeals to the hypothesis that transactions will be aligned with governance structures in a discriminating (mainly, transaction cost economizing) way; (5) regards opportunism as a behavioral assumption of coequal importance with bounded rationality; (6) maintains that any issue that can be posed directly or indirectly as a contracting issue can be examined to advantage in transaction cost economizing terms; and (7) examines the process ramifications of alternative modes of contracting in microanalytic detail.

REFERENCES

Anderson, Erin, and David Schmittlein. 1984. Integration of the sales force: An empirical examination. *The Rand Journal of Economics* 15:385–95.

Arrow, Kenneth. 1974. *The Limits of Organization*. New York: W. W. Norton.

Arrow, Kenneth. 1987. Reflections on the essays. In *Arrow and the Foundations of the Theory of Economic Policy*, ed. George Feiwel, pp. 727–34. New York: NYU Press.

Ashby, W. Ross. 1960. *Design for a Brain*. New York: John Wiley & Sons.

Aumann, Robert. 1985. What is game theory trying to accomplish? In *Frontiers of Economics*, pp. 28–78. ed. Kenneth Arrow and Seppo Hankapohja. Oxford: Basil Blackwell.

Barnard, Chester. 1938. *The Functions of the Executive.* (fifteenth printing, 1962). Cambridge: Harvard University Press.

Barney, Jay, and William Ouchi. 1986. *Organizational Economics*. San Francisco: Jossey-Bass.

Berglof, Eric. 1989. *Capital Structure as a Mechanism of Control*. In *The Firm as a Nexus of Treaties*, ed. Masahiko Aoki, Bo Gustafsson, and Oliver Williamson. London: Sage. chapter 11.

Coase, Ronald. 1952. The nature of the firm. *Economica N.S.* 4 (1937):386–405; reprinted in G. J. Stigler and K. E. Boulding, eds., *Readings in Price Theory*. Homewood, Ill.: Richard D. Irwin.

Coase, Ronald. 1978. Economics and contiguous disciplines. *Journal of Legal Studies* 7:201–11.

Commons, John. 1925. Law and economics. *Yale Law Journal* 34:371–82.

Commons, John. 1934. *Institutional Economics*. Madison: University of Wisconsin Press.

Cyert, Richard, and James March. 1963. *A Behavioral Theory of the Firm*. Englewood Cliffs, N.J.: Prentice-Hall.

Davis, Lance, and Douglass North. 1971. *Institutional Change and American Economic Growth*. Cambridge: Cambridge University Press.

Demsetz, Harold. 1968. Why regulate utilities? *Journal of Law and Economics* 11:55–66.

Ehrlich, Eugen. 1936. *Fundamental Principles of the Sociology of Law*. Cambridge, Mass.: Harvard University Press.

Emerson, Richard. 1962. Power-dependence relations. *American Sociological Review* 27:31–40.

Fama, Eugene. 1980. Agency problems and the theory of the firm. *Journal of Political Economy* 88:288–307.

Galanter, Marc. 1981. Justice in many rooms: Courts, private ordering, and indigenous law. *Journal of Legal Pluralism* 19:1–47.

Gauss, Christian. 1952. Introduction to Machiavelli (1952), pp. 7–32. (Niccolo Machiavelli, *The Prince*. New York: New American Library.)

Gerlach, Michael. 1987. Business alliances and the strategy of the Japanese firm." *California Management Review* 30 (Fall): 126–42.

Gould, Stephen Jay. 1987. *An Urchin in the Storm*. New York: W. W. Norton.

Granovetter, Mark. 1985. Economic action and social structure: the problem of embeddedness. *American Journal of Sociology* 91:481–501.

Grossman, Sanford, and Oliver Hart. 1986. The costs and benefits of ownership:

a theory of vertical and lateral integration. *Journal of Political Economy* 94:691–719.

Hart, H. L. A. 1961. *The Concept of Law.* Oxford: Oxford University Press.

Hayek, Friedrich. 1945. The use of knowledge in society. *American Economic Review* 35:519–30.

Hayek, Friedrich. 1955. *The Counterrevolution of Science.* New York: The Free Press.

Hayek, Friedrich. 1967. *Studies in Philosophy, Politics, and Economics.* London: Routledge & Kegan Paul.

Heide, Jan, and George John. 1988. The role of dependence balancing in safeguarding transaction-specific assets in conventional channels. *Journal of Marketing* 52:20–35.

Helfat, Constance, and David Teece. 1987. Vertical integration and risk reduction. *Journal of Law, Economics, and Organization* 3:47–68.

Jensen, Michael. 1983. Organization theory and methodology. *Accounting Review* 50:319–39.

John, George, and Barton Weitz. 1988. Forward integration into distribution. *Journal of Law, Economics, and Organization* 4:337–56.

Jorde, Thomas, and David Teece. 1988. Innovation, cooperation, and antitrust. Unpublished manuscript, University of California, Berkeley.

Joskow, Paul. 1985. Vertical integration and long-term contracts. *Journal of Law, Economics, and Organization* 1:33–80.

Joskow, Paul. 1987. Contract duration and relationship-specific investments. *American Economic Review* 77:168–85.

Joskow, Paul. 1988. Asset specificity and the structure of vertical relationships: empirical evidence. *Journal of Law, Economics and Organization* 4:95–118.

Joskow, Paul, and Richard Schmalensee. 1983. *Markets for Power.* Cambridge, Mass.: MIT Press.

Keohane, Robert. 1984. *After Hegemony: Cooperation and Discord in the World Political Economy.* Princeton, N.J.: Princeton University Press.

Knight, Frank. 1941. Anthropology and economics. *Journal of Political Economy* 49:247–68.

Kreps, David. 1984. Corporate culture. Unpublished manuscript.

Kreps, David, and Michael Spence. 1985. Modelling the role of history in industrial organization and competition. In *Issues in Contemporary Microeconomics and Welfare,* ed. George Feiwel, pp. 340–79. London: Macmillan.

Llewellyn, Karl. 1931. What price contract? An essay in perspective. *Yale Law Journal* 40:704–51.

Macneil, Ian R. 1974. The many futures of contracts. *Southern California Law Review* 47:691–816.

March, James. 1966. The power of power. In *Varieties of Political Theory,* ed. David Easton, pp. 39–70. Englewood Cliffs, N.J.: Prentice-Hall.

March, James. 1973. Model bias in social action. *Review of Educational Research* 42:413–39.

March, James. 1988. *Decisions and Organizations.* Oxford: Basil Blackwell.

March, James, and Herbert A. Simon. 1958. *Organizations.* New York: John Wiley & Sons.

Marglin, Stephen A. 1974. What do bosses do? The origins and functions of hierarchy in capitalist production. *Review of Radical Political Economic* 6:33–60.

Mathews, R. C. O. 1986. The economics of institutions and the sources of economic growth. *Economic Journal* 96:903–18.

Menger, Karl. 1963. *Problems in Economics and Sociology* (Francis J. Nock, translator). Urbana: University of Illinois Press.

North, Douglass, and Barry Weingast. Constitutions and commitment: the evolution of institutions governing public choice in 17th century England. *Journal of Economic History* (forthcoming).

Perrow, Charles. 1986. *Complex Organizations*, 3d ed. New York: Random House.

Posner, R. A. 1972. The appropriate scope of regulation in the cable television industry. *The Bell Journal of Economics and Management Science* 5:335–58.

Schotter, Andrew. 1981. *The Economic Theory of Social Institutions*. New York: Cambridge University Press.

Scott, W. Richard. 1987. *Organizations*, 2d ed. Englewood Cliffs, N.J.: Prentice-Hall.

Simon, Herbert. 1951. A formal theory of the employment relation. *Econometrica* 19:293–305.

Simon, Herbert. 1955. A behavioral model of rational choice. *Quarterly Journal of Economics* 69:99–118.

Simon, Herbert. 1957a. *Administrative Behavior,* 2d ed. New York: Macmillan.

Simon, Herbert. 1957b. *Models of Man.* New York: John Wiley & Sons.

Simon, Herbert. 1962a. The architecture of complexity. *Proceedings of the American Philosophical Society* 106:467–82.

Simon, Herbert. 1962b. New developments in the theory of the firm. *American Economic Review* 52:1–15.

Simon, Herbert. 1972. Theories of bounded rationality. In *Decision and Organization,* ed. C. B. McGuire and R. Radner, pp. 161–76. Amsterdam: North Holland.

Simon, Herbert. 1978. Rationality as process and as product of thought. *American Economic Review* 68:1–16.

Simon, Herbert. 1984. On the behavioral and rational foundations of economic dynamics. *Journal of Economic Behavior and Organization* 5:35–56.

Stigler, George. 1961. The economics of information. *Journal of Political Economy* 69:213–25.

Stigler, George. 1968. *The Organization of Industry.* Homewood, Ill.: Richard D. Irwin.

Teece, David. 1986. Profiting from technological innovation. *Research Policy* 15:285–305.

Weick, Karl. 1969. *The Social Psychology of Organizing.* Reading, Mass.: Addison-Wesley.

Weingast, Barry, and William Marshall. 1988. The industrial organization of Congress; or, why legislatures, like firms, are not organized as markets. *Journal of Political Economy* 96:132–63.

Weizsacker, C. C. von. 1984. The costs of substitution. *Econometrica* 52:1085–116.

Wiggins, Steven. 1988. The comparative advantage of long-term contracts. Unpublished manuscript, Texas A & M University.

Williamson, Oliver E. 1975. *Markets and Hierarchies: Analysis and Antitrust Implications.* New York: The Free Press.

Williamson, Oliver E. 1985a. *The Economic Institutions of Capitalism.* New York: The Free Press.

Williamson, Oliver E. 1985b. Assessing contract. *Journal of Law, Economics, and Organization* 1:177–208.

Williamson, Oliver E. 1988a. The logic of economic organization. 4:65–93.

Williamson, Oliver E. 1988b. The economics of sociology of organization: promoting a dialogue. In *Industries, Firms, and Jobs,* eds. George Farkas and Paula England, pp. 159–85. New York: Plenum.

Yarborough, Beth, and Robert Yarborough. 1987. Institutions for the governance of opportunism in international trade. *Journal of Law, Economics, and Organization* 3:129–39.

9

Transaction Cost Economics and Organization Theory

OLIVER E. WILLIAMSON

Economic and sociological approaches to economic organization have reached a state of healthy tension. That is to be contrasted with an earlier state of affairs in which the two approaches were largely disjunct, hence ignored one another, or described each other's research agendas and research accomplishments with disdain (Swedberg, 1990, p. 4). Healthy tension involves genuine give-and-take. Neither the obsolescence of organization theory, to which Charles Perrow has recently alluded (1992, p. 162), nor the capitulation of economics, to which James March (tongue-in-cheek) remarks,[1] is implied.

A more respectful relation, perhaps even a sense that economics and organization are engaged in a joint venture, is evident in W. Richard Scott's remark that "while important areas of disagreement remain, more consensus exists than is at first apparent" (1992, p. 3), in game theorist David Kreps's contention that "almost any theory of organization which is addressed by game theory will do more for game theory than game theory will do for it" (1992, p. 1), and in my argument that a science of organization is in progress in which law, economics, and organization are joined.[2]

Joint ventures sometimes evolve into mergers and sometimes unravel. I do not expect that either will happen here. That merger is not in prospect is because economics, organization theory, and law have separate as well as combined agendas. A full-blown merger, moreover, would impoverish the evolving science of organization—which has benefitted from the variety of insights that are revealed by the use of different lenses. I expect that the joint venture will hold until one of the parties has learned enough from the others to go it alone. Progress attended by controversy is what I project for the remainder of the decade.

This paper focuses on connections between transaction cost economics and organization theory and argues that a three-part relation is taking shape. The first and most important of these is that transaction cost economics has been (and will continue to be) massively influenced by concepts and empirical regularities that have their origins in organization theory. Secondly, I sketch the key concepts out of which transaction cost economics works to which organization theorists can (and many do) productively relate. But thirdly, healthy tension survives—as revealed by an examination of phenomena for which rival interpretations have been advanced, remain unsolved, and provoke controversy.

I began this paper with some background on institutional economics, both old and new. A three-level schema for studying economic organization is proposed in the second section. Some of the more important ways in which transaction cost economics has benefited from organization theory are examined in the third section. The key concepts in transaction cost economics are sketched in the fourth section. Empirical regularities, as discerned through the lens of transaction cost economics, that are pertinent to organization theory are discussed in the fifth section. Contested terrain is surveyed in the sixth section. Concluding remarks follow.

INSTITUTIONAL ECONOMICS

Older Traditions

Leading figures in the older institutional economics movement in the United States were Wesley Mitchell, Thorstein Veblen, and John R. Commons. Although many sociologists appear to be sympathetic with the older tradition, there is growing agreement that the approach was "largely descriptive and historically specific" (DiMaggio and Powell, 1991, p. 2) and was not cumulative (Granovetter, 1988, p. 8).

Criticisms of the old institutional economics by economists have been scathing. Thus George Stigler remarks that "the school failed in America for a very simple reason. It had nothing in it except a stance of hostility to the standard theoretical tradition. There was no positive agenda of research" (Stigler, 1983, p. 170). Similar views are expressed by R. C. O. Matthews (1986, p. 903). Ronald Coase concurs: the work of American institutionalists "led to nothing. . . . Without a theory, they had nothing to pass on except a mass of descriptive material waiting for a theory or a fire. So if modern institutionalists have antecedents, it is not what went immediately before" (Coase, 1984, p. 230).

My general agreement with these assessments notwithstanding, I would make an exception for John R. Commons. Not only is the institutional economics tradition at Wisconsin still very much alive (Bromley, 1989), but also the enormous public policy influence of Commons and his students and colleagues deserves to be credited. Andrew Van de Ven's summary of Commons's intellectual contributions is pertinent to the first of these (1993, p. 148):

> Especially worthy of emphasis [about Commons] are his (a) dynamic views of institutions as a response to scarcity and conflicts of interest, (b) original formulation of the transaction as the basic unit of analysis, (c) part-whole analysis of how collective action constrains, liberates, and expands individual action in countless numbers of routine and complementary transactions on the one hand, and how individual wills and power to gain control over limiting or contested factors provide the generative mechanisms for institutional change on the other, and (d) historical appreciation of how customs, legal precedents, and laws of a society evolve to construct a collective standard of prudent reasonable behavior for resolving disputes between conflicting parties in pragmatic and ethical ways.

Albeit in varying degree, transaction cost economics is responsive to Commons in *all four of these respects.*[3]

Commons and his colleagues and students were very influential in politics during and after the Great Depression—in shaping social security, labor legislation, public utility regulation, and, more generally, public policy toward business. Possibly because of its public policy successes, the Wisconsin School was remiss in developing its intellectual foundations. The successive operationalization—from informal into preformal, semiformal, and fully formal modes of analysis—that I associate with transaction cost economics (Williamson, 1993a) never materialized. Instead, the institutional economics of Commons progressed very little beyond the informal stage.

There is also an older institutional economics tradition in Europe. Of special importance was the German Historical School. [Interested readers are advised to consult Terrence Hutchison (1984) and Richard Swedberg (1991) for assessments.] And, of course, there were the great works of Karl Marx.

A later German School, the Ordoliberal or Freiburg School, also warrants remark. As discussed by Heinz Grossekettler (1989), this School was inspired by the work of Walter Eucken, whose student Ludwig Erhard was the German Minister of Economics from 1949 to 1963, Chancellor from 1963 to 1966, and is widely credited with being the political father of the "economic miracle" in West Germany. Grossekettler describes numerous parallels between the Ordoliberal program and those of Property Rights Theory, Transaction Cost Economics, and especially Constitutional Economics (1989, pp. 39, 64–67).

The Ordoliberal program proceeded at a very high level of generality (Grossekettler, 1989, p. 47) and featured the application of lawful principles to the entire economy (Grossekettler, 1989, pp. 46–57). Its great impact on postwar German economic policy notwithstanding, the influence of the School declined after the mid-1960s. Although Grossekettler attributes the decline to the "wide scale of acceptance of the Keynesian theory

. . . [among] young German intellectuals" (1989, pp. 69–70), an additional problem is that the principles of Ordoliberal economics were never given operational content. Specific models were never developed; key trade-offs were never identified; the mechanisms remained very abstract. The parallels with the Wisconsin School—great public policy impact, underdeveloped conceptual framework, loss of intellectual influence—are striking.

The New Institutional Economics

The new institutional economics comes in a variety of flavors and has been variously defined. The economics of property rights—as developed especially by Coase (1959, 1960), Armen Alchian (1961), and Harold Demsetz (1967)—was an early and influential dissent from orthodoxy. An evolutionary as opposed to a technological approach to economic organization was advanced, according to which new property rights were created and enforced as the economic needs arose, if and as these were cost effective.

The definition of ownership rights advanced by Eirik Furubotn and Svetozar Pejovich is broadly pertinent: "By general agreement, the right of ownership of an asset consists of three elements: (a) the right to use the asset . . . , (b) the right to appropriate the returns from the asset . . . , and (c) the right to change the asset's form and/or substance" (174, p. 4). Strong claims on behalf of the property rights approach to economic organization were set out by Coase as follows (1959, p. 14):

> A private enterprise system cannot function unless property rights are created in resources, and when this is done, someone wishing to use a resource has to pay the owner to obtain it. Chaos disappears; and so does the government except that a legal system to define property rights and to arbitrate disputes is, of course, necessary.

As it turns out, these claims overstate the case for the property rights approach. Not only is the definition of property rights sometimes costly—consider the difficult problems of defining intellectual property rights—but also court ordering can be a costly way to proceed. A comparative contractual approach—according to which court ordering is often (but selectively) supplanted by private ordering for purposes of governing contractual relations (Macneil, 1974, 1978; Williamson, 1979, 1991a)—rather than a pure property rights approach, therefore has a great deal to recommend it.

Although the earlier property rights approach and the more recent comparative contractual approach appear to be rival theories of organization, much of that tension is relieved by recognizing that the new institutional economics has actually developed in two complementary parts. One of these parts deals predominantly with background conditions (expanded beyond property rights to include contract laws, norms, customs, conventions, and the like) while the second branch deals with the mechanisms of governance. The two-part definition proposed by Lance Davis and Douglass North (1971, pp. 5–6; emphasis added) is pertinent:

> The *institutional environment* is the set of fundamental political, social and legal ground rules that establishes the basis for production, exchange and distribution. Rules governing elections, property rights, and the right of contract are examples. . . .
>
> An *institutional arrangement* is an arrangement between economic units that governs the ways in which these units can cooperate and/or compete. It . . . [can] provide a structure within which its members can cooperate . . . or [it can] provide a mechanism that can effect a change in laws or property rights.

Interestingly, these two parts correspond very closely with the much earlier division of effort between "economic sociology" and "economic theory" described by Joseph Schumpeter—where economic sociology was expected to study the institutional environment and economic theory was concerned principally with the mechanisms of governance (1989, p. 293). As it turns out, a large number of economists have productively worked on issues relating to the institutional environment. These include a prodigious amount of research by North, who defines institutions as "the humanly devised constraints that structure political, economic, and social interactions. They consist of both informal constraints (sanctions, taboos, customs, traditions, and codes of conduct), and formal rules (constitutions, laws, property rights)" (1991, p. 97). Elsewhere he argues that "institutions consist of a set of constraints on behavior in the form of rules and regulations; a set of procedures to detect deviations from the rules and regulations; and, finally, a set of moral, ethical behavioral norms which define the contours and that constrain the way in which the rules and regulations are specified and enforcement is carried out" (1984, p. 8). Relatedly, Allan Schmid defines institutions as "sets of ordered relationships among people which define their rights, exposures to the rights of others, privileges, and responsibilities" (1972, p. 893); Daniel Bromley contends that institutions fall into two classes: conventions, and rules or entitlements (1989, p. 41); and Andrew Schotter defines institutions as "regularities in behavior which are agreed to by all members of a society and which specify behavior in specific recurrent situations" (1981, p. 9). According to Eirik Furubotn and Rudolf Richter, "Modern institutional economics focuses on the institution of property, and on the system of norms governing the acquisition or transfer of property rights" (1991, p. 3), although they subsequently make significant provision for governance.

This emphasis on property rights, customs, norms, conventions and the like is especially pertinent for purposes of doing intertemporal, international, or cross-cultural comparisons. What the economics of organization is predominantly concerned with, however, is this: holding these background conditions constant, why organize economic activity one way (e.g.

procure from the market) rather than another (e.g. produce to your own needs: hierarchy)? That is the Coasian question (Coase, 1937), is the focus of transaction cost economics, and explains much of the interest of organization theorists and the sociology of organization with the New Institutional Economics. Not only does the study of governance raise different issues, but also much of the predictive content and most of the empirical research in institutional economics has been at the governance level (Matthews, 1986, p. 907).

A THREE-LEVEL SCHEMA

Transaction cost economics is mainly concerned with the governance of contractual relations. Governance does not, however, operate in isolation. The comparative efficacy of alternative modes of governance varies with the institutional environment on the one hand and the attributes of economic actors on the other. A three-level schema is therefore proposed, according to which the object of analysis, governance, is bracketed by more macro features (the institutional environment) and more micro features (the individual). Feedbacks aside (which are underdeveloped in the transaction cost economics set-up), the institutional environment is treated as the locus of shift parameters, changes in which shift the comparative costs of governance, and the individual is where the behavioral assumptions originate.

Roger Friedland and Robert Alford also propose a three-level schema in which environment, governance, and individual are distinguished, but their emphasis is very different. They focus on the individual and argue that the three levels of analysis are "nested, where organization and institution specify progressively higher levels of constraint and opportunity for individual action" (1991, p. 242).

The causal model proposed here is akin to and was suggested by, but is different from, the causal model recently proposed by W. Richard Scott (1992, p. 45), who is also predominantly concerned with governance. There are three main effects in my schema (see Figure 9.1). These are shown by the solid arrows. Secondary effects are drawn as dashed arrows. As indicated, the institutional environment defines the rules of the game. If changes in property rights, contract laws, norms, customs, and the like induce changes in the comparative costs of governance, then a reconfiguration of economic organization is usually implied.

The solid arrow from the individual to governance carries the behavioral assumptions within which transaction cost economics operates, and the circular arrow within the governance sector reflects the proposition that organization, like the law, has a life of its own. The latter is the subject of this section.

Although behavioral assumptions are frequently scanted in economics,

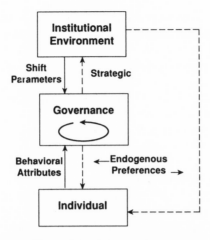

Figure 9.1   A layer schema.

transaction cost economics subscribes to the proposition that economic actors should be described in workably realistic terms (Simon, 1978; Coase, 1984). Interestingly, "outsiders," especially physicists, have long been insistent that a better understanding of the actions of human agents requires more self-conscious attention to the study of how men's minds work (Bridgeman, 1955, p. 450; Waldrop, 1992, p. 142). Herbert Simon concurs (1985, p. 303):

> Nothing is more fundamental in setting out research agenda and informing our research methods than our view of the nature of the human beings whose behavior we are studying. It makes a difference, a very large difference, to our research strategy whether we are studying the nearly omniscient *Homo economicus* of rational choice theory or the boundedly rational *Homo psychologicus* of cognitive psychology. It makes a difference to research, but it also makes a difference for the proper design of political institutions. James Madison was well aware of that, and in the pages of the *Federalist Papers* he opted for this view of the human condition (*Federalist*, No. 55):
>> As there is a degree of depravity in mankind which requires a certain degree of circumspection and distrust, so there are other qualities in human nature which justify a certain portion of esteem and confidence.
> —a balanced and realistic view, we may concede, of bounded human rationality and its accompanying frailties of motive and reason.

Transaction cost economics expressly adopts the proposition that human cognition is subject to bounded rationality—where this is defined as behavior that is "intendedly rational, but only limitedly so" (Simon, 1957a, p. xxiv)—but differs from Simon in its interpretation of the "degree of depravity" to which Madison refers.

Whereas Simon regards the depravity in question as "frailties of motive and reason," transaction cost economics describes it instead as opportunism—to include self-interest seeking with guile. The former is a much more benign interpretation, and many social scientists understandably prefer it. Consider, however, Robert Michels's concluding remarks about oligarchy: "nothing but a serene and frank examination of the oligarchical dangers of democracy will enable us to minimize these dangers" (1962, p. 370). If a serene and frank reference to opportunism alerts us to avoidable dangers which the more benign reference to facilities of motive and reason would not, then there are real hazards in adopting the more benevolent construction. As discussed below, the mitigation of opportunism plays a central role in transaction cost economics.

Opportunism can take blatant, subtle, and natural forms. The blatant form is associated with Niccolò Machiavelli. Because he perceived that the economic agents with whom the Prince was dealing were opportunistic, the Prince was advised to engage in reciprocal and even pre-emptive opportunism—to breach contracts with impugnity whenever "the reasons which made him bind himself no longer exist" (1952, p. 92). The subtle form is strategic and has been described elsewhere as "self-interest seeking with guile" (Williamson, 1975, pp. 26–37; 1985, pp. 46–52, 64–67). The natural form involves tilting the system at the margin. The so-called "dollar-a-year" men in the Office of Production Management, of which there were 250 at the beginning of World War II, were of concern to the Senate Special Committee to Investigate the National Defense Program because (McCullough, 1992, p. 265):

> Such corporate executives in high official roles were too inclined to make decisions for the benefit of their corporations. "They have their own business at heart," [Senator] Truman remarked. The report called them lobbyists "in a very real sense," because their presence inevitably meant favoritism, "human nature being what it is."

Michel Crozier's treatment of bureaucracy makes prominent provision for all forms of opportunism, which he describes as "the active tendency of the human agent to take advantage, in any circumstances, of all available means to further his own privileges" (1964, p. 194).

Feedback effects from governance to the institutional environment can be either instrumental or strategic. An example of the former would be an improvement in contract law, brought about at the request of parties who find that extant law is poorly suited to support the integrity of contract. Strategic changes could take the form of protectionist trade barriers against domestic and/or foreign competition. Feedback from governance to the level of the individual can be interpreted as "endogenous preference" formation (Bowles and Gintis, 1993), due to advertising or other forms of "education." The individual is also influenced by the environment, in that endogenous preferences are the product of social conditioning. Although transaction cost economics can often relate to these secondary effects, other modes of analysis are often more pertinent.

More generally, the Friedland and Alford scheme, the Scott scheme, and the variant that I offer are not mutually exclusive. Which to use when depends on the questions being asked. To repeat, the main case approach to economic organization that I have proposed works out of the heavy line causal relations shown in Figure 9.1, to which the dashed lines represent refinements.

THE VALUE ADDED OF ORGANIZATION THEORY

Richard Swedberg (1987, 1990), Robert Frank (1992), and others have described numerous respects in which economics has been influenced by sociology and organization theory. The value added to which I refer here deals only with those aspects where transaction cost economics has been a direct and significant beneficiary.

The behavioral assumptions to which I refer above—bounded rationality and opportunism—are perhaps the most obvious examples of how transaction cost economics has been shaped by organization theory. But the proposition that organization has a life of its own (the circular arrow in the governance box in Figure 9.1) is also important. And there are yet additional influences as well.

Intertemporal Process Transformations

Describing the firm as a production function invites an engineering approach to organization. The resulting "machine model" of organization emphasizes intended effects to the neglect of unintended effects (March and Simon, 1958, chapter 3). But if organizations have a life of their own, and if the usual economic approach is unable to relate to the intertemporal realities of organization, then—for some purposes at least—an extraeconomic approach may be needed.

Note that I do not propose that the economic approach be abandoned. Rather, the "usual" or orthodox economic approach gives way to an augmented or extended economic approach. That is very different from adopting an altogether different approach—as, for example, that of neural networks.

As it turns out, the economic approach is both very elastic and very powerful. Because it is elastic and because increasing numbers of economists have become persuaded of the need to deal with economic organization "as it is," warts and all, all significant regularities whatsoever—intended and unintended alike—come within the ambit. Because it is very powerful, economics brings added value. Specifically, the "farsighted propensity" or "rational spirit" that economics ascribes to economic actors permits the analysis of previously neglected regularities to be taken a step further. Once the unanticipated consequences are understood, those effects will thereafter be anticipated and the ramifications can be folded back into the organizational design. Unwanted costs will then be mitigated and unanticipated benefits will be enhanced. Better economic performance will ordinarily result.

Unintended effects are frequently delayed and are often subtle. Deep knowledge of the details and intertemporal process transformations that attend organization is therefore needed. Because organization theorists have wider and deeper knowledge of these conditions, economists have much to learn and ought to be deferential. Four specific illustrations are sketched here.

Demands for control   A natural response to perceived failures of performance is to introduce added controls. Such efforts can have both intended and unintended consequences (Merton, 1936; Gouldner, 1954).

One illustration is the employment relation, where an increased emphasis on the reliability of behavior gives rise to added rules (March and Simon, 1958, pp. 38–40). Rules, however, serve not merely as controls but also define minimally acceptable behavior (Cyert and March, 1963). Managers who apply rules to subordinates in a legalistic and mechanical way invite "working to rules," which frustrates effective performance. .

These unintended consequences are picked up by the wider peripheral vision of organization theorists. In the spirit of farsighted contracting, however, the argument can be taken yet a step further. Once apprised of the added consequences, the farsighted economist will make allowance for them by factoring these into the original organizational design. (Some organization theorists might respond that this last is fanciful and unrealistic. That can be decided by examining the data.)

Oligarchy   The Iron Law of Oligarchy holds that "It is organization which gives birth to the dominion of the elected over the electors, of the mandatories over the mandators, of the delegates over the delegators. Who says organization, says oligarchy" (Michels, 1962, p. 365). Accordingly, good intentions notwithstanding, the initial leadership (or its successors) will inevitably develop attachments for the office. Being strategically situated, the leadership will predictably entrench itself by controlling information, manipulating rewards and punishments, and mobilizing resources to defeat rivals. Even worse, the entrenched leadership will use the organization to promote its own agenda at the expense of the membership.

One response would be to eschew organization in favor of anarchy, but that is extreme. The better and deeper lesson is to take all predictable regularities into account at the outset, whereupon it may be possible to mitigate foreseeable oligarchical excesses at the initial design stage.[4]

Identity/capability The proposition that identity matters has been featured in transaction cost economics from the outset. As developed below, identity is usually explained by some form of "asset specificity." The "capabilities" view of the firm (Penrose, 1959; Selznick, 1975; Wernerfelt, 1984; Teece, Pisano, and Shven, 1992) raises related but additional issues.

One way to unpack the "capabilities" view of the firm is to ask what—in addition to an inventory of its physical assets, an accounting for its financial assets, and a census of its workforce—is needed to describe the capabilities of a firm. Features of organization that are arguably important include the following: (i) the communication codes that the firm has developed (Arrow, 1974); (ii) the routines that it employs (Cyert and March, 1963; Nelson and Winter, 1982); (iii) the corporate culture that has taken shape (Kreps, 1990). What do we make of these?

One response is to regard these as spontaneous features of economic organization. As interpreted by institutional theory in sociology, "organizational structures, procedures, and decisions are *largely ritualistic and symbolic,* especially so when it is difficult or impossible to assess the efficacy of organizational decisions on the basis of their tangible outcomes" (Baron and Hannan (1992), p. 57; emphasis added).

If, of course, efficiency consequences are impossible to ascertain, then intentionality has nothing to add. Increasingly, however, some of the subtle efficiency consequences of organization are coming to be better understood, whereupon they are (at least partly) subject to strategic determination. If the benefits of capabilities vary with the attributes of transactions, which arguably they do, then the cost effective thing to do is to *shape* culture, *develop* communication codes, and *manage* routines in a deliberative (transaction specific) way. Implementing the intentionality view will require that the microanalytic attributes that define culture, communication codes, and routines be uncovered, which is an ambitious exercise.

Bureaucratization As compared with the study of market failure, that study of bureaucratic failure is underdeveloped. It is elementary that a well-considered theory of organization will make provision for failures of all kinds.

Albeit underdeveloped, the bureaucratic failure literature is vast, partly because purported failures are described in absolute rather than comparative terms. Unless, however, a superior and feasible form of organization to which to assign a transaction (or related set of transactions) can be identified, the failure in question is effectively irremediable. One of the tasks of transaction cost economics is to assess purported bureaucratic failures in comparative institutional terms.

The basic argument is this: it is easy to show that a particular hierarchical structure is beset with costs, but that is neither here nor there if all feasible forms of organization are beset with the same or equivalent costs. Efforts to ascertain bureaucratic costs that survive comparative institutional scrutiny are reported elsewhere (Williamson, 1975, chapter 7; 1985, chapter 6), but these are very provisional and preliminary. Although intertemporal transformations and complexity are recurrent themes in the study of bureaucratic failure, much more concerted attention to these matters is needed.

Adaptation

The economist Friedrich Hayek maintained that the main problem of economic organization was that of adaptation and argued that this was realized spontaneously through the price system. Changes in the demand or supply of a commodity give rise to price changes, whereupon "*individual* participants . . . [are] able to take the right action" (1945, p. 527; emphasis added). Such price-induced adaptations by individual actors will be referred to as autonomous adaptations.

The organization theorist Chester Barnard also held that adaptation was the central problem of organization. But whereas Hayek emphasized autonomous adaptation of a spontaneous kind, Barnard was concerned with cooperative adaptation of an intentional kind. Formal organization, especially hierarchy, was the instrument through which the "conscious, deliberate, purposeful" cooperation to which Barnard called attention was accomplished (1938, p. 4). Barnard's insights, which have had a lasting effect on organization theory, should have a lasting effect on economics as well.

Transaction cost economics (i) concurs that adaptation is the central problem of economic organization; (ii) regards adaptations of both autonomous and cooperative kinds as important; (iii) maintains that whether adaptations to disturbances ought to be predominantly autonomous, cooperative, or a mixture thereof varies with the attributes of the transactions (especially on the degree to which the investments associated with successive stages of activity are bilaterally or multilaterally dependent); and (iv) argues that each generic from of governance—market, hybrid, and hierarchy—differs systematically in its capacity to adapt in autonomous and cooperative ways. A series of predicted (transaction cost economizing) alignments between transactions and governance structures thereby obtain (Williamson, 1991a), which predictions invite and have been subjected to empirical testing (Joskow, 1988; Shelanski, 1991; Masten, 1992).

Politics

Terry Moe (1990) makes a compelling case for the proposition that public bureaucracies are different. Partly that is because the transactions that are assigned to the public sector are different, but Moe argues additionally that public sector bureaucracies are shaped by politics. Democratic politics requires compromises that are different in kind from those posed in the private sector and poses novel expropriation hazards. Added "inefficiencies" arise in the design of public agencies on both accounts.

The inefficiencies that result from compromise are illustrated by the design of the Occupational Safety and Health Administration (OSHA) (Moe, 1990, p. 126):

> If business firms were allowed to help design OSHA, they would structure it in a way that it could not do its job. They would try to cripple it.
>
> This is not a hypothetical case. Interest groups representing business actually did participate in the design of OSHA, . . . [and] OSHA is an administrative nightmare, in large measure because some of its influential designers fully intended to endow it with structures that would not work.

To be sure, private sector organization is also the product of compromise. Egregious inefficiency in the private sector is checked, however, by competition in both product and capital markets. Note with reference to the latter that the voting rules in the private and public sectors are very different. The private rule is one share one vote, and shares may be concentrated through purchase. The public rule is one person one vote, and the "purchase" of votes is much more cumbersome. Because, moreover, the gains that result from improved efficiency accrue (in the first instance, at least) to private sector owners in proportion to their ownership, private incentives to concentrate ownership and remove inefficiency are greater.

Even setting voting considerations aside, however, there is another factor that induces politicians to design agencies inefficiently. Incumbent politicians who create and design bureaus are aware that the opposition can be expected to win a majority and take control in the future. Agencies will therefore be designed with reference to both immediate benefits (which favors responsive mechanisms) and possible future losses (which often favors crafting inertia into the system). A farsighted majority party will therefore design some degree of (apparent) inefficiency into the agency at the outset—the effect of which will be to frustrate the efforts of successor administrations to reshape the purposes served by an agency.[5]

Embeddedness and Networks

Gary Hamilton and Nicole Biggart take exception with the transaction cost economics interpretation of economic organization because it implicitly assumes that the institutional environment is everywhere the same; namely, that of Western democracies, and most especially that of the United States. They observe that large firms in East Asia differ from United States corporations in significant respects and explain that "organizational practices . . . are fashioned out of preexisting interactional patterns, which in many cases date to preindustrial times. Hence, industrial enterprise is a complex modern adaptation of pre-existing patterns of domination to economic situations in which profit, efficiency, and control usually form the very conditions of existence" (1988, p. S54).

The evidence that East Asian corporations differ is compelling. The argument, however, that transaction cost economics does not have application to East Asian economies goes too far.

The correct argument is that the institutional environment matters and that transaction cost economics, in its preoccupation with governance, has been neglectful of that. Treating the institutional environment as a set of shift parameters—changes in which induce shifts in the comparative costs of governance—is, to a first approximation at least, the obvious response (Williamson, 1991a). That is the interpretation advanced above and shown in Figure 9.1.

The objection could nevertheless be made that this is fine as far as it goes, but that comparative statics—which is a once-for-all exercise—does not go far enough. As Mark Granovetter observes, "More sophisticated . . . analyses of cultural influences . . . make it clear that culture is not a once-for-all influence but an *ongoing process,* continuously constructed and reconstructed during interaction. It not only shapes its members but is also shaped by them, in part for their own strategic reasons" (1985, p. 486).

I do not disagree, but I would observe that "more sophisticated analyses" must be judged by their value added. What are the deeper insights? What are the added implications? Are the effects in question really beyond the reach of economizing reasoning?

Consider, with reference to this last, the embeddedness argument that "concrete relations and structures" generate trust and discourage malfeasance of non-economic or extra-economic kinds (Granovetter, 1985, p. 490):

> Better than a statement that someone is known to be reliable is information from a trusted informant that he has dealt with that individual and found him so. Even better is information from one's own past dealings with that person. This is better information for four reasons: (1) it is cheap; (2) one trusts one's own information best—it is richer, more detailed, and known to be accurate; (3) individuals with whom one has a continuing relation have an economic motivation to be trustworthy, so as not to discourage future transactions; and (4) departing from pure economic motives, continuing economic relations often become overlaid with social content that carries strong expectations of trust and abstention from opportunism.

This last point aside, the entire argument is consistent with, and much of it has been anticipated by, transaction cost reasoning. Transaction cost economics and embeddedness reasoning are evidently complementary in many respects.

A related argument is that transaction cost economics is preoccupied with dyadic relations, whereupon network relations are given short shrift. The former is correct,[6] but the suggestion that network analysis is beyond the reach of transaction cost economics is too strong. For one thing, many of the network effects described by Ray Miles and Charles Snow (1992) correspond very closely to the transaction cost economics treatment of the hybrid form of economic organization (Williamson, 1983, 1991a). For another, as the discussion of Japanese economic organization (see below) reveals, transaction cost economics can be and has been extended to deal with a richer set of network effects.

Discrete Structural Analysis

One possible objection to the use of maximization/marginal analysis is that "Parsimony recommends that we prefer the postulate that men are reasonable to the postulate that they are supremely rational when either of the two assumptions will do our work of inference as well as the other" (Simon, 1978, p. 8). But while one might agree with Simon that satisficing is more reasonable than maximizing, the analytical toolbox out of which satisficing works is, as compared with maximizing apparatus, incomplete and very cumbersome. Thus if one reaches the same outcome through the satisfying postulate as through maximizing, and if the latter is much easier to implement, then economists can be thought of as analytical satisficers: they use a short-cut form of analysis that is simple to implement. Albeit at the expense of realism in assumptions, maximization gets the job done.

A different criticism of marginal analysis is that this glosses over first-order effects of a discrete structural kind. Capitalism and socialism, for example, can be compared in both discrete structural (bureaucratization) and marginal analysis (efficient resource allocation) respects. Interestingly, Oskar Lange (1938, p. 109) conjectured that, as between the two, bureaucratization posed a much more severe danger to socialism than did inefficient resource allocation.

That he was sanguine with respect to the latter was because he had derived the rules for efficient resource allocation (mainly of a marginal cost pricing kind) and was confident that socialist planners and managers could implement them. Joseph Schumpeter (1942) and Abram Bergson (1948) concurred. The study of comparative economic systems over the next fifty years was predominantly an allocative efficiency exercise.

Bureaucracy, by contrast, was mainly ignored. Partly that is because the study of bureaucracy was believed to be beyond the purview of economics and belonged to sociology (Lange, 1938, p. 109). Also, Lange held that "monopolistic capitalism" was beset by even more serious bureaucracy problems (p. 110). If, however, the recent collapse of the former Soviet Union is attributable more to conditions of waste (operating inside the frontier) than to inefficient resource allocation (operating at the wrong place on the frontier), then it was cumulative burdens of bureaucracy—goal distortions, slack, maladaptation, technological stagnation—that spelt its demise.

The lesson here is this: always study first-order (discrete structural) effects before examining second-order (marginalist) refinements. Arguably, moreover, that should be obvious: waste is easily a more serious source of welfare losses than are price induced distortions [cf. Harberger (1954) with Williamson (1968)].

Simon advises similarly. Thus he contends that the main questions are (1978, p. 6):

> Not "how much flood insurance will a man buy?" but "what are the structural conditions that make buying insurance rational or attractive?"
>
> Not "at what levels will wages be fixed" but "when will work be performed under an employment contract rather than a sales contract?"

Friedland and Alford's recent treatment of institutions is also of a discrete structural kind. They contend that "Each of the most important institutional orders of contemporary Western societies has a central logic—a set of material practices and symbolic constructions—which constitutes its organizing principles and which is available to organizations and individuals to elaborate" (1991, p. 248). Transaction cost economics concurs. But whereas Friedland and Alford are concerned with discrete structural logics between institutional orders—capitalism, the state, democracy, the family, etc.—transaction cost economics maintains that distinctive logics within institutional orders also need to be distinguished. Within the institutional order of capitalism, for example, each generic mode of governance—market, hybrid, and hierarchy—possesses its own logic and distinctive cluster of attributes. Of special importance is the proposition that each generic mode of governance is supported by a distinctive form of contract law.

As developed elsewhere (Williamson, 1991a), transaction cost economics holds that classical contract law applies to markets, neoclassical contract law applies to hybrids, and forbearance law is the contract law of hierarchy. As between these three concepts of contract, classical contract law is the most legalistic, neoclassical contract law is somewhat more elastic (Macneil, 1974, 1978), and forbearance law has the property that hierarchy is its own court of ultimate appeal. But for these contract law differences, markets and hierarchies would be indistinguishable in fiat respects.

Recall in this connection that Alchian and Demsetz introduced their analysis of the "classical capitalist firm" with the argument that (172, p. 777): "It is common to see the firm characterized by the power to settle issues by fiat. . . . This is delusion. The firm . . . has no power of fiat, no authority, no disciplinary action any different in the slightest degree from ordinary market contracting." That is a provocative formulation and places the burden on those who hold that firm and market differ in fiat respects to show wherein those differences originate.

The transaction cost economics response is that courts treat interfirm and intrafirm disputes differently, serving as the forum of ultimate appeal for interfirm disputes while refusing to hear identical technical disputes that arise between divisions (regarding transfer prices, delays, quality, and the like). Because hierarchy is its own court of ultimate appeal (Williamson, 1991a), firms can and do exercise fiat that markets cannot. Prior neglect of the discrete structural contract law differences that distinguish alternative modes of governance explains earlier claims that firms and markets are indistinguishable in fiat and control respects.

TRANSACTION COST ECONOMICS, THE STRATEGY

The transaction cost economics program for studying economic organization has been described elsewhere (Williamson, 1975, 1981, 1985, 1988a, 1991a; Klein *et al.*, 1978; Alchian and Woodward, 1987; Davis and Powell, 1992). My purpose here is to sketch the general strategy that is employed by transaction cost economics, with the suggestion that organization theorists could adopt (some already have adopted) parts of it.

The five-part strategy that I describe entails (i) a main case orientation (transaction cost economizing), (ii) choice and explication of the unit of analysis, (iii) a systems view of contracting, (iv) rudimentary trade-off apparatus, and (v) a remediableness test for assessing "failures."

The Main Case

Economic organization being very complex and our understanding being primitive, there is a need to sort the wheat from the chaff. I propose for this purpose that each rival theory of organization should declare the *main case* out of which it works and develop the *refutable implications* that accrue thereto.

Transaction cost economics holds that economizing on transaction costs is mainly responsible for the choice of one form of capitalist organization over another. It thereupon applies this hypothesis to a wide range of phenomena—vertical integration, vertical market restrictions, labor organization, corporate governance, finance, regulation (and deregulation), conglomerate organization, technology transfer, and, more generally, to any issue that can be posed directly or indirectly as a contracting problem. As it turns out, large numbers of problems which on first examination do not appear to be of a contracting kind turn out to have an underlying contracting structure—the oligopoly problem (Williamson, 1975, chapter 12) and the organization of the company town (Williamson, 1985, pp. 35–38) being examples. Comparisons with other—rival or complementary—main case alternatives are invited.

Three of the older main case alternatives are that economic organization is mainly explained by (i) technology, (ii) monopolization, and (iii) efficient risk bearing. More recent main case candidates are (iv) contested exchange between labor and capital, (v) other types of power arguments (e.g. resource dependency), and (vi) path dependency. My brief responses to the first three are that (i) technological non-separabilities and indivisibilities explain only small groups and, at most, large plants, but explain neither multiplant organization nor the organization of technologically separable groups/activities (which should remain autonomous and which should be joined), (ii) monopoly explanations require that monopoly preconditions be satisfied, but most markets are competitively organized, and (iii) although differential risk aversion may apply to many employment relationships, it has much less applicability to trade between firms (where portfolio diversification is more easily accomplished and where smaller firms [for incentive intensity and economizing, but not risk bearing, reasons] are often observed to bear inordinate risk). Responses to the last three are developed more fully below. My brief responses are these: (iv) the failures to which contested exchange refers are often irremediable, (v) resource dependency is a truncated theory of contract, and (vi) although path dependency is an important phenomenon, remediable inefficiency is rarely established.

To be sure, transaction cost economizing does not always operate smoothly or quickly. Thus we should "expect [transaction cost economizing] to be most clearly exhibited in industries where entry is [easy] and where the struggle for survival is [keen]" (Koopmans, 1957, p. 141).[7] Transaction cost economics nevertheless maintains that later, if not sooner, inefficiency in the commercial sector invites its own demise—all the more so as international competition has become more vigorous. Politically imposed impediments (tariffs, quotas, subsidies, rules) can and have, however, delayed the reckoning;[8] and disadvantaged parties (railroad workers, longshoremen, managers) may also be able to delay changes unless compensated by buyouts.

The economizing to which I refer operates through weak-form selection—according to which the fitter, but not necessarily the fittest, in some absolute sense, are selected (Simon, 1983, p. 69).[9] Also, the economizing in question works through a private net benefit calculus. That suits the needs of positive economics—What's going on out there?—rather well, but public policy needs to be more circumspect. As discussed below, the relevant test of whether public policy intervention is warranted is that of remediableness.

These important qualifications notwithstanding, transaction cost economics maintains that economizing is mainly determinative of private sector economic organization and, as indicated, invites comparison with rival main case hypotheses. Nicholas Georgescu-Roegen's views on the purpose of science and the role of prediction are pertinent: "the purpose of science in general is not prediction, but knowledge for its own sake," yet prediction is "the touchstone of scientific knowledge" (1971, p. 37). There being many plausible accounts from which to choose, it is vital that each be prepared to show its hand (offer its predictions).

Unit of Analysis

A variety of units of analysis have been proposed to study economic organization. Simon has proposed that the *decision premise* is the appropriate unit of analysis (1957a, pp. xxx–xxxii). *"Ownership"* is the unit of analysis for the economics of property rights. The *industry* is the unit of analysis in the structure–conduct–performance approach to industrial organization (Bain, 1956; Scherer, 1970). The *individual* has been nominated as the unit of analysis by positive agency theory (Jensen, 1983). Transaction cost economics follows John R. Commons (1924, 1934) and takes the *transaction* to be the basic unit of analysis.

Whatever unit of analysis is selected, the critical dimensions with respect to which that unit of analysis differs need to be identified. Otherwise the unit will remain non-operational. Also, a paradigm problem to which the unit of analysis applies needs to be described. Table 9.1 sets out the relevant comparisons.

As shown, the representative problem with which transaction cost economics deals is that of vertical integration—when should a firm make rather than buy a good or service? The focal dimension on which much of the predictive content of transaction cost economics relies, moreover, is asset specificity, which (as discussed below) is a measure of bilateral dependency. More generally, transaction cost economics is concerned with the governance of contractual relations (which bears a resemblance to the "going concerns" to which Commons referred). As it turns out, economic organization—in intermediate products markets, labor markets, capital markets, regulation, and even the family—involves variations on a few key transaction cost economizing themes. The predictive action turns on the following proposition: transactions, which differ in their attributes, are aligned with governance structures, which differ in their costs and competence, in a discriminating—mainly, transaction cost economizing—way.

The arguments are familiar and are developed elsewhere. Suffice it to observe here that empirical research in organization theory has long suffered from the lack of an appropriate unit of analysis and the operationalization, which is to say, dimensionalization, thereof.

Table 9.1 Comparison of Units of Analysis

Unit of Analysis	Critical Dimensions	Focal Problem
Decision premise	Role; information; idiosyncratic[a]	Human problem solving[b]
Ownership	Eleven characteristics[c]	Externality
Industry	Concentration; barriers to entry	Price-cost margins
Individual	Undeclared	Incentive alignment
Transaction	Frequency; uncertainty; asset specificity	Vertical integration

[a] Simon (1957a, pp. xxx–xxxi).
[b] Newell and Simon (1972).
[c] Bromley (1989, pp. 187–190).

Farsighted Contracting

The preoccupation of economists with direct and intended effects to the neglect of indirect and (often delayed) unintended effects is widely interpreted as a condition of myopia. In fact, however, most economists are actually farsighted. The problem is one of limited peripheral vision.

Tunnel vision is both a strength and a weakness. The strength is that a focused lens, provided that it focuses on core issues, can be very powerful. The limitation is that irregularities which are none the less important will be missed and/or even worse, dismissed.

Transaction cost economics relates to these limitations by drawing on organization theory. Because organization has a life of its own, transaction cost economics (i) asks to be apprised of the more important indirect effects, whereupon (ii) it asks what, given these prospective effects, are the ramifications for efficient governance. A joinder of unanticipated effects (from organization theory) with farsighted contracting (from economics) thereby obtains.

Lest claims of farsightedness be taken to hyper-rationality extremes, transaction cost economics concedes that all complex contracts are unavoidably incomplete. That has both practical and theoretical significance. The practical lesson is this: all of the relevant contracting action cannot be concentrated in the *ex ante* incentive alignment but some spills over into *ex post* governance. The theoretical lesson is that differences among organization forms lose economic significance under a comprehensive contracting set-up because any form of organization can then replicate any other (Hart, 1990).

Transaction cost economics combines incompleteness with farsighted contracting by describing the contracting process as one of "incomplete contracting in its entirety." But for incompleteness, the above-described significance of *ex post* governance would vanish. But for farsightedness, transaction cost economics would be denied access to one of the most important "tricks" in the economist's bag, namely the assumption that economic actors have the ability to look ahead, discern problems and prospects, and factor these back into the organizational/contractual design. "Plausible farsightedness," as against hyper-rationality, will often suffice.

Consider, for example, the issue of threats. Threats are easy to make, but which threats are to be believed? If A says that it will do X if B does Y, but if after B does Y, A's best response is to do Z, then the threat will not be perceived to be credible to a farsighted B. Credible threats are thus those for which a farsighted B perceives that A's *ex post* incentives comport with its claims, because, for example, A has made the requisite kind and amount of investment to support its threats (Dixit, 1980).

Or consider the matter of opportunism. As described above, Machiavelli worked out of a myopic logic, whereupon he advised his Prince to reply to opportunism in kind (get them before they get you). By contrast, the farsighted Prince is advised to look ahead and, if he discerns potential hazards, to take the hazards into account by redesigning the contractual relation—often by devising *ex ante* safeguards that will deter *ex post* opportunism. Accordingly, the wise Prince is advised to give and receive "credible commitments."

To be sure, it is more complicated to think about contract as a triple *(p, k, s)*, where *p* refers to the price at which the trade takes place, *k* refers to the hazards that are associated with the exchange, *s* denotes the safeguards within which the exchange is embedded, and price, hazards, and safeguards are determined simultaneously—than as a scalar, where price alone is determinative. The simple schema shown in Figure 9.2 nevertheless captures much of the relevant action.[10]

It will facilitate comparisons to assume that suppliers are competitively organized and are risk neutral. The prices at which product will be supplied therefore reflect an expected break-even condition. The break-even price that is associated with Node A is p_1. There being no hazards, $k = 0$. And since safeguards are unneeded, $s = 0$.[11]

Node B is more interesting. The contractual hazard here is $\bar{k}$. If the

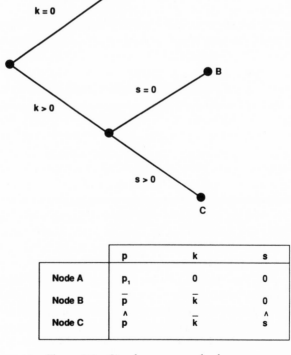

	p	k	s
Node A	p_1	0	0
Node B	$\bar{p}$	$\bar{k}$	0
Node C	$\hat{p}$	$\bar{k}$	$\hat{s}$

Figure 9.2 Simple contractual schema.

buyer is unable or unwilling to provide a safeguard, then $s = 0$. The corresponding break-even price is $\bar{p}$.

Node C poses the same contractual hazard, namely $\bar{k}$. In this case, however, a safeguard in amount $\hat{s}$ is provided. The break-even price that is projected under these conditions is $\hat{p}$. It is elementary that $\hat{p} < \bar{p}$.

Note that Jeffrey Bradach and Robert Eccles contend that "mutual dependence [i.e., $k > 0$] between exchange partners . . . [promotes] trust, [which] contrasts sharply with the argument central to transaction cost economics that . . . dependence . . . fosters opportunistic behavior" (1989, p. 111). What transaction cost economics says, however, is that because opportunistic agents will not self-enforce open-ended promises to behave responsibly, efficient exchange will be realized only if dependencies are *supported* by credible commitments. Wherein is trust implicated if parties to an exchange are farsighted and reflect the relevant hazards in terms of the exchange? [A better price ($\hat{p} < \bar{p}$) will be offered if the hazards ($k > 0$) are mitigated by cost-effective contractual safeguards ($\hat{s} > 0$).]

As it turns out, the farsighted approach to contracting has pervasive ramifications, some of which are developed below.

Trade-Offs

The ideal organization adapts quickly and efficaciously to disturbances of all kinds, but actual organizations experience trade-offs. Thus whereas more decentralized forms of organization (e.g. markets) support high-powered incentives and display outstanding adaptive properties to disturbances of an autonomous kind, they are poorly suited in cooperative adaptation respects. Hierarchy, by contrast, has weaker incentives and is comparatively worse at autonomous adaptation but is comparatively better in cooperative adaptation respects.

Simple transactions (for which $k = 0$)—in intermediate product markets, labor, finance, regulation, and the like—are easy to organize. The requisite adaptations here are preponderantly of an autonomous kind and the market-like option is efficacious (so firms buy rather than make, use spot contracts for labor, use debt rather than equity, eschew regulation, etc.). Problems with markets arise as bilateral dependencies, and the need for cooperative adaptations, build up. Markets give way to hybrids which in turn give way to hierarchies (which is the organization form of last resort) as the needs for cooperative adaptations ($k > 0$) build up.

More generally, the point is this: informed choice among alternative forms of organization entails trade-offs. Identifying and explicating trade-offs is the key to the study of comparative economic organization. Social scientists—economists and organization theorists alike—as well as legal specialists, need to come to terms with that proposition.

Remediableness

Related to this last is the concept of remediableness. If all feasible forms of organization are flawed (Coase, 1964), then references to benign government, costless regulation, omniscient courts, and the like are operationally irrelevant. That does not deny that hypothetical ideals can be useful as a reference standard, but standards are often arbitrary. Is unbounded rationality the relevant standard? How about perfect stewardship, in which event opportunism vanishes?

Lapses into ideal but operationally irrelevant reasoning will be avoided by (i) recognizing that it is impossible to do better than one's best, (ii) insisting that all of the finalists in an organization form competition meet the test of feasibility, (iii) symmetrically exposing the weaknesses as well as the strengths of all proposed feasible forms, and (iv) describing and costing out the mechanisms of any proposed reorganization. Such precautions seem to be reasonable, transparent, even beyond dispute; yet all are frequently violated.

Note in this connection that "inefficiency" is unavoidably associated with contractual hazards. The basic market and hierarchy trade-off that is incurred upon taking transactions out of markets and organizing them internally substitutes one form of inefficiency (bureaucracy) for another (maladaptation). Other examples where one form of inefficiency is used to patch up another are (i) decisions by firms to integrate into adjacent stages of production (or distribution) in a weak intellectual property rights regime, thereby to mitigate the leakage of valued know-how (Teece, 1986), (ii) decisions by manufacturers' agents to incur added expenses, over and above those needed to develop the market, if these added expenses strengthen customer bonds in a cost-effective way, thereby to deter manufacturers from entering and expropriating market development investments (Heide and John, 1988), and (iii) the use of costly bonding to deter franchisees from violating quality norms (Klein and Leffler, 1981). Organization also has a bearing on the distribution of rents as well as asset protection. Concern over rent dissipation influenced the decision by the United States automobile industry firms to integrate into parts (Helper and Levine, 1992) and also helps to explain the resistance by oligopolies to industrial unions.

To be sure, any sacrifice of organizational efficiency, for oligopolistic rent protection reasons or otherwise, poses troublesome public policy issues.[12] A remediableness test is none the less required to ascertain whether public policy should attempt to upset the oligopoly power in question. The issues are discussed further in relation to path dependency below.

ADDED REGULARITIES

It is evident from the foregoing that the comparative contractual approach out of which transaction cost economics works can be and needs to be informed by organization theory. Transaction cost economics, however, is more than a mere user. It pushes the logic of self-interest seeking to deeper levels, of which the concept of credible commitment is one example. More generally, it responds to prospective dysfunctional consequences by proposing improved *ex ante* designs and/or alternative forms of governance. Also, and what concerns me here, transaction cost has helped to discover added regularities that are pertinent to the study of organization. These include (i) the Fundamental Transformation, (ii) the impossibility of selective intervention, (iii) the economics of atmosphere, and (iv) an interpretation of Japanese economic organization.

The Fundamental Transformation[13]

The Fundamental Transformation is the principal transaction cost economics way of demonstrating that "identity matters." It helps to explain how firms take on distinctive identities and why identity matters.

Economists of all persuasions recognize that the terms upon which an initial bargain will be struck depend on whether non-collusive bids can be elicited from more than one qualified supplier. Monopolistic terms will obtain if there is only a single highly qualified supplier, while competitive terms will result if there are many. Transaction cost economics fully accepts this description of *ex ante* bidding competition but insists that the study of contracting be extended to include *ex post* features.

Contrary to earlier practice, transaction cost economics holds that a condition of large numbers bidding at the outset does not necessarily imply that a large numbers bidding condition will obtain thereafter. Whether *ex post* competition is fully efficacious or not depends on whether the good or service in question is supported by durable investments in transaction specific human or physical assets. Where no such specialized investments are incurred, the initial winning bidder realizes no advantage over non-winners. Although it may continue to supply for a long period of time, this is only because, in effect, it is continuously meeting competitive bids from qualified rivals. Rivals cannot be presumed to operate on a parity, however, once substantial investments in transaction specific assets are put in place. Winners in these circumstances enjoy advantages over non-winners, which is to say that parity at the renewal interval is upset. Accordingly, what was a large numbers bidding condition at the outset is effectively transformed into one of bilateral supply thereafter. The reason why significant reliance investments in durable, transaction specific assets introduce contractual asymmetry between the winning bidder on the one hand and non-winners on the other is because economic values would be sacrificed if the ongoing supply relation were to be terminated.

Faceless contracting is thereby supplanted by contracting in which the pairwise identity of the parties matters. Not only would the supplier be unable to realize equivalent value were the specialized assets to be redeployed to other uses, but also a buyer would need to induce potential suppliers to make similar specialized investments were he to seek least-cost supply from an outsider. Such parties therefore have strong incentives to work things out rather than terminate. More generally, farsighted agents will attempt to craft Node C safeguards *ex ante*. As previously indicated, that entails a progression from markets to hybrids and, if that does not suffice, to hierarchies. Given its bureaucratic disabilities, hierarchy is the organizational form of last resort.

The Impossibility of Selective Intervention

Large established firms purportedly have advantages over smaller potential entrants because (Lewis, 1983, p. 1092):

> . . . the leader can at least use [inputs] exactly as the entrant would have . . . , and earn the same profit as the entrant. But typically, the leader can improve on this by coordinating production from his new and existing inputs. Hence [inputs] will be valued more by the dominant firm.

That argument has the following implication: if large firms can everywhere do as well as a collection of smaller firms, through replication, and can sometimes do better, through selective intervention, then large firms ought to grow without limit. That is a variant of the Coasian puzzle "Why is not all production carried on in one big firm?" (1937, p. 340).

The simple answer to that query is that replication and/or selective intervention are impossible. But that merely moves the argument back one stage. What explains these impossibilities?

The underlying difficulty is this: the integrity of rule governance is unavoidably compromised by allowing discretion (Williamson, 1985, chapter 6). Accordingly, any effort to combine rule governance (as in markets) with discretionary governance (hierarchy) experiences trade-offs. The proposal to "Implement the rules with discretion" is simply too facile.

That comes as no surprise to those who approach the study of governance in discrete structural terms—whereupon each generic form of governance possesses distinctive strengths and weaknesses and movements between them entail trade-offs. The puzzle of limits to firm size none the less eluded an answer for fifty years and more (Williamson, 1985, pp. 132–135) and still occasions confusion.

Atmosphere [14]

The unintended effects described in 4 above are of a more local kind than the atmospheric effects examined here. Atmosphere refers to interactions between transactions that are technologically separable but are joined attitudinally and have systems consequences.

Thus suppose that a job can be split into a series of separable functions. Suppose further that differential metering at the margin is attempted with reference to each. What are the consequences?

If functional separability does not imply attitudinal separability, then piecemeal calculativeness can easily be dysfunctional. The risk is that pushing metering at the margin everywhere to the limit will have spillover effects from easy-to-meter on to hard-to-meter activities. If cooperative attitudes are impaired, then transactions that can be metered only with difficulty, but for which consummate cooperation is important, will be discharged in a more perfunctory manner. The neglect of such interaction effects is encouraged by piecemeal calculativeness, which is to say by an insensitivity to atmosphere.

A related issue is the matter of externalities. The question may be put as follows: ought all externalities to be metered which, taken separately, can be metered with net gains? Presumably this turns partly on whether secondary effects obtain when an externality is accorded legitimacy. All kinds of grievances may be "felt," and demands for compensation made accordingly, if what had hitherto been considered to be harmless byproducts of normal social intercourse are suddenly declared to be compensable injuries. The transformation of relationships that will ensue can easily lead to a lower level of satisfaction felt among the parties than prevailed previously—at least transitionally and possibly permanently.

Part of the explanation is that filing claims for petty injuries influences attitudes toward other transactions. My insistence on compensation for A leads you to file claims for B, C, and D, which induces me to seek compensation for E and F, etc. Although an efficiency gain might be realized were it possible to isolate transaction A, the overall impact can easily be negative. Realizing this to be the case, some individuals will be prepared to overlook such injuries. But everyone is not similarly constituted. Society is rearranged to the advantage of those who demand more exacting correspondences between rewards and deeds if metering at the margin is everywhere attempted. Were the issue of compensation to be taken up as a constitutional matter, rather than on a case-by-case basis, a greater tolerance for spillover would commonly be obtained (Schelling, 1978).

Also pertinent is that individuals keep informal social accounts and find the exchange of reciprocal favors among parties with whom uncompensated spillovers exist to be satisfying (Gouldner, 1954). Transforming these casual social accounts into exact and legal obligations may well be destructive of atmosphere and lead to a net loss of satisfaction between the parties. Put differently, pervasive pecuniary relations impair the quality of "contracting"—even if the metering of the transactions in question were costless.[15]

The argument that emerges from the above is not that metering ought to be prohibited but that the calculative approach to organization that is associated with economics can be taken to extremes. An awareness of attitudinal spillovers and non-pecuniary satisfactions serves to check such excesses of calculativeness.

Japanese Economic Organization

Transaction cost economics deals predominantly with dyadic contractual relations. Viewing the firm as a nexus of contracts, the object is to prescribe the best transaction/governance structure between the firm and its intermediate product market suppliers, between the firm and its workers, between the firm and finance, etc. Japanese economic organization appears to be more complicated. Employment, banking, and subcontracting relations need to be examined simultaneously.

The banking, employment, and subcontracting differences between Japanese and United States economic organization have been explicated by Masahiko Aoki (1988, 1990), Banri Asanuma (1989), Erik Berglof (1989), Ronald Dore (1983), Michael Gerlach (1992), James Lincoln (1990), Paul Sheard (1989), and others. I am not only persuaded that these three are joined but believe that transaction cost economics can help to explicate the complementarities (Williamson, 1991b).

Figures 9.3A and B display the nature of the complementarities. Figure 9.3A depicts the contractual hazards that are posed by lifetime employment. These are (i) economic adversity—due, say, to periodic decreases in demand—which makes it costly to offer lifetime employment; (ii) workers who enjoy lifetime employment may treat it as a sinecure and shirk; (iii) workers who are induced by promises of lifetime employment to specialize their assets to a firm are exposed to a breach of contract hazard; (iv) equalitarian pressures develop within firms, whereupon the offer of lifetime employment to key workers (where the justification is strong) spreads to all workers (to include those for whom the justification is weak). Although each of these can be addressed separately, the systems solution shown by Figure 3A is (arguably) more effective still.

Figure 9.3B is somewhat more complicated and interested readers are referred to discussions elsewhere (Williamson, 1991b; Aoki, 1992). Suffice it to observe here that banking and subcontracting (i) are not only supports for the employment relation in the core firm but (ii) are supported by the employment relation and (iii) are supports for each other.

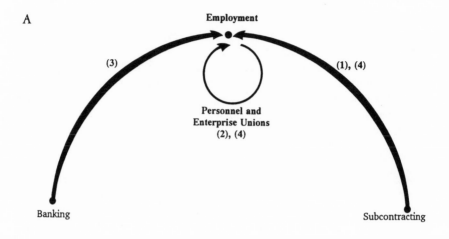

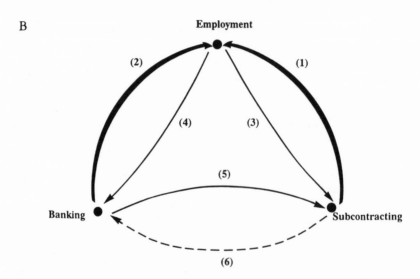

Figure 9.3 (A) Supports for life-time employment against the hazards of (1) adversity, (2) shirking, (3) breach, (4) equalitarianism. Subcontracting reduces (1) and (4), the personnel office and enterprise unions reduce (2) and (4), and banking reduces (3). (B) Japanese corporate connectedness through contracting, where → denotes strong support; → denotes support; - - → denotes weaker support. Benefits are (1) greater homogeneity; (2) greater contract stability; (3) feedback stability; (4) reliably responsive to adversity; (5) financial planning (convergent expectations); (6) no surprises.

UNRESOLVED TENSIONS

The healthy tension to which I referred at the outset has contributed to better and deeper understandings of a variety of phenomena. The matters that concern me here—power, path dependence, the labor managed enterprise, trust, and tosh—are ones for which differences between transaction cost economics and organization theory are great.

Power/Resource Dependence

That efficiency plays such a large role in the economic analysis of organization is because parties are assumed to consent to a contract and do this in a relatively farsighted way. Such voluntarism is widely disputed by sociologists, who "tend to regard systems of exchange as embedded within systems of power and domination (usually regarded as grounded in a class structure in the Marxian tradition) or systems of norms and values" (Baron and Hannan, 1992, p. 14).

The concept of power is very diffuse. Unable to define power, some specialists report that they know it when they see it. That has led others to conclude that power is a "disappointing concept. It tends to become a tautological label for the unexplained variance" (March, 1988, p. 6).

Among the ways in which the term power is used are the following: the power of capital over labor (Bowles and Gintis, 1993); strategic power exercised by established firms in relation to extant and prospective rivals (Shapiro, 1989); special interest power over the political process (Moe, 1990); and resource dependency. Although all are relevant to economic organization, the last is distinctive to organization theory.[16] I examine it.

Two versions of resource dependency can be distinguished. The weak version is that parties who are subject to dependency will try to mitigate it. That is unexceptionable and is akin to the safeguard argument advanced above. There are two significant differences, however: (i) resource dependency nowhere recognizes that price, hazards, and safeguards are determined simultaneously; (ii) resource dependency nowhere remarks that asset specificity (which is the source of contractual hazard) is intentionally chosen because it is the source of productive benefits.

The strong version of resource dependency assumes myopia. The argument here is that myopic parties to contracts are victims of unanticipated and unwanted dependency. Because myopic parties do not perceive the hazards, safeguards will not be provided and the hazards will not be priced out.

Evidence pertinent to the myopic versus farsighted view of contract includes the following. (i) Are suppliers indifferent between two technologies that involve identical investments and have identical (steady state) operating costs, but one of which technologies is much less redeployable than the other? (ii) Is the degree of non-redeployability evident *ex ante* or is it revealed only after an adverse state realization (which induces defection from the spirit of the agreement) has materialized? (iii) Do added *ex ante* safeguards appear as added specificity builds up? (iv) Does contract law doctrine and enforcement reflect one or the other of these concepts of contract? Transaction cost economics answers these queries as follows: (i) the more generic (redeployable) technology will always be used whenever the cetera are paria; (ii) non-redeployability can be discerned *ex ante* and is recognized as such (Masten, 1984; Palay, 1984, 1985; Shelanski, 1993); (iii) added *ex ante* safeguards do appear as asset specificity builds up (Jaskow, 1985, 1988); (iv) because truly unusual events are unforeseeable and can have punitive consequences if contracts are enforced literally, various forms of "excuse" are recognized by the law, but excuse is granted sparingly.[17]

Path Dependency

Transaction cost economics not only subscribes to the proposition that history matters but relies on that proposition to explain the differential strengths and weaknesses of alternative forms of governance. The Fundamental Transformation, for example, is a specific manifestation of the proposition that history matters. (Transactions that are not subject to the Fundamental Transformation are much easier to manage contractually.) The bureaucracy problems that afflict internal organization (entrenchment; coalitions) are also the product of experience and illustrate the proposition that history matters. Were it not that systems drifted away from their initial conditions, efforts to replicate markets within hierarchies (or the reverse) and selectively intervene would be much easier—in which event differences between organization forms would diminish.

The benefits that accrue to experience are also testimony to the proposition that history matters. Tacit knowledge and its consequences (Polanyi, 1962; Marschak, 1968; Arrow, 1974) attest to that. More generally, firm-specific human assets of both spontaneous (e.g. coding economies) and intentional (e.g. learning) kinds are the product of idiosyncratic experience. The entire institutional environment (laws, rules, conventions, norms, etc.) within which the institutions of governance are embedded is the product of history. And although the social conditioning that operates within governance structures [e.g. corporate culture (Kreps, 1990)] is reflexive and often intentional, this too has accidental and temporal features.

That history matters does not, however, imply that only history matters. Intentionality and economizing explain a lot of what is going on out there. Also, most of the path dependency literature emphasizes technology (e.g. the QWERTY typewriter keyboard) rather than the organizational consequences referred to above, Paul David's recent paper (1992) being an exception. I am not persuaded that technological, as against organizational, path dependency is as important as much of that literature suggests. Many of the "inefficiencies" to which the technological path dependency literature refers are of an irremediable kind.

Remediable inefficiencies   As described above, transaction cost economics emphasizes remediable inefficiencies; that is, those conditions for which a feasible alternative can be described which, if introduced, would yield net gains. That is to be distinguished from hypothetical net gains, where the inefficiency in question is judged by comparing an actual alternative with a hypothetical ideal.

To be sure, big disparities between actual and hypothetical sometimes signals opportunities for net gains. But a preoccupation with hypotheticals comes at a cost (Coase, 1964, p. 195; emphasis added):

> Contemplation of an optimal system may provide techniques of analysis that would otherwise have been missed and, in certain special cases, it may go far to providing a solution. But in general its influence has been pernicious. It has directed economists' attention away from the main question, which is how *alternative arrangements will actually work in practice.*

Consider Brian Arthur's (1989) numerical example of path dependency in which the pay-offs to individual firms upon adopting either of two technologies (A or B) depend on the number of prior adoptions of each. Technology A has a higher pay-off than B if there are few prior adoptions, but the advantage switches to technology B if there have been many prior adoptions. The "problem" is that if each potential adopter consults only its own immediate net gain, then each will select A and there will be "lock-in" to an inferior technology. A tyranny of micromotives thereby obtains (Schelling, 1978).

As S. J. Liebowitz and Stephen Margolis observe of this argument, however, whether choice of technology A is inefficient or not depends on what assumptions are made about the state of knowledge (1992, p. 15). Also, even if individual parties could be assumed to know that technology B would become the more efficient choice after thirty or fifty adoptions, the added costs of collective action to deter individuals from choosing technology A would need to be taken into account. If it is unrealistic to assume that individuals possess the relevant knowledge that a switchover (from A to B) will occur upon thirty or fifty adoptions, or if, given that knowledge, the costs of orchestrating collective action are prohibitive, then the inefficiency in question is effectively irremediable through private ordering.

Sometimes, however, public ordering can do better. The issues here are whether (i) the public sector is better informed about network externalities, (ii) the requisite collective action is easier to orchestrate through the public sector (possibly by fiat), and/or (iii) the social net benefit calculus differs from the private in sufficient degree to warrant a different result. Absent *plausible* assumptions that would support a prospective net gain (in either private or social respects), the purported inefficiency is effectively irremediable.

That is regrettable, in that society would have done better if it had better knowledge or if a reorganization could have been accomplished more easily. Hypothetical regrets—the "nirvana economics" to which E. A. G. Robinson (1934) and Harold Demsetz (1969) refer—are neither here nor there. Real costs in relation to real choices is what comparative institutional economics is all about.

Quantitative significance Path dependency, remediable or not, poses a greater challenge if the effects in question are large and lasting rather than small and temporary. It is not easy to document the quantitative significance of path dependency. Arthur provides a series of examples and emphasizes especially the video cassette recorder (where VHS prevailed over the Beta technology [1990, p. 92]) and nuclear power (where light water reactors prevailed over high-temperature, gas-cooled reactors [1990, p. 99]). But while both are interesting examples of path dependency, it is not obvious that the "winning" technology is significantly inferior to the loser, or even, for that matter, whether the winner is inferior at all.

Much the most widely cited case study is that of the typewriter keyboard. The QWERTY keyboard story has been set out by Paul David (1985, 1986). It illustrates "why the study of economic history is a necessity in the making of good economists" (David, 1986, p. 30).

QWERTY refers to the first six letters on the top row of the standard typewriter keyboard. Today's keyboard layout is the same as that which was devised when the typewriter was first invented in 1870. The early mechanical technology was beset by typebar clashes, which clashes were mitigated by the QWERTY keyboard design.

Subsequent developments in typewriter technology relieved problems with typebar clashes, but the QWERTY keyboard persisted in the face of large (reported) discrepancies in typing speed between it and later keyboard designs. Thus the Dvorak Simplified Keyboard (DSK), which was patented in 1932, was so much faster than the standard keyboard that, according to United States Navy experiments, the "increased efficiency obtained with DSK would amortize the cost of retraining a group of typists within the first ten days of their subsequent full-time employment" (David, 1986, p. 33). More recently, the Apple IIC computer comes with a built-in switch which instantly converts its keyboard from QWERTY to DSK: "If as Apple advertising copy says, DSK 'lets you type 20–40% faster,' why did this superior design meet essentially the same resistance . . . ?" (David, 1986, p. 34).

There are several possibilities. These include non-rational behavior, conspiracy among typewriter firms, and path dependency (David, 1986, pp. 34–46). David makes a strong case for the last, but there is a fourth possibility, subsequently raised and examined by Liebowitz and Margolis

(1990): neither the Navy study nor Apple advertising copy can support the astonishing claims made on their behalf. Upon going back to the archives and examining the data, Liebowitz and Margolis conclude that "the standard history of QWERTY versus Dvorak is flawed and incomplete. . . . [The] claims of superiority of the Dvorak keyboard are suspect. The most dramatic claims are traceable to Dvorak himself, and the best documented experiments, as well as recent ergonomic studies, suggest little or no advantage for the Dvorak keyboard" (1990, p. 21). If that assessment stands up, then path dependence has had only modest efficiency effects in the QWERTY keyboard case. Such effects could easily fall below the threshold of remediable inefficiency.

Recent studies of the evolution of particular industries by sociologists also display path dependency. Population ecologists have used the ecological model of density-dependent legitimation and competition to examine the evolutionary process—both in particular industries (e.g., the telephone industry [Barnett and Carroll, 1993]) and in computer simulations. Glenn Carroll and Richard Harrison conclude from the latter that "chance can play a major role in organizational evolution" (1992, p. 26).

Although their simulations do suggest that path dependency has large and lasting effects, Carroll and Harrison do not address the matter of remediability. Until a feasible reorganization of the decision process for choosing technologies can be described, the effect of which is to yield expected net private or social gains, it seems premature to describe their experiments as a test of the "relative roles of chance and rationality" (Carroll and Harrison, 1992, p. 12). Large but irremediable inefficiencies nevertheless do raise serious issues for modelling economic organization.[18]

Perspectives   David contends and I am persuaded that "there are many more QWERTY worlds lying out there" (1986, p. 47). An unchanged keyboard layout does not, however, strike me as the most important economic attribute of typewriter development from 1870 to the present. What about improvements in the mechanical technology? What about the electric typewriter? What about personal computers and laser printers? Why did these prevail in the face of path dependency? Were other "structurally superior" technologies (as defined by Carroll and Harrison) bypassed? If, with lags and hitches, the more efficient technologies have regularly supplanted less efficient technologies, should not that be featured? Possibly the response is that "everyone knows" that economizing is the main case: "It goes without saying that economizing is the main case to which path dependency, monopolizing, efficient risk bearing, etc. are qualifications."

The persistent neglect of economizing reasoning suggests otherwise. Thus the "inhospitality tradition" in antitrust proceeded with sublime confidence that non-standard and unfamiliar business practices had little or no efficiency rationale but mainly had monopoly purpose and effect. Similarly, the vast inefficiencies that brought down the economies of the Soviet

Union and Eastern Europe may now be obvious, but that could never have been gleaned from the postwar literature on comparative economic systems or from CIA intelligence estimates. The preoccupation in the area of business strategy with clever "plans, ploys, and positioning" to the neglect of economizing is likewise testimony to the widespread tendency to disregard efficiency (Williamson, 1991b). And the view that the "effective organization is (1) *garrulous*, (2) *clumsy*, *(3) superstitious*, (4) *hypocritical*, (5) *monstrous*, (6) *octopoid*, (7) *wandering*, and (8) *grouchy*" (Weick, 1977, pp. 193–194; emphasis in original) is reconciled with economizing only with effort. More recent "social construction of industry" arguments reduce economizing to insignificance.[19]

If economizing really does get at the fundamentals, then that condition ought to be continuously featured. Some progress has been made (Zald, 1986), but there is little reason to be complacent.

Worker-Managed Enterprises[20]

John Bonin and Louis Putterman define a worker-managed firm as (1987, p. 2):

> . . . a productive enterprise the ultimate decision-making rights over which are held by member-workers, on the basis of equality of those rights regardless of job, skill grade, or capital contribution. A full definition would state that no non-workers have a direct say in enterprising decisions, and that no workers are denied an equal say in those decisions. This definition does not imply that any particular set of decisions must be made by the full working group, nor does it imply a particular choice rule, such as majority voting. It says nothing about financing structures other than that financiers are not accorded direct decision-making powers in the enterprise by virtue of their non-labor contributions, and it does not say anything about how income is distributed among workers. On all of these matters, all that is implied is that ultimate decision-making rights are vested in the workers, and only in the workers. Thus, the basic definition centers on an allocation of governance rights, and is simultaneously economic and political.

This definition does not preclude hierarchical structure, specialized decision-making, a leadership élite, or marginal product payment schemes. It merely stipulates that finance can have no decision rights in the labor-managed enterprise. The question is whether these financial restrictions come at a cost. Putterman evidently believes that they do not, since he elsewhere endorses Roger McCain's proposal that the labor-managed enterprise be financed in part by "risk participation bonds," where these purportedly differ from "ordinary equity" only in that "its owner can have no voting control over enterprise decisions, or over the election of enterprise management" (Putterman, 1984, p. 189). Since "the labor-managed firm whose objective is to maximize profit-per-worker, having both ordinary and 'risk participation' bonds at its disposal, would 'attain the same allocation of resources as would a capitalist corporation, under comparable circumstances and informationally efficient markets' " (1984, p. 189), Putterman concludes that the labor-managed firm is on a parity.

The argument illustrates the hazards of addressing issues of economic organization within a framework that ignores, hence effectively suppresses, the role of governance. Operating, as he does, out of a firm-as-production-function framework, McCain (1977) is only concerned with examining the marginal conditions that obtain under two different set-ups, under both of which the firm is described as a production function.

Governance issues never arise and hence are not amenable to analysis within this orthodox framework. If, however, a critical—indeed, I would say, the critical—attribute of equity is the ability to exercise contingent control by concentrating votes and taking over the board of directors, then McCain's demonstration that allocative efficiency is identical under standard equity and risk participation bonds is simply inapposite.

Indeed, if risk participation finance is available on more adverse terms than standard equity because holders are provided with less security against mismanagement and expropriation, then the constraints that Bonin and Putterman have built into the worker-managed firm come at a cost. To be sure, the worker-managed firm may be able to offset financial disabilities by offering compensating advantages. If those advantages are not uniform but vary among firms and industries, then the net gains of the worker-maanaged firm will vary accordingly.

I submit that firms that can be mainly financed with debt are the obvious candidates for worker-management. Thus, if there is little equity-like capital at stake, then there is little reason for equity to ask or expect that preemptive control over the board of directors will be awarded to equity as a contractual safeguard. The question then is what types of firms best qualify for a preponderance of debt financing?

As discussed elsewhere, peer group forms of organization can and do operate well in small enterprises where the membership has been carefully screened and is committed to democratic ideals (Williamson, 1975, chapter 3). Also, the partnership form of organization works well in professional organizations, such as law and accounting firms, where the need for firm-specific physical capital is small (Hansmann, 1988). There being little need for equity capital to support investment in such firms, the control of these firms naturally accrues to those who supply specialized human assets (Williamson, 1989, pp. 24–26). These exceptions aside, 'third forms' experience serious incentive disabilities.[21]

Trust

There is a growing tendency, among economists and sociologists alike, to describe trust in calculative terms: both rational choice sociologists (Coleman, 1990) and game theorists (Dasgupta, 1988) treat trust as a subclass of risk. I concur with Granovetter that to craft credible commitments (through the use of bonds, hostages, information disclosure rules, specialized dispute settlement mechanisms, and the like) is to create functional substitutes for trust (Granovetter, 1985, p. 487). Albeit vitally important to economic organization, such substitutes should not be confused with (real) trust.[22]

That calculativeness plays a larger role in economics than in the other social sciences is evident from my discussion of farsighted contracting. But calculativeness can also be taken to excesses, which is the main point in my discussion of atmosphere (*see* above). Sometimes, however, an altogether different orientation is needed. Thus whereas the response to excesses of monitoring is to *be more sophisticatedly calculative* (take the dysfunctional effects into account), there are other circumstances where the response is to *avoid being calculative*.

As I have argued elsewhere (Williamson, 1993a), relations that are subject to continuous Bayesian updating of probabilities based on experience are thoroughly calculative. And because commercial relations are invariably calculative, the concept of calculated risk (rather than calculated trust) should be used to describe commercial transactions.

Continuous experience rating need not obtain everywhere, however. Indeed, because some personal relations are unique and because continuous updating, even if only of a low-grade kind, can have corrosive effects,[23] certain personal relations are treated in a nearly non-calculative way. That is accomplished by a discrete structural reclassification, according to which personal relations are dealt with on an all-or-none, rather than a continuous updating, basis.

The upshot is that personal trust relations and commercial/calculative risk relations differ in kind. Commercial relations are in no way denigrated as a result (Robbins, 1933, pp. 179–180).

Tosh

The legal philosopher, Lon Fuller, distinguished between "essentials" and "tosh," where the former involves an examination of the "rational core" (1978, pp. 359–362) and tosh is preoccupied with "superfluous rituals, rules of procedure without clear purpose, [and] needless precautions preserved through habit" (1978, p. 356). According to Fuller, to focus on the latter would "abandon any hope of fruitful analysis" (1978, p. 360).

I think that this last goes too far: a place should be made for tosh, but tosh should be kept in its place.[24] Consider in this connection the Friedland and Alford interpretation of Clifford Geertz's description of Balinese cockfights (1991, pp. 247–248; emphasis added):

> Enormous sums of money can change hands at each match, sums that are *irrational* from an individualistic, utilitarian perspective. The higher the sums, the more *evenly matched* the cocks are arranged to be, and the more likely

the odds on which the bet is made are even. The greater the sum of money at stake, the more the decision to bet is not individualistic and utilitarian, but collective—one bets with one's kin or village—and status-oriented.

That there are social pressures to support one's kin to village is a sociological argument. Absent these pressures, the concentration of bets on evenly matched cocks would be difficult to explain. It does not, however, follow that it is "irrational" to bet enormous sums on evenly matched cocks. Given the social context, it has become non-viable, as a betting matter, to fight unevenly matched cocks.

Thus suppose that the objective odds for a proposed match are 4:1. Considerations of local pride may reduce the effective odds of 3:2. Such a match will not attract much betting because those from the village with the lesser cock who view it from an individualistic, acquisitive perspective will make only perfunctory bets. Accordingly, the only interesting matches are those *where social pressures are relieved by the even odds.*[25] The "symbolic construction of reality" to which Friedland and Alford refer thus has real consequences. It delimits the feasible set within which rationality operates; but rationality is fully operative thereafter.

One interpretation of this is that tosh has discrete structural effects and that rationality, operating through the marginal calculus, applies thereafter. Indeed, that seems to fit the Balinese cockfight rather well. Whether the social construction of reality has such important consequences more generally is then the question. My sense is that it varies with the circumstances.

Tosh is arguably more important in non-commercial circumstances—state, family, religion—than in the commercial sector, although the Hamilton and Biggart (1988) examination of differences in corporate forms in Far East Asia might be offered as a contradiction. Hamilton and Biggart, however, go well beyond tosh (as described by Fuller) to implicate the institutional environment—to include property rights, contract law, politics, and the like.

Thus although both tosh (superfluous rituals) and the institutional environment refer to background conditions, the one should not be confused with the other. Tosh is a source of interesting variety and adds spice to life. Core features of the institutional environment, as defined by North (1986, 1991) and others (Sundaram and Black, 1992), are arguably more important, however, to the study of comparative economic organization.[26]

CONCLUSIONS

The science of organization to which Barnard made reference (1938, p. 290) over fifty years ago has made major strides in the past ten and twenty years. All of the social sciences have a stake in this, but none more than economics and organization theory.

If the schematic set out in Figure 9.1 is an accurate way to characterize much of what is going on, then the economics of governance needs to be informed both from the level of the institutional environment (where sociology has a lot to contribute) and from the level of the individual (where psychology is implicated). The intertemporal process transformations that take place within the institutions of governance (with respect to which organization theory has a lot to say) are also pertinent. The overall schema works out of the rational spirit approach that is associated with economics.[27]

This multilevel approach relieves some, perhaps much, of the strain to which Baron and Hannan refer: "we think it important to understand the different assumptions and forms of reasoning used in contemporary sociology versus economics. . . . These disciplinary differences . . . represent major barriers to intellectual trade between economics and sociology" (1992, p. 13). If, however, deep knowledge at several levels is needed and is beyond the competence of any one discipline, and if a systems conception can be devised in which intellectual trade among levels can be accomplished, then some of the worst misunderstandings of the past can be put behind us.

I summarize here what I see to be some of the principal respects in which the healthy tension to which I referred at the outset has supported intellectual trade, of which more is in prospect.

Organization Theory Supports for Transaction Cost Economics

Behavioral assumptions   Organization theory's insistence on workably realistic, as opposed to analytically convenient, behavioral assumptions is a healthy antidote. Transaction cost economics responds by describing economic actors in terms of bounded rationality and opportunism.

Adaptation   The cooperative adaptation emphasized by Barnard is joined with the autonomous adaptation of Hayek, with the result that transaction cost economics makes an appropriate place for both market and hierarchy.

Unanticipated consequences   The subtle and unintended consequences of control and organization need to be uncovered, whereupon provision can be made for these in the *ex ante* organizational design.

Politics   Because property rights in the public arena are shaped by democratic politics, provision needs to be made for these in the *ex ante* organizational design of public sector bureaus.

Embeddedness   The first-order response to the proposition that embeddedness matters is to regard the institutional environment as a locus of shift parameters, changes in which change the comparative costs of governance.

Discrete structural analysis Each generic form of organization is described as a syndrome of attributes and possesses its own logic. These discreteness features need to be discovered and explicated both within and between sectors.

Transaction Cost Economics Supports for Organization Theory

Unit of analysis Any theory of organization that fails to name the unit of analysis out of which it works and thereafter identify the critical dimensions with respect to which that unit of analysis varies is non-operational at best and could be bankrupt.

The main case All rival theories of organization are asked to nominate the main case, develop the refutable implications that accrue thereto, and examine the data. Economizing on transaction costs is the transaction cost economics candidate.

Farsighted contracting Looking ahead, recognizing hazards, and folding these back into the design of governance is often feasible and explains a very considerable amount of organizational variety.

Trade-offs Because each mode of governance is a syndrome of attributes, the move from one mode to another involves trade-offs. The key trade-offs need to be stated and explicated.

Remediableness Relevant choices among feasible forms of organization are what the analysis of comparative economic organization is all about.

NOTES

This paper is reprinted from *Industrial and Corporate Change*, Vol. 2, Number 2 (1993), 107–56. Reproduced with permission from Oxford University Press.

This paper has benefited from oral presentations to the Macro Organization Behavior Society at the October 1992 meeting at Northwestern, the Stanford Center for Organizational Research, the Institutional Analysis Workshop at the University of California, Berkeley, and the "Handbook of Economic Sociology Conference" at the Russell Sage Foundation in February 1993. Helpful comments by James Baron, Paul DiMaggio, David Levine, Neil Smelser, and Richard Swedberg are gratefully acknowledged.

I am also grateful to the conference organizers and to the Russell Sage Foundation for permission to publish this version of the paper here. (A somewhat revised version will appear in the *Handbook*.)

1. James March advised the Fourth International Conference of the Society for the Advancement of Socio-Economics that economics had been so fully re-

formed that the audience should "declare victory and go home" (Coughlin, 1992, p. 23).

2. Richard Posner comes out differently. He argues that "organization-theory . . . [adds] nothing to economics that the literature on information economics had not added years earlier" (1993, p. 84).

3. Briefly, the transaction cost economics responses are: (i) institutions respond to scarcity as economizing devices, (ii) the transaction is expressly adopted as the basic unit of analysis, (iii) conflicts are recognized and relieved by the creation of credible commitments/*ex post* governance apparatus, and (iv) the institutional environment is treated as a set of shift parameters that change the comparative costs of governance. Although these may be incomplete responses, the spirit of the transaction cost economics enterprise nevertheless makes serious contact with Commons's prescription.

4. Oligarchy is usually applied to composite organization, but it applies to subdivisions as well. Whether a firm should make or buy is thus a matter for which oligarchy has a bearing. If the decision to take a transaction out of the market and organize it internally is attended by subsequent information distortions and subgoal pursuit, then that should be taken into account at the outset (Williamson, 1975, chapter 7; 1985, chapter 6). Not only do operating costs rise but also a constituency develops that favor the renewal of internal facilities. An obvious response is to demand high hurdle rates for new projects, thereby to protect against the unremarked but predictable distortions (added costs; advocacy efforts) to which internal (as compared with market) procurement is differentially subject.

   The argument applies to public sector projects as well. Because of the deferred and undisclosed but nevertheless predictable distortions to which "organization" is subject, new projects and regulatory proposals should be required to display large (apparent) net gains.

5. That is an interesting and important argument. Politics really is different. But it is not as though there is no private sector counterpart. The more general argument is this: weak property rights regimes—both public and private— invite farsighted parties to provide added protections. The issues are discussed further in conjunction with remediableness (see below).

   Note, as a comparative institutional matter, that secure totalitarian regimes can, according to this logic, be expected to design more efficient public agencies. That is neither here nor there if democratic values are held to be paramount—in which event the apparent inefficiencies of agencies under a democracy are simply a cost of this form of governance.

6. Interdependencies among dyadic contracting relations and the possible manipulation thereof have, however, been examined (Williamson, 1985, pp. 318–319). Also see the discussion of appropriability below.

7. The statement is a weakened variant on Tjalling Koopmans. Where he refers to "profit maximization," "easiest," and "keenest," I have substituted transaction cost economizing, easy, and keen.

8. Joe Mokyr observes that resistance to innovation "occurred in many periods and places but seems to have been neglected by most historians" (1990, p. 178). He nevertheless gives a number of examples in which established interests, often with the use of the political process, set out to defeat new technologies. In the end, however, the effect was not to defeat but to delay machines

that pressed pinheads, an improved slide rest lathe, the ribbon loom, the flying shuttle, the use of arabic numerals, and the use of the printing press (Mokyr, 1990, pp. 178–179). That, of course, is not dispositive. There may be many cases in which superior technologies were in fact defeated—of which the type-writer keyboard (see below) is purportedly an example. Assuming, however, that the appropriate criterion for judging superiority is that of remediability (see below), I register grave doubts that significant technological or organiza-tional efficiencies can be delayed indefinitely.

9. The Schumpeterian process of "handing on"—which entails "a fall in the price of the product to the new level of costs" (Schumpeter, 1947, p. 155) and purportedly works whenever rivals are alert to new opportunities and are not prevented by purposive restrictions from adopting them—is pertinent. The ef-ficacy of handing on varies with the circumstances. When are rivals *more* alert? What are the underlying information assumptions? Are there other capi-tal market and/or organizational concerns?

10. The remainder of this subsection is based on Williamson (1993a).

11. Another way of putting it is that (transition problems aside), each party can go its own way without cost to the other. Competition provides a safeguard.

12. This has public policy ramifications. As between two oligopolies, one of which engages in rent-protective measures while the other does not, and assuming that they are identical in other respects, the dissolution of the rent-protective oligopoly will yield larger welfare gains.

13. This subsection is based on Williamson (1985, pp. 61–63).

14. This subsection is based on Williamson (1993a).

15. The buying of "rounds" in English pubs is an example. Would a costless meter lead to a superior result? Suppose that everyone privately disclosed a willing-ness to pay and that successive bids were solicited until a breakeven result was projected. Suppose that the results of the final solicitation either are kept secret or posted, depending on preferences, and that rounds are thereafter delivered to the table on request. Monthly bills are sent out in accordance with the breakeven condition. How is camaraderie effected?

16. Friedland and Alford (1991, p. 235) identify resource dependency as one of the two dominant theories of organization (the other being population ecology).

17. Because contracts are incomplete and contain gaps, errors, omissions, and the like, and because the immediate parties may not be able to reconcile their differences when an unanticipated disturbance arises, parties to a contract will sometimes ask courts to be excused from performance. Because, moreover, literal enforcement can pose unacceptably severe contractual hazards—the ef-fects of which are to discourage contracting (in favor of vertical integration) and/or to discourage potentially cost-effective investments in specialized assets—some relief from strict enforcement recommends itself. How much re-lief is then the question. Were excuse to be granted routinely whenever adver-sity occurred, then incentives to think through contracts, choose technologies judiciously, share risks efficiently, and avert adversity would be impaired. Ac-cordingly, transaction cost economics recommends that (i) provision be made for excuse but (ii) excuse should be awarded sparingly—which it evidently is (Farnsworth, 1968, p. 885; Buxbaum, 1985).

18. I have argued that dominant firm industries in which chance plays a role do

warrant public policy intervention (Williamson, 1975, chapter 11), but whether net gains would really be realized by implementing that proposal (especially as international competition becomes more intensive) is problematic.

19. The "new sociology of organization" holds that "even in identical economic and technical conditions, outcomes may differ dramatically if social structures are different" (Granovetter, 1992, p. 9). The "social construction of industry" argument is developed in a major book by Patrick McGuire, Mark Granovetter, and Michael Schwartz on the origins of the American electric power industry. That book has been described as follows (McGuire et al., 1992, pp. 1–2):

> Building on detailed historical research, . . . this book treats the origins of the electrical utility industry from a sociological perspective. The idea that industries, like other economic institutions, are "socially constructed," derives from Granovetter's work on "embeddedness" (1985) and presents an alternative to the new institutional economics, which contends that economic institutions should be understood as the efficient solutions to economic problems. . . .
>
> We believe that the way the utility industry developed from its inception in the 1880s was not the only technologically practical one, nor the most efficient. It arose because a set of powerful actors accessed certain techniques and applied them in a highly visible and profitable way. Those techniques resulted from the shared personal understandings, social connections, organizational conditions, and historical opportunities available to these actors. This success, in turn, triggered pressures for uniformity across regions, even when this excluded viable and possibly more efficient alternative technologies and organizational forms.
>
> Our argument resembles that made by economists Paul David and Brian Arthur on the "lock-in" of inefficient technologies (such as the QWERTY keyboard . . .), but draws on the sociology of knowledge and of social structure.

20. This subsection is based on Williamson (1989, pp. 41–43).

21. The limits of third forms of organizing *large* enterprises with *variegated* membership are severe in both theory and fact. To be sure, some students of economic organization remain sanguine (Horvat, 1991). The evidence from Eastern Europe has not, however, been supportive. Maciej Iwanek (1991, p. 12) remarks of the Polish experience that "except [among] advocates of workers' management, nobody believes that the . . . governance scheme of state-owned enterprises [by workers' management] creates strong incentives"; Manuel Hinds (1990, p. 28) concludes that "absenteeism, shirking, and lack of initiative are pervasive in the self-managed firm"; Janos Kornai (1990, p. 144) counsels that "it would be intellectually dishonest to hide the evidence concerning the weakness of third forms."

22. Note that the trust that Granovetter ascribes to ongoing relations can go either way—frequent suggestions to the contrary notwithstanding. That is because experience can be either good (more confidence) or bad (less confidence), which, if contracts of both kinds are renewed, will show up in differential contracting (Crocker and Reynolds, 1993).

23. Not only can intendedly non-calculative relations be upset by type I error, according to which a true relation is incorrectly classified as false, but calculativeness may be subject to (involuntary) positive feedback. Intendedly non-

calculative relations that are continuously subject to being reclassified as calculative are, in effect, calculative.

24. The evolution of cooperation between opposed armies or gangs that are purportedly engaged in "deadly combat" is illustrated by Robert Axelrod's examination of "The Live-and-Let-Live System in Trench Warfare in World War I" (1984, pp. 73–87). Interesting and important as the live-and-let-live rituals were, these non-violent practices should not be mistaken for the main case. Rather, these rituals were the exception to the main case, which was that British and German troops were at war.

25. Richard M. Coughlin contends that the "essence" of the socio-economic approach proposed by Amitai Etzioni is that (1992, p. 3):

> Human behavior must be understood in terms of the fusion of individually-based and communally-based forces, which Etzioni labels the *I and We*. The *I* represents the individual acting in pursuit of his or her own pleasure; the *We* stands for the obligations and restraints imposed by the collectivity.

That is close to the interpretation that I advance here to interpret the Balinese cock fights.

26. This is pertinent, among other things, to the study of the multinational enterprise. As Anant Sundaram and J. Stewart Black observe, MNEs "pursue different entry/involvement strategies in different markets and for different products at any given time" (1992, p. 740). Their argument, that transaction cost economics "is inadequate for explaining simultaneously different entry modes because . . . asset specificity . . . [is] largely the same the world over" (1992, p. 740) assumes that the governance level operates independently of the institutional environment under a transaction cost set-up. That is mistaken.

27. I borrow the term "rational spirit" from Kenneth Arrow (1974, p. 16). The rational spirit approach holds that there is a *logic* to organization and that this logic is mainly discerned by the relentless application of economic reasoning (subject, however, to cognitive constraints). The rational spirit approach is akin to but somewhat weaker (in that is eschews stronger forms of utility maximization) than the "rational choice" approach associated with James Coleman (1990).

REFERENCES

Alchian, A. (1961), *Some Economics of Property*. RAND D-2316. RAND Corporation: Santa Monica.

Alchian, A. and H. Demsetz (1972), Production, Information Costs, and Economic Organization, *American Economic Review*, 62 (December), 777–795.

Alchian, A. and S. Woodward (1987), Reflections on the Theory of the Firm, *Journal of Institutional and Theoretical Economics*, 143 (March), 110–136.

Aoki, M. (1988), *Information, Incentives, and Bargaining in the Japanese Economy*. Cambridge University Press: New York.

Aoki, M. (1990), Toward an Economic Model of the Japanese Firm, *Journal of Economic Literature*, 28 (March), 1–27.

Aoki, M. (1992), The Japanese Firm as a System of Attributes: A Survey and Research Agenda, unpublished manuscript.

Arrow, K. J. (1974). *The Limits of Organization,* 1st edn. W. W. Norton: New York.

Arthur, B. (1989), Competing Technologies, Increasing Returns, and Lock-In by Historical Events, *Economic Journal,* 99 (March), 116–131.

Arthur, B. (1990), Positive Feedbacks in the Economy, *Scientific American* (February), 92–99.

Asanuma, B. (1989), Manufacturer-Supplier Relationships in Japan and The Concept of Relationship-Specific Skill, *Journal of Japanese and International Economies,* 3, 1–30.

Axelrod, R. (1984), *The Evolution of Cooperation.* Basic Books: New York.

Bain, J. (1956), *Barriers to New Competition.* John Wiley & Sons: New York.

Barnard, C. (1938). *The Functions of the Executive.* Harvard University Press (fifteenth printing, 1962): Cambridge, MA.

Barnett, W. and G. Carroll (1993), How Institutional Constraints Affected the Organization of the Early American Telephone Industry, *Journal of Law, Economics, and Organization,* 9 (April).

Baron, J. and M. Hannan (1992), The Impact of Economics on Contemporary Sociology, unpublished manuscript.

Becker, G. (1976), *The Economic Approach to Human Behavior.* University of Chicago Press: Chicago.

Berglof, E. (1989), Capital Structure as a Mechanism of Control—A Comparison of Financial Systems, in M. Aoki, B. Gustafsson, and O. Williamson (eds), *The Firm as a Nexus of Treaties.* Sage: London, pp. 237–262.

Bergson, A. (1948), Socialist Economies, in Howard Ellis (ed.), *Survey of Contemporary Economies.* Philadelphia: Blakiston, pp. 430–458.

Bonin, J. and L. Putterman (1987), *Economics of Cooperation and Labor Managed Economies.* Cambridge University Press: New York.

Bowles, S. and H. Gintis (1993), The Revenge of Homo Economicus: Contested Exchange and the Revival of Political Economy, *Journal of Economic Perspectives* (Winter).

Bradach, J. and R. Eccles (1989), Price, Authority, and Trust, *American Review of Sociology,* 15, 97–118.

Bridgeman, P. (1955), *Reflections of a Physicist,* 2nd edn. Philosophical Library: New York.

Bromley, D. (1989), *Economic Interests and Institutions.* Basil Blackwell: New York.

Buxbaum, R. (1985), Modification and Adaptation of Contracts: American Legal Developments, *Studies in Transnational Law,* 3, 31–54.

Carroll, G. and J. R. Harrison (1992), Chance and Rationality in Organizational Evolution, unpublished manuscript.

Coase, R. H. (1937), The Nature of the Firm, *Economica,* 4, 386–405.

Coase, R. H. (1959), The Federal Communications Commission, *Journal of Law and Economics,* 2 (October), 1–40.

Coase, R. H. (1960), The Problem of Social Cost, *Journal of Law and Economics,* 3 (October), 1–44.

Coase, R. H. (1964), The Regulated Industries: Discussion, *American Economic Review,* 54 (May), 194–197.

Coase, R. H. (1972), Industrial Organization: A Proposal for Research, in V. R. Fuchs (ed.), *Policy Issues and Research Opportunities in Industrial Organization.* National Bureau of Economic Research: New York, pp. 59–73.

Coase, R. H. (1984), The New Institutional Economics, *Journal of Institutional and Theoretical Economics*, 140 (March), 229–231.

Coleman, J. (1982). *The Asymmetric Society*. Syracuse University Press: Syracuse, NY.

Coleman, J. (1990), *The Foundations of Social Theory*. Harvard University Press: Cambridge, MA.

Commons, J. R. (1924), *Legal Foundations of Capitalism*. Macmillan: New York.

Commons, J. R. (1934), *Institutional Economics*. University of Wisconsin Press: Madison.

Coughlin, R. (1992), Interdisciplinary Nature of Socio-Economics, unpublished manuscript.

Crocker, K. and K. Reynolds (1993), The Efficiency of Incomplete Contracts: An Empirical Analysis of Air Force Engine Procurement, *Rand Journal of Economics* (Spring).

Crozier, M. (1964), *The Bureaucratic Phenomenon*. University of Chicago Press: Chicago.

Cyert, R. M. and J. G. March (1963), *A Behavioral Theory of the Firm*. Prentice-Hall: Englewood Cliffs, NJ.

Dasgupta, P. (1988), Trust as a Commodity, in D. Gambetta (ed.), *Trust: The Making and Breaking of Cooperative Relations*. Basil Blackwell: Oxford, pp. 49–72.

David, P. (1985), Clio in the Economics of QWERTY, *American Economic Review*, 75 (May), 332–337.

David, P. (1986), Understanding the Economics of QWERTY: The Necessity of History, in W. N. Parker (ed.), *Economic History and the Modern Economist*. Basil Blackwell: New York.

David, P. (1992), Heroes, Herds, and Hysteresis in Technological History, *Industrial and Corporate Change*, 1, 129–180.

Davis, G. F. and W. W. Powell (1992), Organization-Environment Relations, in M. Dunnette (ed.), *Handbook of Industrial and Organizational Psychology*, Vol. 3 (2nd edn). Consulting Psychologists Press: New York, pp. 315–375.

Davis, L. E. and D. C. North (1971), *Institutional Change and American Economic Growth*. Cambridge University Press: Cambridge.

Demsetz, H. (1967), Toward a Theory of Property Rights, *American Economic Review*, 57 (May), 347–359.

Demsetz, H. (1969), Information and Efficiency: Another Viewpoint, *Journal of Law and Economics*, 12 (April), 1–22.

DiMaggio, P. and W. Powell (1991), Introduction, in Walter Powell and Paul DiMaggio (eds), *The New Institutionalism in Organizational Analysis*. University of Chicago Press: Chicago, pp. 1–38.

Dixit, A. (1980), The Role of Investment in Entry Deterrence, *Economic Journal*, 90 (March), 95–106.

Dore, R. (1983), Goodwill and the Spirit of Market Capitalism, *British Journal of Sociology*, 34 (December), 459–482.

Farnsworth, E. A. (1968), Disputes Over Omissions in Contracts, *Columbia Law Review*, 68 (May), 860–891.

Frank, R. (1992), Melding Sociology and Economics, *Journal of Economic Literature*, 30 (March), 147–170.

Friedland, R. and R. Alford (1991), Bringing Society Back In: Symbols, Practices, and Institutional Contradictions, in Walter Powell and Paul DiMaggio (eds),

The New Institutionalism in Organizational Analysis. University of Chicago Press: Chicago, pp. 232–266.

Fuller, L. L. (1978), The Forms and Limits of Adjudication, *Harvard Law Review*, 92, 353–409.

Fuller, L. L. (1981), Human Interaction and the Law, in Kenneth I. Winston (ed.), *The Principles of Social Order: Selected Essays on Lon L. Fuller.* Duke University Press, Durham, NC, pp. 212–246.

Furubotn, E. and S. Pejovich (1974), *The Economics of Property Rights.* Ballinger: Cambridge, MA.

Furubotn, E. and R. Richter (1991), *The New Institutional Economics.* Texas A&M University Press: College Station, TX.

Georgescu-Roegen, N. (1971), *The Entropy Law and Economic Process.* Harvard University Press: Cambridge, MA.

Gerlach, M. (1992), *Alliance Capitalism.* University of California Press: Berkeley, CA.

Gouldner, A. W. (1954), *Industrial Bureaturacy.* Free Press: Glencoe, IL.

Granovetter, M. (1985), Economic Action and Social Structure: The Problem of Embeddedness, *American Journal of Sociology,* 91 (November), 481–501.

Granovetter, M. (1988), The Sociological and Economic Approaches to Labor Market Analysis, in George Farkas and Paula England (eds), *Industries, Firms, and Jobs.* Plenum: New York, pp. 187–218.

Granovetter, M. (1990), The Old and the New Economic Sociology: A History and an Agenda, in Roger Frieldand and A. F. Robertson (eds), *Beyond the Marketplace.* Aldine: New York.

Granovetter, M. (1992), Economic Institutions as Social Constructions: A Framework for Analysis, *Acta Sociologica,* 35, 3–11.

Grossekettler, H. (1989), On Designing an Economic Order: The Contributions of the Freiburg School, in Donald Walker (ed.), *Perspectives on the History of Economic Thought, Vol. II.* Edward Elgar: Aldershot, pp. 38–84.

Hamilton, G. and N. Biggart (1988) Market, Culture, and Authority, *American Journal of Sociology* (Supplement), 94, S52–S94.

Hansmann, H. (1988), The Ownership of the Firm, *Journal of Law, Economics, and Organization,* 4, 267–303.

Harberger, A. (1954), Monopoly and Resource Allocation, *American Economic Review,* 44 (May), 77–87.

Hart, O. (1990), An Economist's Perspective on the Theory of the Firm, in Oliver Williamson (ed.), *Organization Theory.* Oxford University Press: New York, pp. 154–171.

Hayek, F. (1945), The Use of Knowledge in Society, *American Economic Review,* 35 (September), 519–530.

Hechter, M. (1987), *Principles of Group Solidarity.* University of California Press: Berkeley, CA.

Heide, J. and G. John (1988), The Role of Dependence Balancing in Safeguarding Transaction-Specific Assets in Conventional Channels, *Journal of Marketing,* 52 (January), 20–35.

Helper, S. and D. Levine (1992), Long-Term Supplier Relations and Product-Market Structure, *Journal of Law,* Economics, and Organization, 8 (October), 561–581.

Hinds, M. (1990), Issues in the Introduction of Market Forces in Eastern European Socialist Economies, The World Bank. Report No. IDP-0057.

Harvat, B. (1991), Review of Janos Kornai, The Road to a Free Economy, *Journal of Economic Behavior and Organization*, 15 (May), 408–410.

Hutchison, T. (1984). Institutional Economics Old and New, *Journal of Institutional and Theoretical Economics*, 140 (March), 20–29.

Iwanek, M. (1991), Issues of Institutions Transformations and Ownership Changes in Poland, *Journal of Institutional and Theoretical Economics*, 147, 83–95.

Jensen, M. (1983), Organization Theory and Methodology, *Accounting Review*, 50 (April), 319–339.

Joskow, P. L. (1985), Vertical Integration and Long-Term Contracts, *Journal of Law, Economics, and Organization*, 1 (Spring), 33–80.

Joskow, P. L. (1988), Asset Specificity and the Structure of Vertical Relationships: Empirical Evidence, *Journal of Law, Economics, and Organization*, 4 (Spring), 95–117.

Klein, B., R. A. Crowford, and A. A. Alchian (1978), Vertical Integration, Appropriable Rents, and the Competitive Contracting Process, *Journal of Law and Economics*, 21 (October), 297–326.

Koopmans, T. (1957), *Three Essays on the State of Economic Science*. McGraw-Hill Book Company: New York.

Kornai, J. (1990), The Affinity Between Ownership Forms and Coordination Mechanisms: The Common Experience of Reform in Socialist Countries, *Journal of Economic Perspectives*, 4 (Summer), 131–147.

Kreps, D. M. (1990), Corporate Culture and Economic Theory, in James Alt and Kenneth Shepsle (eds), *Perspectives on Positive Political Economy*. Cambridge University Press: New York, pp. 90–143.

Kreps, D. M. (1992), (How) Can Game Theory Lead to a Unified Theory of Organization? unpublished manuscript.

Lange, O. (1938), On the Theory of Economic Socialism, in Benjamin Lippincott (ed.), *On the Economic Theory of Socialism*. University of Minnesota Press: Minneapolis, pp. 55–143.

Lewis, T. (1983), Preemption, Divestiture, and Forward Contracting, *American Economic Review*, 73, (December), 1092–1101.

Liebowitz, S. J. (1992), Path Dependency, Lock-In, and History, unpublished manuscript.

Liebowitz, S. J. and S. Margolis (1990), The Fable of the Keys, *Journal of Law and Economics*, 33 (April), 1–26.

Lincoln, J. (1990), Japanese Organization and Organization Theory, *Research in Organizational Behavior*, 12, 255–294.

Llewellyn, K. N. (1931), What Price Contract? An Essay in Perspective, *Yale Law Journal*, 40 (May), 704–751.

McCain, R. (1977), On the Optimal Financial Environment for Worker Cooperatives, *Zeitschrift für Nationalekonomie*, 37, 355–384.

McCullough, D. (1992), *Truman*. Simon & Schuster: New York.

McGuire, P., M. Granovetter, and M. Schwartz (1992), The Social Construction of Industry (a book prospectus).

Machiavelli, N. (1952), *The Prince*. New American Library: New York.

Macneil, I. R. (1974), The Many Futures of Contracts, *Southern California Law Review*, 47 (May), 691–816.

Macneil, I. R. (1978), Contracts: Adjustments of Long-Term Economic Relations Under Classical, Neoclassical, and Relational Contract Law, *Northwestern University Law Review*, 72, 854–906.

March, J. G. (1988, *Decisions and Organizations*. Basil Blackwell: Oxford.

March, J. G. and H. A. Simon (1958), *Organizations*. John Wiley & Sons: New York.

Marschak, J. (1968, Economics of Inquiring, Communicating, Deciding, *American Economic Review*, 58 (May), 1–18.

Masten, S. (1984), The Organization of Production: Evidence from the Aerospace Industry, *Journal of Law and Economics*, 27 (October), 403–418.

Masten, S. (1992), Transaction Costs, Mistakes, and Performance: Assessing the Importance of Governance, *Management and Decision Sciences*, in press.

Matthews, R. C. O. (1986), The Economics of Institutions and the Sources of Economic Growth, *Economic Journal*, 96 (December), 903–918.

Merton, R. (1936), The Unanticipated Consequences of Purposive Social Action, *American Sociological Review*, 1, 894–904.

Michels, R. (1962), *Political Parties*. Free Press: Glencoe, IL.

Miles, R. and C. Snow (1992), Causes of Failure in Network Organizations, *California Management Review*, 34 (Summer), 53–72.

Moe, T. (1990), Political Institutions: The Neglected Side of the Story: Comment, *Journal of Law, Economics, and Organization*, 6 (Special Issue), 213–254.

Mokyr, J. (1990), *The Lever of Riches*. Oxford University Press: New York.

Nelson, R. R. and S. G. Winter (1982), *An Evolutionary Theory of Economic Change*. Harvard University Press: Cambridge, MA.

Newell, A. and H. Simon (1972), *Human Problem Solving*. Prentice-Hall: Englewood Cliffs, NJ.

North, D. (1986), The New Institutional Economics, *Journal of Institutional and Theoretical Economics*, 142, 230–237.

North, D. (1991), Institutions, *Journal of Economic Perspectives*, 5 (Winter), 97–112.

Palay, T. (1984), Comparative Institutional Economics: The Governance of Rail Freight Contracting, *Journal of Legal Studies*, 13 (June), 265–288.

Palay, T. (1985), 'The Avoidance of Regulatory Constraints: The Use of Informal Contracts, *Journal of Law, Economics, and Organization*, 1 (Spring).

Parsons, T. and N. Smelser (1956), *Economy and Society*. New York: The Free Press.

Penrose, E. (1959), *The Theory of Growth of the Firm*. New York: John Wiley & Sons.

Perrow, C. (1992), Review of the New Competition, *Administrative Science Quarterly*, 37 (March), 162–166.

Pfeffer, J. (1981), *Power in Organizations*. Marshfield, MA: Pitman Publishing.

Polanyi, M. (1962), *Personal Knowledge: Towards a Post-Critical Philosophy*. Harper & Row: New York.

Posner, R. (1993), The New Institutional Economics Meets Law and Economics, *Journal of Institutional and Theoretical Economics*, 149 (March), 73–87.

Putterman, L. (1984). On Some Recent Explanations of Why Capital Hires Labor, *Economic Inquiry*, 22, 171–187.

Robbins, Lionel (ed.) (1933), *The Common Sense of Political Economy, and Selected Papers on Economic Theory*, by Philip Wicksteed. G. Routledge and Sons, Ltd.: London.

Robinson, E. A. G. (1934), The Problem of Management and the Size of Firms, *Economic Journal*, 44 (June), 240–254.

Schelling, T. C. (1978), *Micromotives and Macrobehavior*. Norton: New York.

Scherer, F. M. (1970), *Industrial Market Structure and Economic Performance*. Rand McNally & Company: Chicago.

Schotter, A. (1981), *The Economic Theory of Social Institutions*. Cambridge University Press: New York.

Schmid, A. (1972), Analytical Institutional Economics, *American Journal of Agricultural Economics*, 54, 893–901.

Schumpeter, J. A. (1942), *Capitalism, Socialism, and Democracy*. Harper & Row: New York.

Schumpeter, J. A. (1947), The Creative Response in Economic History, *Journal of Economic History*, 7 (November), 149–159.

Schumpeter, J. A. (1989), *Essays on Entrepreneurs. Innovations, Business Cycles, and the Evolution of Capitalism*. New Brunswick: Transaction Publishers.

Scott, W. R. (1992), Institutions and Organizations: Toward a Theoretical Synthesis, unpublished manuscript.

Selznick, P. (1949), *TVA and the Grass Roots*. University of California Press: Berkeley, CA.

Selznick, P. (1957), *Leadership in administration*. Harper & Row: New York.

Shapiro, C. (1989), The Theory of Business Strategy, *Rand Journal of Economics*, 20 (Spring), 125–137.

Sheard, P. (1989), The Main Bank System and Corporate Monitoring in Japan, *Journal of Economic Behavior and Organization*, 11 (May), 399–422.

Shelanski, H. (1991), Empirical Research in Transaction Cost Economics: A Survey and Assessment, unpublished manuscript, University of California, Berkeley.

Shelanski, H. (1993), Transfer Pricing, unpublished Ph.D. Dissertation, University of California, Berkeley.

Simon, H. (1957a), *Administrative Behavior*. Macmillan: New York, 2nd edn.

Simon, H. (1957b), *Models of Man*. John Wiley & Sons: New York.

Simon, H. (1978), Rationality as Process and as Product of Thought, *American Economic Review*, 68 (May), 1–16.

Simon, H. (1983), *Reason in Human Affairs*. Stanford University Press: Stanford.

Simon, H. (1985), Human Nature in Politics: The Dialogue of Psychology with Political Science, *American Political Science Review*, 79, 293–304.

Simon, H. (1991), Organizations and Markets, *Journal of Economic Perspectives*, 5 (Spring), 25–44.

Stigler, G. J. (1968), *The Organization of Industry*. Richard D. Irwin: Homewood, IL.

Stigler, G. J. (1983), Comments in Edmund Kitch (ed.), The Fire of Truth: A Remembrance of Law and Economics at Chicago, 1932–1970, *Journal of Law and Economics*, 26 (April), 163–234.

Sundaram, A. and J. S. Black (1992), The Environment and Internal Organization of Multinational Enterprise, *Academy of Management Review*, 17 (October), 729–757.

Swedberg, R. (1987), Economic Sociology: Past and Present, *Current Sociology*, 35, 1–221.

Swedberg, R. (1990), *Economics and Sociology: On Redefining Their Boundaries*. Princeton University Press: Princeton, NJ.

Swedberg, R. (1991), Major Traditions of Economic Sociology, *Annual Review of Sociology,* 17, 251–276.

Teece, D. J. (1986), Profiting From Technological Innovation, *Research Policy,* 15 (December), 285–305.

Teece, D. J., G. Pisano, and A. Shuen (1990), Firm Capabilities, Resources, and the Concept of Strategy (unpublished manuscript, University of California, Berkeley).

Van de Ven, A. (1993), The Institutional Theory of John R. Commons: A Review and Commentary, *Academy of Management Review,* 18 (January), 139–152.

Waldrop, M. M. (1992), *Complexity.* New York: Simon & Schuster.

Weick, K. E. (I1977), Re-Punctuating the Problem, in Paul S. Goodman, Johannes M. Pennings (eds), *New Perspectives on Organizational Effectiveness.* Jossey-Bass: San Francisco, pp. 193–225.

Wernerfelt, B. (1984), A Resource-Based View of the Firm, *Strategic management Journal,* 5, 171–180.

Williamson, O. E. (1968), Economies as an Antitrust Defense: The Welfare Trade-offs, *American Economic Review,* 58 (March), 18–35.

Williamson, O. E. (1975), *Markets and Hierarchies: Analysis and Antitrust Implications.* Free Press: New York.

Williamson, O. E. (1979), Transaction-Cost Economics: The Governance of Contractual Relations, *Journal of Law and Economics,* 22 (October), 233–261.

Williamson, O. E. (1981), The Economics of Organization: The Transaction Cost Approach, *American Journal of Sociology,* 87 (November), 548–577.

Williamson, O. E. (1983), Credible Commitments: Using Hostages to Support Exchange, *American Economic Review,* 73 (September), 519–540.

Williamson, O. E. (1985), *The Economic Institutions of Capitalism.* Free Press: New York.

Williamson, O. E. (1988a), The Logic of Economic Organization, *Journal of Law, Economics, and Organization,* 4 (Spring), 65–93.

Williamson, O. E. (1988b), The Economics and Sociology of Organization: Promoting a Dialogue, in G. Farkas and P. England (eds), *Industries, Firms, and Jobs.* Plenum: New York, pp. 159–185.

Williamson, O. E. (1989), Internal Economic Organization, in O. E. Williamson, S.-E. Sjostrand, and J. Johanson (eds), *Perspectives on the Economics of Organization.* Lund University Press: Lund, Sweden, pp. 7–48.

Williamson, O. E. (1991a), Comparative Economic Organization: The Analysis of Discrete Structural Alternatives, *Administrative Science Quarterly,* 36 (June), 269–296.

Williamson, O. E. (1991b), Economic Institutions: Spontaneous and Intentional Governance, *Journal of Law, Economics, and Organization,* 7 (Special Issue), 159–187.

Williamson, O. E. (1991c), Strategizing, Economizing, and Economic Organization, *Strategic Management Journal,* 12, 75–94.

Williamson, O. E. (1993a), Calculativeness, Trust, and Economic Organization, *Journal of Law and Economics* 36 (April), 221–270.

Williamson, O. E. (1993b), The Evolving Science of Organization, *Journal of Institutional and Theoretical Economics,* 149 (March), 36–63.

Zald, M. (1987), Review Essay: The New Institutional Economics, *American Journal of Sociology,* 93 (November), 701–708.

Index

Wages. *See* Incentives or inducements
Waterman, Robert H., 40
Wilson, James Q., 40
"Wolves," 108, 109, 111, 112

Zald, Mayer, 9
Zone of acceptance, 176, 180, 183
Zone of indifference, 105–7, 107–8,
    177